TAKE
IT IN

TAKE IT IN

DO THE INNER WORK.
CREATE YOUR BEST DAMN LIFE.

GISELLE
LA POMPE-MOORE

RIDER

Rider, an imprint of Ebury Publishing,
20 Vauxhall Bridge Road,
London SW1V 2SA

Rider is part of the Penguin Random House group of companies
whose addresses can be found at global.penguinrandomhouse.com

First published in Great Britain by Rider in 2022

www.penguin.co.uk

A CIP catalogue record for this book is available from the British Library

ISBN 9781846047077

Printed and bound in Great Britain by Clays Ltd, Elcograf S.p.A.

The authorised representative in the EEA is Penguin Random House
Ireland, Morrison Chambers, 32 Nassau Street, Dublin D02 YH68

Penguin Random House is committed to a sustainable future for our
business, our readers and our planet. This book is made from
Forest Stewardship Council® certified paper

The events described in this book are based on the experiences and recollections
of the author. To preserve patient confidentiality names and other identifying
features have been changed. The anecdotes described are not based on any one
specific individual but rather a selection of composite characters drawing
on the various experiences of the author. Although a character has been given
a name, such as "Maddie", this is for narrative flow rather than because
it represents just one person. Any similarities are purely coincidental.

For my mother, Lystra La Pompe
The continuity of your love has been the fuel for my existence

CONTENTS

Get the Stuff You Want

INTRODUCTION

B elieve it or not, we are all spiritual beings. Every single one of us. If you're alive on this planet, circa now, then you're a spiritual being. That's right, even if you can't get through more than 2.5 minutes of meditation or don't know when the next full moon is, you are a spiritual being. The best news? When you recognise this by living a spirit-informed life, you can see your greater purpose, power and potential. You probably weren't expecting a quote from a French priest to kick off this book, but here we are. Pierre Teilhard de Chardin said, 'We are not human beings having a spiritual experience. We are spiritual beings having a human experience.' And isn't this just the exploding head emoji translated into philosophical text? The meeting place between an 'a-ha' moment and a mini epiphany. It's my brand of spirituality in a nutshell and seeing it this way is a quickfire route to being able to create your reality in some astonishing and meaningful ways.

For me, modern spirituality or being spirit-informed is about dealing with life here on Earth, where the people, messiness, beauty and ups-and-downs are. That's what makes it accessible, do-able and pretty life-changing for every single one of us. It's how we can navigate life and whatever it throws at *us* and we're being thrown a *lot*. Beyond that, we get to see that stepping into a life that feels really damn good to be in isn't as unbelievable as we might have thought. Spirituality is basically like the scarf your mum made you take on a night out, that you thought you didn't need, but that really helped you out later when it started to get chilly.

OK, SO WHAT'S BEING SPIRIT-INFORMED THEN?

I'll start with what it isn't. Spirituality isn't something that some of us have access to and others don't, and it isn't something that you will find neatly packaged up in an overpriced wellness shop. It doesn't require you to search for your intuition on Google maps or shell out for a Facebook ad to find your spirit guides. Spirituality can include, but isn't limited to, buying crystals, tracking the moon or understanding tarot. You don't need to know what your rising sign is and sign up for an astrology app's daily notifications to be spiritual. It isn't a snakes and ladders game of finding some kind of unattainable level of bliss, nor is it about flexing your spiritual prowess in a competition to be the most enlightened.

Rather annoyingly, it's often dismissed as a cute hobby that belongs in New Age retailers, but it's actually just good old-fashioned survival. More of us are finding our way into the non-judgemental-won't-reject-you arms of spirituality because it's rough living on this planet right now. There's only so much

Netflix and trying to offset your Amazon guilt that can distract you from chronic stress, a political climate that's uncertain to say the least, environmental threats to our planet, racism, the plethora of injustices that were highlighted during the COVID-19 pandemic and harmful levels of divisive rhetoric.

On a brighter note, spirituality is just who you *are*. We are all spiritual beings, but this isn't about love and lighting our way out of real life. Being spirit-informed is deeply and profoundly tethered to our humanness. We can now open our phones with facial recognition, instantly share a photo of our lunch to a global audience on social media and shout demands at Alexa and Siri, who have the artificial intelligence to run our lives; it's obviously time to advance from the version of spirituality that looks like packing up a bag and looking for inner peace on the other side of a mountain. It's time to move away from the spirituality that's filled with gatekeepers, hierarchy, superstition, privilege and a ton of confusing concepts – and that's the seed I hope to plant for you here.

No, but really, what exactly *is it?*

If you ask anyone for a definition of spirituality, you'll probably be met with a significant pause and shifting eyes. It's a hard one to sum up into words, but being able to define it is key to navigating your own interpretation of it. The one I've landed on and what we'll work through in this book, is:

Being spirit-informed is grounded in your human experience. It's the personal practices you use to connect to anything that guides you to return back to *you* and create.

Let's unpack that:

1. **Being spirit-informed is grounded in your human experience:** Most of this work comes from just living your life and working with everything that comes up. There aren't any shortcuts or hacks to side-step that; it's just you, existing. The only way to return back to *you* and create is to learn, understand and grow through your life experiences.

2. **It's the personal practices you use:** Your spiritual path is yours to curate and the practices you choose can be both exhaustive and ever-changing. For many, this looks like doing the inner work and some self-care. But it can also include energy healing, crystals, meditation, journalling, prayer, breathwork, witchcraft, divination, yoga, grounding, chanting and much more. The only requirements are that they benefit you and help you to connect. It need not look like anyone else's version of spirituality nor does it need to be complex or long.

3. **To connect to anything that guides you:** The emphasis is on the 'anything' because what you choose to connect to isn't anyone's business but your own. You'll see throughout the book that I call it spirit, but you can call it source, the divine, the universe, God, Goddess, light, the name of a deity or anything else that resonates. It's also fine if you're unsure about what you believe in right now; it's just something beyond (but also, within) you that's all-seeing, all-knowing and makes you feel held.

4. **To return back to *you*:** This is it, the feeling that's akin to fresh out of the womb wholeness. This is your true,

authentic self, you recognising that you're a spiritual being. The version of you that resides underneath who you *think* you are. This is where all the answers to the questions you have about your existence start to make some sense. This is your soul-level self and the version of you that's not confined to your body.

5. **And create:** When you're stepping into and seeing the world as who you really are, ready and waiting to make bold moves, up-level, love yourself without conditions and do the inner work, that's how you create your best damn life.

WHO GAVE ME PERMISSION TO WRITE THIS BOOK?

Seeing as we're about to spend a significant amount of time together, first and foremost, I'm definitely not a guru and I'm not perfect. I make mistakes, gossip, swear, stay up till 3am watching crime dramas, spend indecent amounts of money on false lashes and believe I should have been a meme-maker. No-one's trying to get you to become a martyr in the name of living a spirit-informed life, so do your thing – this is a judgement-free zone.

Officially, I'm a trauma-sensitive meditation teacher, tarot reader, Reiki master teacher and akashic records practitioner, and I'm always knowledge-seeking. Unofficially, I'm a space holder and a London-raised gal in her thirties, who left over a decade-worth of work in the fashion and beauty industry and is just trying to grow through life's episodes. I spend most of my time doing one-to-one sessions, group workshops and talks for people just like you – thousands of incredible people who I've had the privilege and honour to work with and witness as they make sense of what being a spiritual being in a human body is all about. From 18 months old to 80 years old, London to Bahrain, New York to Toronto, Mumbai to Krugersdorp, whether the focus is on getting over an ex, leaving a draining workplace or getting to know your intuition, spiritual practices have been a powerful ally for each and every one of them and I hope they will be for you too. This work has been the most precious gift because while each of my clients is uniquely different, with all kinds of diverse life experiences, we all have the same hopes, fears, questions and doubts. It's daily evidence of our shared humanity.

This isn't just what I *do* though, it's always been who I am. I was well aware that my churning childhood thoughts on human existence were somewhat different to my classmates, who were sticking pencils up their left nostril to incite brutal nose bleeds. These thoughts were exacerbated by the very unwelcome intrusion of seeing visions and having premonitions in my dreams. Dreams that had no place in my Catholic school, so I put them to the back of my mind. There's nothing quite like having a vivid vision of your paternal grandmother dying mid-class, then going home to find out that she did indeed die, to put you off anything spirit-based. I tuned out and focused on more important and innocuous things like learning dance routines and trying to understand boys instead. In my pre-teens, I still found myself being attracted to crystal bracelets and reading the heavy spiritual and self-help books on my auntie Wilma's bookshelf, which I didn't really understand, but was fascinated by. Then when I entered the ever so bewildering age of 15, I started reading about the law of attraction and in a desperate attempt to pass my G CSEs I tried my hand at manifesting and making my own rituals. It worked. It always worked and I started to understand that maybe I was onto something pretty powerful.

Unfortunately, it wasn't all about passing exams and manifesting everything from a move to NYC to meeting Sarah Jessica Parker. I live and breathe this work because I had to. My entire life is like a billboard-sized trigger warning, so viewer discretion is advised here. My mum spent three months in ICU after a routine hysterectomy went awry and nearly died as a result. I don't have a relationship with my dad and spent most of my life believing that he didn't love me. I was raped when I was 15 and my body stored all of that trauma for another 15 years until I recalled it on a retreat. I spent seven years in an emotionally and mentally abusive relationship. I've faced racial microaggressions just by existing, appalling treatment in most of the workplaces I've been in and have been stalked by anxiety attacks for years. Oh, and I was diagnosed with multiple sclerosis a month after I signed the contract for this very book that you're reading. Being spirit-informed is why I'm still here. Surviving, smiling, belly-deep laughing and thriving through all of it. I'm not preaching from a snake oil pedestal of 'healing' myself and asking you to buy whatever I'm selling so you can do the same. I still have rough days, but they are peppered into an enchanting life, and while there's no quick fix to creating your best life, all I do and still do every single day is the work that I share in this book and I am beyond grateful for it.

Of course, spirituality isn't a panacea and I've had a team of people and resources who've supported me on my healing journey. But, doing the inner work has been my constant during a life that at times felt incredibly hard to be in. It's why I didn't give up and even on the days that I didn't want to get out of bed, I saw a glimmer of possibility peeking out of my duvet. My practices are probably the only reason why I don't over-identify with any of the things I've been through. I know I am *not* all of those things. They're things I've experienced. Things I've lived with. Things I've moved into deep layers of healing with. Things I work on comprehending because I know that underneath it all I'm a light-filled being, just trying to show up for these human experiences (even the shitty ones) and advance through them. I've seen first-hand the role that spirituality has played in my clients' lives and it gives me goosebumps to see the inner world they've created and the shifts they've made in their outer world.

I certainly don't have all the answers, but I will work damn hard to inspire, prompt, guide and sometimes annoy you into finding your own. This book is less spiritual awakening and more about realising you have the power to create. It reminds me of when I come home at the end of a long day, disrobe, free the crystals from my bra, lie on the sofa and just breathe. We've been spiritually deceived into believing that we should hand over our autonomy to teachers, speakers and practitioners. That it's only then that we can 'find' ourselves even if we don't agree with everything they say. That our healing *only* comes via juices that don't work with everyone's digestive system, holding our arms in weird poses, meditating for a precise number of minutes, repeating a phrase over and over again or being told what to say and what not to say. That's not what's going on here. I want you to think critically about every single word in this book, to take what aligns with you the most, question what you're unsure of and discard what doesn't work for you. This still doesn't give me (or, anyone) the right to say harmful things or to assume that you can figure it out alone. It's just a reminder that your thoughts and choices always come first, because I have never lived in the uniqueness of your mind, body and soul. Inner work is full-spectrum work and this requires it to be physical, mental, emotional and spiritual. While I'm not an expert on life, I am an expert at staying in my lane and this book will be speaking primarily to the spiritual, because I won't do you the disservice of speaking on topics I don't know enough about. There might be some overlap, but fundamentally this is about the foundation of who you are. Being spirit-informed holds the pieces of who we are together and as you journey through this book, keep utilising the physical, mental and emotional practices, services, practitioners and people that will best support your spiritual growth. To assist with that, I'd really encourage you to check out the resources (page 269) before you dive into the book, where you'll find some tools to support you, including guidance on working through this with a therapist or other professional help.

WHAT IS THIS BOOK ABOUT?

This isn't yet another 65-step guide on how to manifest, but it's a route to create the life that you never thought would be possible for you. To do this, I wanted to keep things nice and simple, plus as the Sagittarian that I am, bluntness is my forte. So, the book is divided up into three parts:

1. *Look At Your Stuff*
2. *Work On Your Stuff*
3. *Get the Stuff You Want*

Consider it a cosmic soup that's mixed up with what I've lived through, worked with my clients on and the wisdom I've translated and channelled from spirit. Spirit is kind of my ghost-writer. Before every chapter, I go off and meditate, or chat to spirit (more on this later) and ask what I need to share with you. I'm well aware of how wild this sounds, but I then receive messages through streams of consciousness that I write down or see. I spend some time living the chapters and exploring concepts in my sessions, before writing it all up in a way that'll make sense to you.

Just in case you have triskaidekaphobia (fear of the number 13) and clocked that there are 13 chapters in this book and subsequently cursed my name, it's a deliberate choice. In *The Original Rider Waite Tarot Deck*, Death is the 13th card. I don't like to play favourites, but this is one of the richest cards in the deck for me. It's the card that often terrifies people, when in actual fact it's about soul-activating, story-releasing, letting go of who you thought you should be, ready for spirit-informed living and next-level transformation. It's a rebirth, a rechoosing, a recentring and most importantly an intense remembering. It's the pulse that beats through these chapters.

In the first section, we'll be **looking at your stuff,** and this is the awareness and introspection that accounts for so much of spirituality. I'll be guiding you to take it in so you can get to the core of both who you really are and who you *think* you are. To see all the stuff you might be carrying that might hold you back from seeing the spirit in you. When you can see that your life experiences shape how you respond and react to the world around you, you can then define your own relationship with spirit, that makes the most sense for your life.

Then you'll move onto **working on your stuff** and let's take a minute to look at the word 'work' here. There's a lot of eye-rolling at those who announce that they're 'doing the work'. This is not the work we associate with our day jobs, household chores or anything we often have a lot of resistance around, though. This isn't about spending days on end in solitude with your journal and your thoughts and never leaving the house. This is simply about the commitment and devotion to stepping fully into who you are, reclaiming your power and showing up for yourself every single day. Inner work is about having compassion, allowing yourself to feel everything you need to feel and having the courage and resilience to keep on going. It breathes through you both when you're loving life and also when things feel a bit stickier. You'll flow through seasons of 'doing the work' and seasons of 'living the work', and you get to call the shots on when you just need to pause and go out for dinner instead of pulling cards and processing. In this section, you'll explore how to connect to your intuition in a very doable way, find enjoyment even in life's pretty grim moments and give yourself an all-access pass to chilling.

Unfortunately, you can't skip ahead to **get the stuff you want** and I know the temptation is *so* real. Manifesting and creating the life you want isn't all about a Pinterest board full of fun things you wish you could buy. The *stuff* you want can be as expansive as you'd like. It can be not worrying if people are talking about you whenever you leave the house, having the confidence to change careers or just being able to tell people no. It's also how you witness the world around you. OK sure, it can also include the leather beauty from Saint Laurent that you've had your eye on. We'll explore your ability to create, how to connect to spirit, widen the scope of what manifesting is and kick out all of the myths you might have around finding your purpose.

Weaved into the pages of this book are some exercises and mini rituals. Being spirit-informed is a practice which, you guessed it, needs to be practised. While you'll have a fantastic time from just reading the book and ignoring the exercises, I did make a wildly bold statement about creating your best damn life and to get there the work has to be based on your *own* stuff. These are the exercises that I've done myself for over 17 years and the ones that have really helped all of my clients too. There's no way that you can miss or skip them, as they'll be right in your face. You'll spot the exercises as they'll all begin with **PAUSE, TAKE IT IN, AND** . . . so even if the page is unputdownable, take a breath, stop reading, take in what you just read, grab your journal or start a note on your phone and try to do the practice. As I said, you know yourself better than I can imagine you, so despite all of this, if anything doesn't feel good for where you're at, skip it or come back to it when you're feeling more resourced. Always listen to you, before me. The practices are short, effective and well-worth doing, if you are able. These pauses are also a lesson in themselves about rethinking the pause. We so often allow our minds and society to create these pauses in our lives that stop us from taking risks, reaching beyond our comfort zones and going against the grain. This big fear of being unsettled that makes us stop growing. The other side of that – the sacred, fierce, powerful side – is letting pauses be an arena for creation, integration and stillness where we return back to ourselves and invite spirit to the party. In other words, try your best to do the exercises, as your own self-inquiry is truly what doing this work is all about.

Doing inner work isn't just about personal responsibility. For some of you this might be solo work, but it doesn't have to be. It definitely isn't for me. To this day, I continue to work with an army of people, including a trauma therapist, breathwork facilitator, nutritionist, medical doctors, yoga teachers and, of course, my soul team of friends and family. Give people the permission to facilitate and accompany you; you're worthy of receiving that and you don't have to carry everything alone. Do whatever you need to do that will support and assist you in your own spiritual journey. This is also about collective responsibility, as a *lot* of change needs to happen on a societal level. Many of us have been harmed by the world around us and the people in it, so this is never all about you. When you look at your stuff, work on your stuff and get the stuff you want, that also includes going out into the world and sharing that. Collectives of change-makers, shift-creators and people who just demand more from the world around them all start from somewhere. Systems need to change, collective healing needs to happen, but they don't just come from thin air. They come from everyone doing their own inner work by taking it in and then bringing it out. That's how society changes. Every single person can make a difference, *you* make a difference and it's my deepest intention that some of that can start here.

Look At Your Stuff

ONE

What Stuff Are You Carrying?

There's a certain category of film that usually rates below 4.2 on IMDb, ripe for evenings when the indecision of finding something else to watch becomes too much to bear. After investing upwards of 50 minutes into the movie, the action-filled scene that bordered on improbable suddenly ends and the sweat-soaked character jolts up in bed, declaring that it was all a dream. *Seriously,* if only you could get a time refund for moments like this.

It's a pretty similar feeling to the idea that you're not who you *think* you are or you're so much more than who you think you are. It kind of sounds like a rip-off, right? Surely, it can't be *that* simple. It sounds rather frustrating, just like the 'it was all a dream' energy in those cinematic let-downs. But, it's true. There's so much internal mingling that happens in our heads. Thoughts of not being worthy enough bump into all the reasons why you shouldn't speak up. Whispers of why you can't do something grind up against why you don't think you'll ever thrive in your career. Then just as you believe that the networking mixer in your mind is wrapping up, you fall asleep listing all the bad decisions you've made since the day of your birth. It's a lot, but what causes us the most exhaustion is the belief that this is who we are. That we are only the ruminating thoughts, what we look like in the mirror or all of the adjectives that make up our bios. This isn't who we are, though, and it's not only a spiritual mic drop; it's also the way to make manifesting and spirituality feel more doable.

So, buckle up, grab your snacks, get your 'behind the wheel' playlist going and pee before you leave, because we're going on a trip. The kind of trip that's a lifetime in the making, the one where you can't stop researching routes and luxury hotels to do overnighters in, so a plane ticket ends up being cheaper than a couple of days in a car. Ready to go? The destination you can enter into your GPS is **creation**. We're going here, because the fact that you can *only* control your inner reality is actually your greatest superpower. When you work on your inner self, your outer reality shows up to match it. Basically, even in a world that feels distressingly out of our control, we can create our reality and, no, it doesn't involve you living in a blissfully ignorant bubble. You'll be in the thick of it with the rest of us; it's just your experience of it that will change. Creation isn't a literal destination where you arrive, stretch out your legs and say the work is done. It's an ever-evolving and episodic trip, where there'll be times when you feel like you've created your best damn life and times when, well, it'll just feel like you're entrenched in an abyss of your own misery.

Living a spirit-informed life leads to creation. It's that simple. That's the route. We stay in the car with spirit beside us, going and growing towards it. It wouldn't be a road trip unless there were some obstacles, though. Maybe you run out of petrol, there's some roadworks or a motorway full of traffic. All the things that determine how smooth a ride the trip to creation will be. All the thoughts, fears, experiences and beliefs that you *think* you are and identify primarily as, but you're actually not. All your stuff. That's it. No secret held under lock and key. No translation app to understand. We spend our lives carrying stuff around with us. It's piled up in the car with us, so sometimes it slows the car down, makes the route feel foggy or the destination feel like it's impossible to reach. Why does your stuff do that? Because, when you're transforming by way of the inner work, it's frightening. When you're spirit-informed, you're in the energy that arises when you return back to *you*. The road trip to creation is uncertain, it's unknown and we just don't know what life looks like when we're there, because it's not how we're used to being in the world. Just know this — you are *not* what you carry, but depending on what you have in there, it might make you believe that creation isn't possible for you.

YOU ARE NOT YOUR STUFF

While the pile of stuff we carry around is made up of both inner and outer stuff, it's not separate, individual piles, but more like an infusion of sorts. The inner stuff is the self-criticism saying you're not good enough and you never will be. It's the voice that makes an appearance in the fitting room, remarking that you should have refused that slice of cake at lunch. It's all the labels that society places on you. It's the part of you that thrives on self-sabotage. It's the part of you that might feel more nauseous than when you're experiencing mid-flight turbulence because you want to engage deeper in spirituality. It's the stuff that makes you terrified of returning back to *you* and wants you to go back to your usual life, as you've had enough with all this talk of growing. It's the stuff that looks like not wanting to be loud about who you are because what if you're mocked for it. A lot of our stuff is the seemingly bottomless pile of limiting beliefs, doubts and fears that we carry. The thoughts that probably led to you reading this book, the beliefs that have reached their expiry date, the fears that exhaust and frustrate you. They live within us like unwelcome visitors, coming out to play to pull us back and make us shrivel up. They're the stick we continually beat ourselves up with and it can be so confronting to look at it all.

In the past, some of the stuff that had the biggest impact on my life was that I had an 'issue' with money. I fully believed that money would never be something that I could accumulate or grasp. I hung onto it like it was my entire personal brand. All the inner work I did was around money, all the personal development books were about money. I spent nights in bed doing EFT tapping on my meridian points while I recited that I was a money magnet. This is where the outer stuff intersects and why it can't be separated up, because my money beliefs were quite obviously shaped by not having any money growing up. I'm from east London, the east London that came before it was both cool and expensive to reside there. I come from the east London where screams of 'ten for a fiver' in cockney accents rang out from the fruit and veg markets every weekend. I didn't have an understanding of money; we didn't really speak about it and I had all the toys I wanted. I didn't question why my Barbie had a bicycle instead of the sports car I asked for, but when you're an only child your imagination rivals every toy around anyway.

It was only when my parents broke up and we had to register

as homeless and live in temporary accommodation that I was slapped in the face with the unwelcome reality that we had no money. Still, I worked my way through college, university and beyond, so I didn't look at my stuff around it for a while, until I realised that it gave a salty flavour to absolutely everything in my life. I operated through the world with a filter of never being able to be someone who had money. My family even had a syndicate for the National Lottery, believing that those all-important six numbers would change our reality. The reality that was my grandparents and parents coming from the West Indies to the UK with nothing but their luggage and dreams. Working day in, day out, to be able to build a life here, a life that had a ceiling. A limit. Winning the lottery had to be the only way out. I jumped on the bandwagon too, insisting that with a couple of affirmations and visualising myself as a millionaire that I'd quickly be one.

Truth time – there's no amount of visualisation that can outwit systemic racism, poverty and personal experience. I came to realise that I didn't actually have a 'problem' with money, I didn't have a so-called lack or scarcity mindset and I didn't have a money 'block'. I'm just a Black woman and daughter of immigrants, who grew up in Tower Hamlets, London, which has the highest rate of child poverty in the UK. That's it. There would never be any three-step approach to manifesting money or impaired trust in the universe that would lead me to a full bank account without acknowledging and working through that first. This is the kind of outer stuff that spiritual teachings don't give much credit to as the focus usually goes straight to the ego. This limits us when we start to divide ourselves up into separate labels and boxes. An inclusive approach to manifesting or spirituality has to take our real experiences and circumstances into consideration.

Our outer stuff is just as important as all the untruths going around in our minds. The pile of outer stuff includes the conditioning and modelling that makes you believe that you're not of use unless you're doing acts of service, because that's what you witnessed growing up. It's the childhood in which you moved from school to school, so now feel uncomfortable being in the same place for too long. It's the economic, political and social realities of life that have shaped how you're treated in the world. There's so much bypassing rhetoric that happens in the spiritual space, which says things like, if you don't have a great relationship with money then you need to work on your ego, as that's what defines how you think about money. To then label someone as having a 'money mindset problem' or, even worse, 'it's just their ego talking' is limiting and reductive as it doesn't take into account that maybe they spent most of their life in financial insecurity. If we work with that model, it's easy to assume that everyone who has a great relationship with money has 'checked their ego' or done the work, when they may not have done either – they simply grew up with more money.

This work needs to be more practical and realistic for it to make sense of the complexity and differences of our shared human experience. It needs to be all-encompassing and balanced; instead of labelling ourselves into split parts of ego, inner child, shadow and so on. Parts that seem separate to ourselves, that we shout at, blame, think we need to reign in and whip into shape. Parts that not everyone will even be able to define, yet they've been made to feel like compulsory studies for accessing spirituality. We're quick to therapise, pathologise, label and box each other up, which adds to the feeling of something being wrong with us, when there isn't. This work has to work for everyone. So, in the most uncomplicated way, everything that we've witnessed and experienced in our human bodies is what all this stuff is.

It's like when you head to check-in at the airport, and are asked if you packed your bags yourself and if you're carrying anyone else's stuff. The truth? We're always carrying other people's stuff. In fact, we're covered and soaking wet with it. When we came into this lifetime, we weren't carrying anything, but other people and society started piling stuff in there. Load after load of it, seeping into us and becoming a domino effect of stuff that ripples out beyond them and even us. My father's dad was abusive, so he didn't get to receive the paternal love that can charge a heart up; in turn, he didn't know how to express his own love. That's his stuff. It boiled into mine because I never felt connected to him, never knew what it felt like to sit in the security of a father-daughter relationship. That then became me learning how to regain trust and belief in men, to be able to love myself even in the face of uncertainty about someone's love for me. That's my stuff. Look at how the dominoes fall. The dominoes that give us the chance to see that it was never about us, to not excuse the pain that was caused but to have empathy for what they were carrying that led to it.

That's why it's so important to recognise the outer stuff we're carrying is mixed with the inner stuff. Outer stuff is also other people's rules and expectations, which we allow to be our own stories. If an ex-partner told you that you were too loud, you then believe that you're too loud. If an employer says that you're lazy, you then agree that you must be lazy. It's also the reliance on the outer world and looking for joy only in the things around us. It's the judgements we've experienced because of the colour of our skin, age, gender and who we're sexually attracted to. It's the stuff we carry that makes us want to keep people away and say no to their support, as we think we have to carry it alone as a sign of our strength; when we don't. Someone will always help you carry your stuff, if you allow them to.

PAUSE, TAKE IT IN, AND . . .
Know Your Stuff

Write out some of the inner and outer stuff you're carrying in each of the sections below:

- Relationship with myself
- Work, career and money
- Relationships with other people

Here are some examples to assist you:

I believe that I will never be in a loving relationship because of what's happened to me in the past . . .

I have a fear that I can't make money doing what I love . . .

I think that I'm not smart enough to share my voice . . .

I always tie my worth to my productivity . . .

Don't Shame Your Stuff

Let's get something straight here, we're not stopping off at judgement station. When I use the word 'obstacle' in relationship to your stuff, it isn't a negative nor a burden. It's something that might come up as a challenge, but can be transmuted into an opportunity. You don't need to label your stuff in any way that will make you shame or judge it. We just have it. As you sit with the stuff you're carrying, be gentle with yourself. It didn't just pop into your head one day, it's not a 'you problem' – it came from your human experiences. I find reality TV, namely *The Real Housewives* franchise and dating contests to be a solid barometer on most topics. I've lost count of the times when someone has been dismissed for having 'too much baggage'. Baggage implies that there's a problem, that you've almost lived a bit *too* much for some people's liking. It suggests that some people have baggage and others don't. But we all have stuff. If you've lived a life, you have stuff. We need to stop the shared shame that we've attached to just existing. Plus, do you know how much unexpected magic one can find in the lost baggage department at the airport?

Think of it this way, you're walking home with some blue Ikea bags (how iconic). All filled with stuff, maybe some frozen meatballs, saccharine-scented candles and artificial terrariums. How you carry this stuff impacts how you navigate your journey home. Some of us might get a ride home, for a quicker trip. Some might risk it all and get on public transport, and experience the compassion of a stranger lending them a seat. Some might end up carrying a split bag at chest height, which then obstructs their view and causes them to trip over. Some might be carrying a bag of delicate ceramics, which makes them walk slower and carefully. It's not about how heavy or light your stuff is, but what your stuff consists of and how it makes you feel.

We look at what's in there because our stuff determines how we see, respond and move through the world around us. If people-pleasing is your go-to and you struggle to choose yourself first, that's part of your stuff. When you see yourself *as* a people-pleaser, identify with that label and judge yourself for it; it's an obstacle that's handed to you for you to grow through, if you so desire. This growth might look like releasing the label and saying, 'actually, I'm not a people-pleaser, based on my stuff, I just put people's comfort above my own, so I'm learning how to prioritise myself.' The stuff you carry are not problems, they're opportunities to see who you are underneath, so you can choose if you are resourced enough to overcome them and move into creation.

So many industries thrive on us labelling ourselves as flawed, and sell us back fixes, products and solutions with a whiff of superiority. Your stuff isn't 'blocking your blessings' and you don't need to pay someone to 'remove them'. We must also be mindful as while looking at and working on your stuff can be incredibly healing, there's nothing wrong with you. Never allow anyone to use your stuff as a way to hold authority over you. It's unacceptable if anyone, spiritual teachers and coaches included, says that you have to 'remove some of your limiting beliefs' if you simply don't agree with them, don't want to do something or question them. In fact, feel free to delete anyone who passive-aggressively tells you that you need to 'do the work' if they don't like what you say. It's your choice and yours only.

Having a chat with yourself about the stuff you're carrying is a meaningful way to step out of self-blame and into understanding. For this, you need to pull out the receipts. It might be a mental folder or something physical, but this is almost the comeback for your stuff. If you're scared of letting people in, in case you get hurt, because you've been hurt before, what are your receipts to prove that the opposite is true? You might write a list of friends or family who haven't hurt you or were really glad when you asked for support. You might think about the fact that just because you've been hurt by specific people in the past, everyone is different and you have no evidence that this will happen again, as the future isn't here yet. If some of the stuff you're carrying is a lack of pleasure in your life because you find it easier to be busy with work, what are your receipts for the opposite? You could list all the things that make you smile but go unnoticed, like your morning coffee or weekend walks; you can find the things you found pleasurable in the past and see if you need to experience some new fun things. The receipts we bring up can provide some clarification and let us see the opportunity instead of blaming ourselves for having the stuff in the first place.

PAUSE, TAKE IT IN, AND . . .
Fact Check Your Stuff

Look at some of the stuff that you wrote down in the exercise on page 10. For each one, ask yourself:

1. Where did this come from?
2. What receipts do I have, to prove that the opposite might be true?
3. What might it be here to teach me?
4. How would it feel if I stopped believing this?

THE ROAD TO CREATION

When we're hanging out on our road trip, the stuff we carry makes us want to look for the lovely country lane, aka the road of least resistance, rather than the road to creation. As we move from one experience to the next, the country lane feels more tempting. It's the road of what we believe is possible and most comfortable, especially when we believe that safety and sameness are one and the same, even if doing the same thing isn't in our best interest. The country lane is a chill ride, there's some sweet things outside the window, you might have to wait for some sheep to pass, but you get to breathe in all that unpolluted air while you do so. It's the kind of lane that you know as intimately as the characters of a much-loved show that you watch on repeat.

If you don't know anyone from your hometown who's decided to split their time between three cities in the world, that might be a story you carry. You'll believe that it's not possible for you either. The country lane you drive down will be the one where you get a stable, nice job and constantly say the infamous words of Wes Nelson from *Love Island*, 'I'm happy, but I could be happier.' Instead, looking at your stuff might make you realise that the story from your hometown is not *your* story, and that maybe you're supposed to be the first one to do the bold thing. That might be the push to drive down the road to creation and make it happen. The road to creation is an unexpected one – there are challenges and maybe a congestion charge; we have no idea what's around every street corner, but the destination is always epic.

Now that you have some idea of the stuff you're carrying, the ways to work through it all are exclusive to you. I remember when my best friend, Becky, decided to wear my Adidas Gazelles to her yoga class. We wear the same shoe size, but she came back with blisters. We didn't account for the fact that my feet were broader, our toenails may be formed differently and the arch of our heels mismatched. Just as we can't assume that everything you're carrying can be worked through in the same way, with the same tools. The work is personal. I had to do a lot of work on not leaving situations too early with men. Truthfully, midway through a date I'm planning an exit strategy and ready to get the hell out of there. I've also worked with therapists to understand what red flags (for me) actually are and when I'm just a bit scared. So, my work is in needing to stay a bit longer.

My regular client Danielle often stays in one-sided situations for longer than she should, due to fear of expressing her needs and wanting to be liked. She can't heed the same advice I give myself, as staying will not always serve her. The same for people in abusive or toxic relationships. That's why seeing what stuff we're carrying, and deeply understanding, is the only way to begin to unpack it in a way that works for us. It's also key to not reading a one-size-fits-all quote online and blindly following it. Given my stuff, a quote set against a pretty aesthetic background that says to dump someone who doesn't look at you a certain way, will convince me to jump to the dump, even though they're a really lovely human. Depending on our stuff, we'll always look for a way to co-sign and confirm whatever we have in there. But this might not always work in our favour. If you believe that you're unlovable, an 'if they *really* love you then they will . . .' nugget might convince you that someone doesn't love you, unless it's in the specific way that the article says. The stuff we carry makes us look out for assumptions instead of evidence, to prove that the untrue stories we have about ourselves are indeed true. When you intimately know your stuff, you understand that this particular advice will either benefit you or it won't. It's why I don't believe in formulas, processes and strict steps and rules to follow in this work; what works for someone else may not work for you. Remember: the same pair of shoes will not fit everyone who wears the same shoe size.

You don't even have to be ready to look at all your stuff today, tomorrow or anytime soon, if you don't feel resourced enough. Once we're aware of our stuff, that alone can be the invitation into it being transformed into something else. The goal is not to completely remove your stuff and have a blank slate; you might end up having more compassion with it, forgiving yourself for some of the things you said to yourself or it just might not feel so unbearable to carry. When you're struggling, don't expect it to feel the same as any other time you might have experienced hard things before.

There have been moments in my life when I've worked through a hard experience alone, but there have been traumatic experiences when I reached out and got help. The practices that assisted you before might not assist you this time, so check in and see how you're feeling and let that be the guide to how you respond. Sometimes we just cannot deal with something and that is OK. You also never, ever have to do anything that you really don't want to do, in order to 'grow'. That isn't a sign of strength. Your agency is your power. Spirit isn't keeping track on the actions you choose to take, so trust what comes up for you and what your capacity is. This is where it's important to recognise the crossover between spirituality and mental health. If your stuff stems from trauma, abuse, depression or just feels too heavy to carry alone, bring support and resources in (there's some at the back of this book). You can also rest what came up for you and come back to it when you feel called to. There's something very significant that Glennon Doyle says in *Untamed*:

'I know this, but I don't know it today'. Remind yourself of this on the days when you know that comparing yourself to a celebrity will make you feel awful, but you do it anyway. Sometimes all we can do is just let it be. There's always tomorrow to look at it. In that moment, have some compassion and softness for yourself instead.

Sometimes the relationship we have with our stuff is an opportunity to love ourselves – I know you want to gag at that little self-love mention, but hear me out. When I was growing up, my mum had a duffel bag full of hair rollers, tools and products. There was always a white and green bottle of Sofn'free moisturiser nestled in there, the same familiar bottle I saw when walking into the Black hair shops in Dalston. Although my brain and tongue were always tangled with how to pronounce the name, as I watched my mum spread it over her hair it soon became a childhood affirmation. 'Sofn'free. I can be soft and free.'

This is a memo to be soft with yourself when you judge yourself for your stuff, regret doing something that you didn't want to do, feel paralysed by fear or angry at yourself for having doubts. Your mind wants to hungrily eat all of your pain, so it can fix it, understand it, diminish yourself because of it and get attached to it. It doesn't see that it's the heart's job to love that pain up.

How can you be soft and free? How can you release the need to overthink it and find the why of it? Can you instead wrap yourself up in a weighted blanket by letting your stuff just be there? To have compassion because you are the way you are because of all the stuff that you're carrying, but knowing it isn't all that you are. Maybe within your pain and stories you can see an opportunity to love yourself more fully and deeply.

This is what a daily commitment to yourself looks like. It's a promise to show up for yourself, so you can throw out the pressure of needing to fix the stuff you've uncovered here. Awareness is the majority of the work and the remaining piece is what you actually do with it. When you're shooting for awareness, you're able to see that this is the stuff you've been carrying, to acknowledge that there's a part of you that's been running all this over and over in your head without ever getting to the much-anticipated series finale. You can then remove the self-berating that comes when you're not eyes-wide-open aware of your stuff and being gentle with yourself because of it. You can release the mistruths of there being something wrong with you. Your stuff is what you're carrying, it isn't all that you are. Just the fact that you're even aware is honestly most of the work. When you get to this awareness, you know what it's about when you resist looking at something like your bank account, for example, or immediately spend any income because you're accustomed to seeing a low number in there. You're able to see that this stems from the inner and outer stuff you carry about money. Nothing bad, problematic or negative, not an issue, not a new label to give yourself. Just some stuff. Stuff that was born out of your experience in your human body. Stuff that will feel easier to be with, even if it takes a while and some collective or systemic work to do so.

Being spirit-informed is to recognise that you're a spiritual being, just because you're here. Spirituality isn't a private member's club, because we are *all* spiritual beings, as we *all* exist. If Earth is your address, then you've been in the club since you were born. It's who you *really* are, the authentic, bold, confident, in-your-worth, heart-bursting-open, audacious, powerful, intuitive, gasses yourself up, willing to grow, soft, unapologetic being. It's the energy you're in when you're ready to take risks and level up. It's the soul-level part of you that continues to exist even when your physical body doesn't. This is why it's so important to hold and acknowledge all your stuff, because this is the place where we create from. This is what it feels like to return back to *you*. It's from this place that we get to ask ourselves:

How would it feel if I said to myself that I choose to believe that I'm good enough, worthy enough, brave enough?

You may not fully believe it, but you can set the intention to get there, to allow your stuff to move and teach you, because sometimes it's just too heavy to carry the opposite. In these moments, when we aren't there yet, we can ask spirit to help us carry some of it.

PAUSE, TAKE IT IN, AND . . .
Hand it Over to Spirit

You can close your eyes if that feels comfortable and say something like this, or even better, write your own:

Spirit, please guide me into seeing that all the stuff I'm carrying is not who I am. I honour not only how hard it feels to carry all of this, but I'm grateful for the opportunity to grow through whatever I'm going through. Please show me the direction I need to travel in so I can return back to who I am underneath it all. I ask that you show me how I can find greater compassion and understanding for myself, to love myself through it all, and to help me carry it all when I'm not sure how to. Thank you.

Having the courage and willingness to look at your stuff is spir-it's push to show you that you have the power to create an extraordinarily rich life. We're never given any stuff to carry that we can't overcome; it doesn't mean that we have to, but it's an opportunity to. To have courage means sitting in all of it and knowing that we'll find some kind of peace, resolution or magic from doing it. We work incredibly hard to flee from feeling any pain without realising that pain eventually ends and life moves on. It continues and, as it does, the possibility for hope and change will come crashing in like unexpected seaside waves that reach your knees. It's the same reason why we allow our-selves to be distracted by staying friends with people we don't actually like, watching 12 seasons of not-so-funny sitcoms and working overtime without any compensation. We're scared of what we'll have to feel if the distractions end and we're left with ourselves. All the demanding thoughts, fears, doubts and beliefs; all the things we've pushed down as we were afraid that it would be too painful to feel. But what's left behind is who we are. It allows there to be integration with all our stuff, instead of the in-fighting we love to do with ourselves. There will be parts of who you are that you may not always understand, and parts that might confuse you. There will be parts of you that you're obsessed with at times and grateful for at others. They're all special pieces of you and they're all designed to help in your spiritual growth and that's ultimately why we're here. To grow and to create.

TWO

It's Not Always a Smooth Ride

In late 2018, I found myself lying on the itchy carpet of a Santa Monica crystal shop. As the past-life regression practitioner guided us through some grounding breaths, I was very aware of the chunk of amethyst I had carefully placed in my Agent Provocateur bra, making a dent in my nipple. I was also aware that in a room full of people clad in galaxy-printed yoga pants, that my midi-dress was probably not the appropriate attire for traversing my subconscious mind. Little did I know that this would be the very night that I'd stop being so afraid of death.

The grand old D-word. When you look at the size and length of the word, in relation to the breadth of this page you're reading, it's just five letters. Kind of like a piece of microplastic floating in the ocean. But, the heaviness, fear and anxiety of the word actually feels like the ocean itself. We may not think about it every day, but the fear of dying lingers on us, like perfume-tainted jumpers that still smell of tuberose even after three spin cycles. Our fear of pain governs our decisions, our reluctance to suffer stops us in motion and our refusal to feel anything other than good, results in stagnancy. All because on some level the inevitability of death freaks us the hell out and reminds us of how we really can't control anything that happens outside of us. I have an open mind about everything and always believe in other people's spiritual experiences, but I don't put my entire BMI behind anything unless I've experienced it myself. I'd read about past lives and the concept of reincarnation before, but I had to weigh this up with what Father Peter said at church every Sunday when I was younger. In no uncertain terms, we were told that we have one life, we die, we turn to dust and then we'll end up in heaven or hell. I always pictured heaven and hell like two rooms in a nightclub, one filled with air-conditioned fun and the other filled with all the bothersome kids in my class. There wasn't any space for reincarnation here, and as Eminem said, 'You only get one shot, do not miss your chance to blow, this opportunity comes once in a lifetime.' Or, does it?

LIFE AFTER LIFE

During my past-life regression, I had one of the most vivid visualisations I've ever encountered. I discovered that in one of my past lives my name was Mahala, which means 'tender' and is of Hebrew origin. I was in a verdant forest surrounded by babies and pregnant women, and I seemed to be a doula. Fast forward to now and it makes all the sense in the world, as I've always been a bit *too* curious about childbirth, much to the annoyance of my friends who unexpectedly receive texts with open-legged shots of crowning, bloody and vernix-coated babies. Clearly all this time

I've just been filling the shoes of my inner past-life doula. This was the first in a series of mind-boggling experiences of exploring my past lives and those of my clients and using the knowledge to make sense of and guide us through this one.

During an akashic records session (where I connect to a vibrational archive of your soul and its journey through your different lifetimes, to gain insight and guidance, kind of like a spiritual Siri), my client Aria wanted to discuss her career. She was struggling in her role as a PR manager and didn't trust that her ideas were relevant unless she was told they were. She had employers who told her she was pessimistic and she found herself craving positive feedback. I asked the records what was going on here and spirit showed me a past life where Aria was an artist who enjoyed spending much of her time in solitude, but struggled to show her work publicly in case it wasn't admired. This past life helped her to release some of the fears she was carrying as it prompted her to see that if her soul has experienced so much more than she thought, she could live and work more confidently now, without the need to be affirmed by others.

Past lives aren't just cool stories to share during the lull of dinner party chatter. They made me fully understand life, fear and death in a way that I hadn't before. I understood that my soul continues – it ain't going nowhere – and while it can't consciously remember all the exciting and probably very traumatic lives I had before this one, it will continue to be here even when the female, size 8–12 (depending on the year), 5ft 5in, British-born, physical me dies. That's just the body my soul is wrapped in for this current lifetime. With that understanding, I started to see death as something that works in a bit of a circle. Something transformational. That with every death comes an inevitable rebirth. Not necessarily in a direct way, but there's always a rebirth. To live is to die and to die is to live. I was always terrified of ending up in an oversized coffin wearing a mediocre outfit that someone had chosen for my body to inhabit for the rest of eternity. I was terrified of the end being painful and lonely, because only so many people can die serenely in their sleep. I was terrified of everyone I loved dying and leaving me desperately alone and trying to figure out how to adult successfully.

Then I slowly started to release my fear. While I'm not ready to die and I'm not ready for my loved ones to die, there's an inevitability about life and also death. It's going to happen. It's not something that's easy to grasp or like, it isn't something that's easy to accept, but it's going to happen. We can hold and support each other through the painful impact that death has on us, while we also try to release some of the crushing fear of it. Well, less the fear of dying and more the impact that the fear has on how we live. It reminds me of something that Ram Dass said: 'The caterpillar doesn't say "well now I'm going to climb into this cocoon and come out a butterfly." It's just an inevitable process, it's inevitable, it's just happening, it's got to happen that way.'

PAUSE, TAKE IT IN, AND . . .
Feel Alive

Just breathe in your own time, in your own way, for a few minutes. As you breathe, connect to the vastness of who you are. Step out of everything you were just doing and reading and tune into how it feels to be alive. Right now. In this moment.

To not feel good all the time, to not know what's coming and to not have control is to be alive. We don't like that suffering, misery, fear and pain are part of the agreement of being in this human experience. We've got ourselves into a bit of a pickle, as we believe that we signed a happiness contract on our way into this life. We believe that we were contractually obligated to feel good and we spend our entire lives searching for it like a discounted candle in TK Maxx. Everything around us convinces us that we're only here to be happy. So, we live in a never-ending spinning class of wanting. Wanting more things, more stuff and more people to make us feel good. We pick the country lane not only because it's familiar and safe, but because the world and other people benefit from us picking that lane. When we're always in the 'I'm kinda happy, but I could be happier' energy we will do whatever it takes to not be there. The world would stop if we weren't praying for external things to fulfil this need. Imagine if we didn't believe that we needed a Net-a-Porter box full of clothes to be happy. That we didn't need a £30,000 wedding to be happy or to continuously search for a perfect job.

Think about all the things you do in an attempt to be happy, an emotion that is subject to change and is as unique as a fingerprint in how each of us defines and experiences it. If we were all going to have happiness here, then why isn't everyone always happy? If we were obligated to have happiness, surely we should all be suing for breach of contract by now. We didn't sign any contracts to be here. We're here to learn through our stuff, to be students not professors of life. Being a student is experiential. We can't jump straight to graduation; we have to go through the conveyor belt of Starbucks coffees and late nights believing that crying is the only way to reach the essay word count. To feel good in life is also to experience sadness, to be in love we have to know heartbreak, to feel peace we absolutely need to feel fear. We'll continue to be disappointed in life if we see it as anything other than something to feel into, be curious about and grow through. Something to just be in. There's plenty of love, happiness and joy up for grabs here, but we need to be OK with experiencing the opposite too. When we become attached to this fantastical feel-good contract, we will inevitably think that there's something wrong with us when we're unhappy and afraid. We slip into blame easier than sliding our feet into a tan sandal, believing that we must have done something to end up in this state of unease. We're quick to think that we're being punished when something goes awry: 'Here we are yet again, more ridiculous things happening to me, because they always do. Why me?' But, why not you? Why not any of us? Diamonds don't ask this when they're grown out of incredible pressure and heat, nor do volcanoes that violently erupt and in turn create more than 80 per cent of the Earth's surface, or babies who pass through pelvic bones, or the female octopuses that engage in all kinds of self-destructive behaviours after they lay their eggs, like starving to death or eating parts of their own tentacles. It's rough out here, but all the pain and uncertainty of it is why the universe exists. The pressure, pain and fear of it all facilitates transformation. It brings new life.

We've quite literally been dying since the moment we got here, as it's not this one moment at the end. As we live, we are in the process of dying and living is so damn wonderful, yet we are so afraid to live. The fear of death births all the other fears we have. In the same way that we have such little control over knowing when and how we'll die, our fear of not being in control also causes us to not live the life we've always wanted to. When we release the idea that our road trip will always be a smooth ride and instead couple up with the fears we have of what's next, we can grow through the obstacles we're handed. Our fears are like the sneaky pair of shoes at the bottom of a suitcase that contributes at least 6kg to your 23kg baggage allowance. They take up a lot of weight in the stuff we carry and I sum them up as the Three 'U's — fear of the Unknown, Unexpected and Uncertain. The emotions we hate being in because we want to know that we will be safe and, of course, happy. When we're carrying the Three 'U's we don't know if any of that will be true.

PAUSE, TAKE IT IN, AND . . .
Know Your Fears

In each of the sections below, write out your biggest fears and doubts, and see how they're impacting your life:

- Relationship with myself
- Work, career and money
- Relationship with others

Here are some examples to assist you:

I'm afraid that if I'm vulnerable with others I'll be rejected, so I'm not letting people support me . . .

I'm scared of sharing my spiritual side with people in case they laugh at me, but I really want to be open about who I am . . .

I just want to know if this job is right for me . . .

YOU CAN'T CONTROL WHAT'S OUTSIDE THE CAR

I recite the words of Nina Simone to myself at least once a day: 'I'll tell you what freedom is to me: no fear. I mean really, no fear!'* I say it so often because it's the thread making its way through all my client work. Forget all our physical, mental and emotional differences; one thing that unites us all is fear. The fear might look very dissimilar from me to you to someone else, but we all have it. When I'm doing one-to-one sessions, especially grounded tarot readings, my clients come with at least one fear, a very normal fear. The fear might be worrying whether they've made the right decisions in their life, fear that they'll fail in their job, fear that their partner is no longer in love with them, fear that they won't make enough money to have an easygoing lifestyle, fear of the unknown, fear of uncertainty, fear of the unexpected and even fear of what will come up in the actual tarot reading.

You name it, there's most likely a fear accompanying it. You want the relief of being told that everything will be OK, that *you'll* be OK. The certainty of having someone tell you that your life will work out just fine and loosen the grip that fear has. While your fears feel excruciatingly real, they are fake news, false facts and just truly untrue. Let's take my emetophobia (fear of vomiting), which is placed in all Three 'U's. I haven't thrown up since I was four years old and I have no intention of ever doing it again. My fear of throwing up is *very* real, because

* *Nina: A Historical Perspective* directed by Peter Roddis, 1972

why else do I hibernate during norovirus outbreaks, carry Pepto-Bismol and activated charcoal in my bag, and wince at the mere thought of street food? What lies beneath my phobia is neither true or real. I assume that if I throw up, I just won't stop. That I will be remembered as the unfortunate woman who was wedded to the toilet bowl for the rest of her adult life. I assume that if I vomit then all manner of despicable things will happen to me, that I will panic, choke, lose control and eventually die on the bathroom floor.

If you've ever doubted your creativity, simply look at the Olympian efforts your mind makes to jump to unrealistic conclusions, to prove how creative you actually are — catastrophic delusions at their very finest, 'dress-rehearsing tragedy,' as Brené Brown says. In other words, this is the very definition of fake news, because I don't even remember what it's like to throw up. Casual and well-meaning vomiters always assure me that it's pretty unpleasant but by no means life-altering, so I actually have no receipts to support my fear. So, the work to step out of these fears we carry, or to at least get comfortable with them, is to date them a bit, explore and understand them. But most importantly to feel into the resistance of them. As hard as it is, we can survive not feeling good for a bit. We're always one text, email or breaking news notification away from something jarring.

While shifting our perception of fear can create profound shifts in our lives, the starting point is always to feel whatever you need to first. Never minimise just how hard it feels to be in your fears or any of the stuff you're struggling with. The same goes for other people — when someone is scared, don't dismiss it, tell them to rise above it or, even worse, that being human is all an illusion and we have tons of lifetimes left. Not a single person wants to hear that even if you think it might help. Instead, let them in and hear their pain and fears, if you have the capacity to.

Have a picnic with all your emotions and make room for not even knowing what you're feeling. Just allow them all to be there. It's only then that you can move on to what's next. The 'next' is yours to define as there's no shelf life on emotions; you can be in them for as long as you need to. Cosied in on this picnic blanket of feelings are empty spaces that are longing for the warmth of people to support, hold and witness what you're going through. Let them in too. When we stand up and explore what's next, we can start to feel the hunger-pang sensation that rises up and out of us, the rumblings that allow us to see that maybe our stuff can be a catalyst for growth and wisdom. Something that can teach us. Something that makes us human. Something that feels *real* heavy, but we get to sit back and see that we are *more* than the situation and fear that we're in. That even when we're so deeply tethered to how grim and scary something is, we have within us this innate ability for change.

PAUSE, TAKE IT IN, AND . . .
Pinpoint Your Emotions

Google search an image of an 'Emotions Wheel'. Keep it as a reference when you notice you're feeling some resistance, fear or are just a bit stuck and use it to pinpoint some of the emotions you're experiencing. Label them, notice how they feel in your body. Our feelings aren't always what is true, but give yourself permission to be in them.

When you are desperate to be in control of the experiences that happen 'outside the car', know that there are two outcomes in every life situation: what you would like to happen and what you would not like to happen. There's a sense of security when we focus on what we *would* like to happen. When we spend all our energy focusing on what we don't want to happen, we don't want to act, in case it happens. We don't send the text, sky dive, move house, tell a friend that they've hurt us or speak up at work. We forget that within these two outcomes there's a world of possibilities. Whether it's what you wanted to happen or not, you'll travel through them both and learn something either way. Within what you wanted to happen could be a bunch of unknown things that you didn't ask for or expect. At other times we'll find out when we make a decision, trusting that there aren't any right or wrong ones, decisions are just decisions. Spirit will pivot, adapt and quite literally shape-shift you to where you're supposed to be. There will always be something there, even if the experience feels downright brutal.

One of my clients was working through exactly that. She had nearly every material thing she wanted in life, but was stuck in the Three 'U's and didn't know what to do next. She was doubting her ability to make any decision about her future and also if it would be an aligned one. It's the same fear of making the wrong decision that stops a lot of us from moving forward. We explored every option we possibly could, discussing the fears she had about moving cities because she was worried she'd pick the wrong one and regret it, and the worry she had about being able to start a family. Our session ended in the same place of just not knowing what would happen and being OK with not knowing what will happen. It's our work to find some level of peace with it. We have to find the space for uncertainty to exist without the need to find the answer.

The answer can sometimes be felt into and processed, but sometimes we just won't know until the future arrives.

We resist what worries us and what we can't control because we have an in-built system of protection. As troublesome and inconvenient as it feels when you're in it, we're designed to be kept safe and alive, which is quite lovely to be honest. From your body responding to stress by initiating the fight-or-flight response because it has sniffed out a threat, to autoimmune diseases that cause your immune system to get all confused and start attacking your own body by mistake. The intention is pure, although there's a tendency for confusion.

The stuff we carry causes us to believe in the myth that we're safest in the familiar, in what we know and what we can control. Whenever you get close to creating, that's when the trash-talk you say to yourself gets louder and you'll do anything to avoid making a decision. Recognising this, all we can do is date our fears, talk them out and journal them at length. To make so much room for them that we exhaust ourselves with all the possible outcomes and realise that we will never have certainty about what will happen when we make the decision. But, what's the alternative? You stay in fear or you just see what happens? Fears take away our hopefulness and make us question everything so that we stop trying to get the stuff we want. We stop everything. We stop wanting more, different and better. We stop moving. There's little optimism when fear comes knocking at the door. The only antidote for it is faith and trusting that spirit will always reveal what's next, when you need to know what's next. We just never know what will be waiting for us on the other side of our fears. Not living or moving forward doesn't work for us, because we just don't know what's coming. Instead, we assemble our tools of softness when we have courage over fear. These tools are to hold ourselves, to breathe, to allow our community, loved ones and space holders to be with us when we do what is difficult. To love ourselves through the stickiness that life offers us.

When a fear feels like it's becoming bigger than you, and starting to change your behaviours or actions, here's a question to ask yourself: so, what would I do if I wasn't afraid? It's a question that opens up a wardrobe of Narnia-esque possibilities, giving us the opportunity to see how much bigger life could look without fear, to see a glimpse of the freedom we could have without it. If I wasn't afraid of throwing up, I would be able to eat anything I wanted when I travel, I wouldn't have palpitations around drunk people, worry about taking every single medication and be able to be excited about any future pregnancies without needing to see how likely I'll be to get hyperemesis gravidarum. I would be free. If you weren't afraid of failing, how would you live your life? If you weren't afraid of what people thought of you, what would you do? How magic-filled could your life be if you weren't afraid? Knowing that within the question lies the answer that we fear. In so many ways we're afraid of getting the stuff we want, because it's scary to believe that we have the power to create it. It's hard to think about living an uncertain life, when we believe that we have certainty and contentment in the life we live in now, because we presume we know what to expect in it. As much as we can go into what we would do if we weren't afraid, we can also push into what's the worst that could happen. Hanging out there is sometimes exactly what we need to play with to realise it might not be as disastrous a life as we think it'll be. Stepping out of our fears requires change and, as we know, change does not sound like safety. It's safer to believe that we can't make things happen, to stay in the smallness that we're conditioned to be in. It's easier to believe that life is about all the things we might potentially lose, instead of all we can gain when we take a walk outside of our fears.

PAUSE, TAKE IT IN, AND . . .
Explore Your Fears

Date your fears and see what comes up as you spend some time with them. Ask yourself for each one:

1. Where did this fear come from?
2. What receipts do I have, to prove that the opposite is true?
3. So, what would I do if I weren't afraid?

AVOIDING ISN'T LIVING

It's when we shift away from the idea that we're only here to experience the good stuff that we can start living and actually get to *more* of the good stuff. It's like a cruel joke, but because we're so afraid of the Three 'U's we do just about anything to avoid them. We fight for our right to know what's coming and to feel good, with as much vigour as Floyd Mayweather inching towards a win. It feels easier to fight for that than to step out of the ring and say that we are here to experience life in its entirety with every single beautiful and gross human emotion. Using these experiences to draw us closer to creation. We can't be sanitised versions of human beings as to do so means we are *not* humans and this isn't an episode of *Black Mirror*. Our intuition, authenticity and inner power are who we are, and that always goes beyond what we can see, believe and conceive. When your mind says that you will never get over being ghosted by the person you were dating and your body backs it up by unleashing a mason jar full of tears, this isn't all there is. Spirit can always see more than that. Spirit can always see your potential as a being that will never cease to exist. It sees what you have been through in this life right here, your past lives and probably the ones to come.

When you go inwards, listen to who you really are and examine the stuff that's in the way. If what you hear is to do something larger-than-life, then it's because you know you can. If what you hear is that you'll get through something, it's because you know you can. If what you hear under the noise is that you'll get over this moment, it's because you know in your core what's waiting on the other side. All we have to do is listen to that inner truth, as it will always show us who we are, even when we want to avoid it.

The one thing that I love to avoid is vulnerability, especially with men. That's part of my stuff I carry around with me. I continue to work on it so most of the time it feels lighter than a powerlifter lifting a 1.5kg dumbbell. However, there's many times when vulnerability lives rent-free in my box of things that make me feel absolutely terrified. I was once influenced by *The New York Times* Tiny Love Stories column and decided to write a 100-word story about a man that I had feelings for. I mean, I detailed that he felt like home, so you can imagine that the resistance I felt to sharing it with him was enough to make all my internal organs violently spasm. The fear of not knowing how he would respond, what would happen or if I'd be rejected was too much. But I live what I teach and I trusted him, so when resistance comes knocking, best believe I'll answer the door. I knew that regardless of what happened, there would be something for me to learn, if I stopped wrestling with fear. I sent it to him. I then proceeded to put my phone on airplane mode, hid under and nearly suffocated myself with my duvet, in case he could physically see that I was online. As I waited for his response, I affirmed 'I can do brave shit' to myself like a three-year-old trying broccoli for the first time. My mind catapulted into an imagined reality where I would receive a scathing response that would lead to a heartbreak so severe that it would surely lead to a ruptured artery. He responded. He matched my sentiment and as a result of me doing what I was so afraid to do, I let in intimacy and connection. I let myself live. Did it feel good at any point until he responded? Of course not. But what was the alternative? I could have allowed my fear to stop me from feeling a greater level of togetherness with someone. My fear could have stopped me from experiencing why we're here. Which is, to live. I chose courage instead, even though I hated every single second of it.

I may not be there yet with releasing my fear of throwing up and I'm still pushing myself to be more vulnerable, but I face each one as they arise. I look at it. I work on it. I hold myself when it feels impossible to move through it. I see the beauty in what comes when I do so. I observe the transformation. My enthusiasm is helped by continuing to couple up with fear. Even the smallest acts can prepare us for the bigger ones.

My daily method of finding peace with not feeling good comes when I have my two-minute freezing cold shower by way of the Wim Hof Method. A practice that started with 15 seconds of me screaming into my shower curtain, then 30 seconds of me realising that it wasn't as bad as I thought it would be. Then onto 45 seconds of my body telling me that it kind of likes it, then one minute of understanding that my fear of the cold wasn't as bad as the cold itself. Now, as the freezing water lands on my shivering skin I'm reminded again that I can do brave shit. As I wait for the clock to countdown and wonder why I put myself through this fleeting moment of foolishness, I remember why I do it. I do it for the long-lasting benefits of what comes next. I do it because after the fear, after it not feeling good, I feel energised and exhilarated. I feel alive.

THREE

There You Are Again

We often have this internal itchiness that just can't be reached. It's not as annoying as the inopportune itch that always seems to be bang in the middle of your back. No, the internal one is more subtle, more akin to the fuzzy sound of music playing in a fitting room that's too far from the shop floor speakers. This inner itch convinces us that something is not quite right. That the only way to relieve it is to search for a special tool that can reach within us and get to it. It's not your friend's stiletto nails, but insert what you believe will make you feel happy, fulfilled and alive here. It's the stuff that we go searching for because we believe it will soothe the itch that makes it impossible for us to just, *be*. It's the feeling that makes us believe that we'd be these better, shinier, more delightful versions of ourselves, *when* something happens. The something is like a deck of possibility cards. When we shuffle through the deck, most of us might land on the *when* I lose weight, *when* my skin clears up, *when* I'm not in pain, *when* I find my partner, *when* I get my dream job, *when* I move cities or *when* I do anything that I think will be my route to living my best damn life card. Just waiting for something, anything, to happen so we can be happy and not face the unsatisfied self that's asking for our attention.

Imagine if you had to wait for a bus to come to make you happy. You have no idea when the bus is coming; actually, you don't even know *if* the bus will come, but you wait. You ignore the feeling of the sauna-like sun on your skin, the children pulling funny faces as the cars pass by, the stranger smiling intensely at you, the taste of the bitter-sweet coffee on your tongue. You miss it all. Everything that's happening in the present moment, as well as all the things that could make you feel better right now. Mainly because you think it's waiting for you on the bus. A bus that might never arrive. Sounds far-fetched, but we do it all the time. Always waiting for *when*. I spent so much of my life rotating through the carousel of when. As I moved from one fashion job with a toxic boss to another, I convinced myself that *when* I found the dream job I'd be treated better. I hyped myself up on *Sex and the City* and convinced myself that I could only be my most fabulous self *when* I moved to New York City. I made that happen, but subsequently left because I couldn't afford to live there. Back in London I couldn't find work beyond weekend shifts at a lingerie shop and writing $30 articles for a wedding blog, but I believed that *when* I moved back to NYC, I'd find my sparkle again. I moved back and found myself facing relentless panic attacks and a worsening relationship. I left again and when I found myself in yet another appalling job, I knew there had to be something more. The search was over. I ran out of both *whens* and energy. Because, the itch was never going to be scratched until I reached in and relieved it myself. It would never come from any of the exhausting options listed here. I had to discover what within me wanted my attention.

I'm not going to give you my best impression of being a host on a late-night shopping channel, convincing you to call in to find the solution to all this, as it's quite simple. I thought I could find myself in these various cities, jobs, things and circumstances. But, the only constant in my endless searching was me. I was there through all of it, like the ex who pops back up to say happy birthday or even worse, 'hey stranger'. There I was, again. Over and over again. What I was running from always met me upon arrival of whatever experience I believed would be a balm for my woes. What I was running from was myself. Jon Kabat-Zinn even titled his book, *Wherever You Go, There You Are*, as when we unearth this, there's so much that we can discover. I didn't find the illusive sparkle that I took to searching for like a trench coat with all its buttons at a sample sale. I didn't find it, because I didn't have it before I moved to NYC or before my hundredth attempt at finding a workplace that would treat me with a modicum of respect. It was never about the sparkle, I was just desperate for a feeling of relief. The sweet satisfaction of having the inner itch taken care of.

What's happening here is a diversion. In the basement of our being there is something within us that isn't OK and it's this feeling that we're trying to escape from. So, we divert from ourselves and into the distractions that tend to be outside of us in the job, relationship, moving cities, all of it.

Steering us away from what wants to be felt and soothed, because it doesn't feel safe to be in the basement. We want to be anywhere else, so obviously anywhere else looks like all the things that we can't find inside of us and all the things that haven't happened yet. Then we engage in the hunt, that frantic, bordering on obsessive, fast-paced energy to scratch the inner itch. I was up every night until 2am feverishly looking at Manhattan apartments and looking for scenes of NYC in any film I could find. One client maxes out on dating app swipes to find the woman who he hopes will cure his hurt. Another takes on extra work and checks emails until midnight, craving a promotion to take the grief away. Another ran for miles each day, ignoring the soreness of her thighs to get to the body that she hoped would pay her back in self-acceptance. Diversions that we expect will suppress the dissatisfaction today and give us more satisfaction in the future. I preoccupied myself with the *when*, to replace the sadness of the stuff I was carrying. We create diversions that get us further away from ourselves, because in that moment our hearts are hurting. We want to create a fantasy life, or busy ourselves until it doesn't hurt anymore. Inside of us, the itch is waving its arms and shouting, 'Hey, I need something right now, please look at me, it's in here, not out there.' If we stopped, inquired and asked ourselves why we're diverting, we might be able to soothe what needed to be soothed, instead of expecting a new city or person to. When we don't, the same thing that wants soothing will just meet us whenever *when* gets here or in any way that we try to divert.

PAUSE, TAKE IT IN, AND . . .
Tune In

For the next five minutes or so, close your eyes (if that feels comfortable for you), find a soothing instrumental playlist and connect to yourself. Just spend some time here loosely connecting with the following questions, to see what comes to mind:

1. What within me wants my attention right now?
2. Does anything want to be felt or soothed?
3. What are my mind, body and soul craving in this moment?

IT'S NOT ALWAYS OUT THERE

Once we've taken the time to explore what within us wants our attention, we can be more inquisitive about the choices that we make. When you're looking for the perfect job, what are you really looking for? Is it a feeling of fulfilment or purpose? When you've been looking for a relationship, do you want a feeling of love or acceptance? When you've wanted to pack up all your stuff and move to another place, were you hoping for freedom and more confidence? We rarely set the intentions to receive these things without being attached to the physical way that we'd like to attain it. Apart from keeping myself and my loved ones safe, the main intention I set during COVID-19 was for peace. While I didn't feel that way all day every day, peace became my lockdown buddy. I knew that if my focus was on seeing my friends in order to have peace, travelling some-where idyllic to have peace or being able to book in for a massage to get peace, then I would still be waiting for it. Those things were out of my control; I had no idea if or when they would happen. If those were my intentions, then I'd still be naively waiting for peace to send me an email. Of course, friends, travel and massages *can* bring peace, but not always, as we can't control what's outside of us. Travelling with masks, tests and health anxiety doesn't sound peaceful to me. Having to get to a spa on the London underground is the opposite of peace and I will never know what mood my friends might be in when I see them, so peace is uncertain there too. But, what I do know is that I can try to find peace within, without waiting for the world to give it to me first. Taking a few deep breaths, practising self-Reiki, looking at my stuff, and massaging myself with body oils that leave a slippery sheen on my bedsheets are my peace – and it's ready for me *now*, not in the illusive *when*.

There's something really compelling about being able to cultivate peace, calm and joy within. This questioning of what needs your attention can then become the pre-cursor for calling in support. For me that included working with a therapist (see page 269), who I wasn't expecting to give me peace, but rather to help me work on my stuff that was in the way of me getting there myself. If in the midst of hunting for distractions, you stop, pause and see that it's not about the external thing, you might grab a friend and go for a walk. You're not expecting your friend to give you the feeling, but to assist in getting you to the feeling. Once you connect to how these emotions feel and truly embody them, you start to see them from a different perspective. There no longer needs to be this insurmountable goal of doing whatever it takes to find the feeling, especially when the diversions don't actually make you feel good. We are human, though, and our spiritual and physical selves pour into one another. This isn't about transcending that. We need things and we need people, because we are not islands. We all deserve to have a supportive and encouraging work environment that lights us up and where our efforts are respected. There's nothing wrong with moving from city to city and experiencing the beauty of newness. What trips us up is using them to divert us away from what wants to be felt. Or, expecting it to look and feel a certain way that will then become the remedy to our unease. When we do that, we pop open a bottle of inevitable disappointment, as what needed soothing is still waving at you but in a different job, better home, five-star resort or a new lover holding your hand. It's still there and when it's still there we put so much pressure on the outer thing to make us feel an inner thing. We can't even summon the pleasure of receiving it, because we're still seeing it through the filter of the dissatisfaction and unease that we're feeling, so we move onto something else.

When we can't see ourselves, we want the world to show us. We miss out on the world inside of us that's already filled with love, affection and possibility. When we stay in the narrative that only things outside of us can show us who we are, we diminish our ability to give ourselves what we're longing for. When you're about to text one of the periphery folks you had a dreadful date with who've now found their permanent abode in your contact list, under 'Photographer from Tinder' or if you're real fancy 'Anonymous from Raya', how can you check in first? You can still hold onto wanting the love and affection that is yours to have in this lifetime, but when it's midnight on a Tuesday and there are no solid options, how can you give it to yourself instead or get it from a more suitable place? The itch can be scratched by lighting a candle, writing a list of all the reasons why you're such an incredible person, placing a hand on your heart and taking some deep breaths instead of being under the weight of someone you don't actually like. Or, calling your platonic life partner of a best friend and saying that you're not doing too good. How would it feel to move from *that* place? To move from here means that we can accept who we are in this moment and not wait for something or someone to change or fix that. We have this nuisance of an idea that who we are today couldn't possibly be as good as who we might be in the future. Especially if the version of you that exists today feels like they're lacking, missing or in need of something. Enough of that.

PAUSE, TAKE IT IN, AND . . .
Find the Feeling

In your mind, journal or phone, list three special moments in your life when you felt at peace, alive or exhilarated. It could have been a place you visited, an experience you had, a way that a person made you feel. Then for each one, explore the ways that you can find that feeling again now. Here's an example:

I felt a real sense of adventure when I travelled around South America – I can find this feeling now by trying some new online courses, learning a new language or even playing tourist in my own town.

In reflection

Seriously, just think about all the products that thrive on selling you the shininess of who you could be if you bought into them. It's because we place most of our attention on these intermediary

almost middle-person-seeming things – the job, person, course
or even a healing, become the fairy-tale go-betweens that will
fast track us to where we'd like to be. To Uber us right to our
happiness. We then find ourselves attached to and in relationship
with the go-betweens instead of being in relationship with ourselves. This is especially true with our appearance. I spent much
of my life working in fashion and beauty, two industries that are
firmly fixated upon the way we look. While there's unparalleled
levels of glee that can be found when your index finger makes its
way into a tub of mascarpone-like moisturiser, working in this
field takes a toll. I was surrounded by the outer chatter of the
people I worked with, people I wrote for and people changing
next to me in clothing shop fitting rooms. The voices that would
then rise up from deep within us and yell out that we are not good
enough, slim enough, pretty enough, dewy enough and flawless
enough. Voices that sound so believable we mistake them for our
own. These voices never belonged to us. They were seeds planted
within us by the society we live in. Fed by unrealistic and often
Eurocentric beauty standards and watered by patriarchal conditioning. For me, my internal chatter was louder than being too
close to the stage at Glastonbury. All the faces of the Black
women I saw in the media when I was growing up were flawless.
I was always aware of how woefully underrepresented we were,
so when there was one of us in a magazine, film or music video, it
was like they had plucked out only the brightest daffodil in the
field. I was often the only Black woman in every office I was in
and the pressure was immense. I wanted to overachieve and I did
the same in my beauty routine. I grew out of my teenage acne,
but I wanted pore-less, perfect, filtered skin, and skincare products were my Uber straight there.

There's no greater wake-up call than finding yourself at Sephora in Union Square and being told that you can pick from an assortment of free gifts because you spent over $350 in the past month. I don't even want to talk about it, so just imagine that there's an upside-down smiley face here instead. What I will say is that you can find one of your greatest lessons in an Urban Decay eyeshadow palette. I realised that there wasn't hope in a jar and instead looked to my spiritual practices. At the intersection of skincare and spirituality, I found acceptance with the way I looked. Fast forward to now and in some of my sessions I help people to find peace or at least neutrality with their skin and appearance. Usually my clients have acne, psoriasis, dermatitis or are struggling to accept the way they look. Most of them have spent thousands of pounds on skincare products, appointments with dermatologists and radical overhauls of their diets. Going within is often the last resort. When I ask them to tell me their skin story, their stories merge into one. They aren't living anymore. They recite examples of the times they've not slept at a new partner's house in case they catch them without make-up on, hiding in the harsh lights of shopping centres, not eating anything fun in case it causes a breakout, refusing to do presentations at work and skipping exercise as the sweat may exacerbate a skin condition. The rest of their stories often begin with, 'But, when my skin is healed then I can . . .' and what follows is a long list of just living. I always reply with, 'So, what happens if your skin doesn't heal?' and it's often a question they've never considered. Whether it's your skin healing, travelling somewhere or anything that becomes the middle person, none of it is a transportation device to anything. What within you wants to be healed will still be there.

PAUSE, TAKE IT IN, AND . . .
See Yourself

Schedule a reminder in your calendar to do this mirror practice. Go to your bathroom or a full-length mirror. Light some candles if you'd prefer to have the lights off and put your favourite song on. Until the song finishes, spend some time gazing at your face and body. Really look at yourself, and it's OK if you have some resistance at first. Take some deep breaths and be gentle. Notice any thoughts that come up without judgement. Just be with yourself, without attaching anything to it other than greeting yourself as you are today.

* If this practice feels too uncomfortable for you, then please skip it and just spend a moment with your hand on your heart, taking a few deep breaths.

BEFORE THE WHEN

While you wait for all these things to happen, you're basically saying that the life you have in this moment is just not good enough, but the life in a month's time will be. Every day we miss out on life in favour of a life that is uncertain. All we're here to do is live. It's not always going to be cute – in fact it's the opposite most of the time – but there's so much good stuff when we choose to be in it, and not chase what we wish it would be. We can reframe this by centring on the time Before the When and instead of it feeling like you're either waiting or on the hunt and scrambling for diversions, let this be a container to facilitate healing. In this time you're probably going to feel like shit, that's a given. It will feel hard to be in, it will feel uncertain and you'll want answers. It's an in-between time when you're ready to get out of where you've been, but you're not yet where you want to be. When you look at what's in the basement that you're desperate to flee, then you can work on what needs healing and feeling there. You can use this time to investigate and re-choose what comes next. Making small steps to keep you moving on the road to creation. In this container, build on your enough-ness and realising your brilliance, or as I prefer to call it, putting yourself on your own damn honours list. According to gov.uk, which is surely the unseasoned cucumber sandwich of websites, the Queen's Birthday Honours List 'recognises the outstanding achievement of people across the United Kingdom.' When did you last celebrate your outstanding achievements? By outstanding I mean just making it through the day and continuing to show up for yourself, as well as all the big things. It's so easy to belittle our accomplishments in favour of having someone else notice it, but it colours our desires.

We always want to be authenticated for who we are and rightly so, but proceed with awareness. We've all had those tepid friendships when you rush to text your 'friend' your good news and all they can emit is a 'that's cool', without so much as an exclamation point for added decoration. It doesn't feel very good. We want people in our lives to gas us up and shout compliments at us with all the gusto of a stadium packed with football fans. When we can lift each other up, we can all rise and step into our greatness. One of my annoyances of choice to force upon my friends is sending them Leslie Knope compliments. Amy Poehler played the lead character in NBC's *Parks and Recreation* and she was always showering her best friend in the most creative and extra compliments you've ever heard.

I've woken my friends up with quotes such as 'You're a beautiful, talented, brilliant, powerful musk-ox' and 'You poetic, noble land-mermaid.' I highly recommend it for making someone's day, but before that, you need to gas yourself up. When we do that, we can see that we are good old-fashioned love radiating and existing in human form, and no I'm not being over-dramatic. With that, we don't focus on living a life just to receive admiration or other measures of external success. We can have both. At the very least, we don't want to cry in a corner when someone replies to our news with a gif (perish the thought). There's an equilibrium that comes with knowing where it doesn't help you to focus *only* on other people commending you and wanting to be seen for the magical being that you are.

Using this time Before the When to authenticate yourself, also helps you to get clear on your intentions. When I'm giving a talk to a hundred people, if I don't receive a thank you or a 'You did great sweetie' that's OK. I do this work because I love it and to be of service. If my intention is to be adored, then I need to rethink my priorities and try out for *The Voice* instead. I'm forever grateful for the kind words that people send to me after sessions and events, but if I don't receive them, I don't erase the time and energy I put into what I do. I will still haul my tired self into bed and say, 'You showed up today, Gigi, you gave all that you had and you did your best.' Sometimes that's all we need to give ourselves; the softness that reminds us that we can have pride in what we've done whether others give it to us or not. The same goes for our expectations and measures of success. Our only business is to do the thing we've been called to do. If only two people came to my workshop that doesn't lessen my work. It's also true if a work project didn't get the results you hoped for or your personal trainer shook their head at you when you couldn't make it through the last squat. You're still plenty enough. Celebrate the fact that you pushed through and stayed up late to get the project done, thank yourself for getting through the 11 squats you did, which were 11 more than you could do at one point. We can always strive to go further, but in the meantime know that you can gas yourself up in the absence of someone else doing so.

PAUSE, TAKE IT IN, AND . . .
Find Something New

Find a new, exciting, non-productive hobby or practice. If you're finding yourself diverting into distractions, or on the hunt, then find a nourishing one instead. Look for something that feels restorative or energising, but that doesn't make you attach any energy around it being 'the fix'. It could be a practice to help you feel what's coming up or just a softer alternative to some of the things that aren't working for you at the moment.

The healing comes when we can see that the road we're travelling on right now has something to offer us. That, yes, there might well be obstacles but if we're up for feeling and moving through them, we can construct a tomorrow that makes sense for who we are today. Would you still want to move to LA if you had soothed the part of you that wanted soothing? Maybe after spending some time exploring where you're diverting, you'd see that you have a desire to rest. You might then make changes in your life to meet that need. Then, as you feel more rested it might lead to you deciding that you don't even want to move, because it was never about LA. It was always about what's beneath the desire for it. With self-inquiry we can give ourselves what we've been hoping will relieve our internal itch. If you've been pinning all your aspirations on finding a soulmate before you can feel loved, then explore your experiences in relationships. What actions and behaviours made you feel loved and accepted? What have you witnessed in friendships and from family that made you feel this, even if you haven't experienced it romantically? If none of the above applies, I know there's a famous couple you're obsessed with. What traits do you see in them? If you've been hoping for the most impeccable job to land for you, then look back and think about how you want to feel at the end of each day. Let this be the intelligence to give yourself what you need right now, before or irrespective of these outer pieces working out.

When I was going through a heavy, 'I'm not lovable' phase and believed that I wouldn't be lovable until someone chose me, I wrote how I wanted a partner to make me feel and how they'd express their love for me. I explored the classic book by Gary Chapman, *The 5 Love Languages: The Secret To Love That Lasts.* I realised that I wasn't giving myself any of them, so I met my needs instead of waiting. I got myself gifts, spent quality time with myself, did physical touch, used plenty of words of affirmation and even acts of service, like doing the admin I always put off and later regret. I also realised that my friends and family gave me so much of these. When my clients are feeling uncomfortable with where they currently live, we think about the feelings they hope to have if they lived somewhere else. This is often adventure, so we work on finding it exactly where they are now, even if it's in a sleepy town somewhere. This could look like anything from trying a new restaurant or gym class every week, to speaking to at least one new person. If they still choose to move after this then fantastic, but if not, then they still meet the core need. Even with the inner aspects, if we want to feel supported then how do we a) support ourselves and b) ask others how they can support us, instead of waiting for support from something we don't know will happen. If you want to feel accepted, then how do you work towards accepting yourself and expressing where you don't feel accepted? This doesn't mean that you don't go for the outer thing, it just means that you can feel resourced enough before you do it, so you can deal with whatever meets you when you get there.

While this is all important work that can make such a difference, there are times when life can *only* change when something outside of us happens and we should always wait and want that, especially if we're not safe. Finding practices and support to help you navigate the time Before the When is everything. What we're looking at here is not allowing the thing to have all your energy. We can always look to what's next as this is where we grow, but it's almost mathematical. We want the experiences, places, people and jobs to **add** to a soothed self. Not to divert us away from what wants our attention right now. When we want it to **subtract** or **replace** the sadness, pain or unhappiness of our current life, then the sum often doesn't add up. A part of being spirit-informed is in seeing that this starts with you then reverberates out. Wanting different and more comes by connecting to how you can give yourself this without *only* expecting it from something outside of you. So, can you allow yourself to see that you are enough today, in this moment, because this is the only version of you that exists?

FOUR

So Blessed, So Favoured

In primary school, I remember my teacher informing my mum that I was reading at the level of someone twice my age. I was the fastest 60m sprinter out of all the girls in my year and I was also the Head Girl, so I got to sit on a bench instead of the blue, plastic-covered foam mats. At secondary school, I found myself in the gifted and talented class. Although those labels really piled on the pressure, they prepped me for a lifetime of feeling that I was incredibly special. When I researched my North Node in Aquarius in Jan Spiller's book *Astrology for the Soul*, it said 'Aquarius North Node people were kings and queens in past lives, or entertainers – people accustomed to being "special".' I felt very seen and it's now a running joke with my loved ones and workshop attendees. Now, let's be honest with each other. I'm going to assume that you either laughed, rolled your eyes or thought that I need to look up the word humble in the dictionary. Sure, we can do that, the definition is 'Not proud or not believing that you are important; ordinary.' Remind me again why being humble is such a prized trait? It seems to be at the top of the list if you're British too.

Forever apologising for our existence with rambling versions of 'I'm *so* sorry.'

We've been absolutely bamboozled. We didn't come here to be ordinary and unimportant. When I say that I *know* I'm special, I'm not more or less special than you. There is a level of equality that comes with seeing how special we are. When we can't accept this, we start finding all kinds of mental hierarchies with the people around us. We are all *plenty* special and the only thing holding any of us back is the refusal to own it. Until we know our worth and stop apologising for our confidence, then we can close this book and call it quits with all this creation stuff. I remind myself of the importance of this every day, as either plastered on my phone's lock screen or just in the back of my mind are the words, 'I am blessed and highly favoured'. It's my retort for when everyone I know asks how I managed to pull off most of the things that have occurred in my life. It's also one of the lines I remembered from my former church-going years, actually I don't think I heard it at my very restrained Catholic church; it was probably on a U.S. super-church sermon I saw on TV or an Etsy calligraphy poster. Anyway, the original verse in Luke 1:28 (New King James Version) says, 'And having come in, the angel said to her, "Rejoice, highly favoured *one*, the Lord *is* with you; blessed *are* you among women!"' This is in reference to the angel Gabriel announcing the birth of Christ to Mary and when Mary rightly questioned this, the angel later said, 'For with God nothing is impossible.' Regardless of what you believe in, because it really is not what's important here, call it spirit, God, universe, whatever. When I have this constant faith and trust in my ability to make shit happen and remark on how blessed and highly favoured, I am; it's because I trust. I trust in spirit, but I also just trust in my own damn self and I'm unapologetic about that and so should you be. It's kind of like the secret recipe to that exquisite sauce found in Shake Shack Shroom Burgers. Knowing your worth is vital for getting the stuff you want and returning back to *you*. I mean, I've manifested a lot, even when my self-worth felt like the chunk of hair stuck in the shower drain, but once my manifestations arrived, I didn't know what to do with them. I couldn't really enjoy anything as I was stuck in a loop of not believing that I did it and that I just wasn't *good* enough to have it. I wasn't showing up in my worth in the world I created and that's no fun when you've been hauling your vision boards around town for years. Lacy Phillips, of To Be Magnetic, speaks a lot on the relationship between worth and manifesting via her online workshops, but whether it's related to manifesting or not, knowing your worth is a fundamental spiritual principle.

WHAT'S CONFIDENCE, ANYWAY?

Confidence and worth are non-identical twins; same but different. I'm intentionally not going to define them because it's not for me to do so. We've been packaged up what feels like an all-inclusive Mediterranean holiday when it comes to what these terms mean. That we're all supposed to fit into these neat, tidy boxes of what confidence should look like. Depending on where you find the messaging, confidence might be sold as being outspoken, bare-faced and walking around in a permanent power stance. While being in your worth might look like having a Facebook feed flooded with quotes about having impenetrable boundaries and constantly using the click-your-fingers-in-a-Z-formation gif, this isn't for all of us. It's not who we all *are*. You are the only one who gets to define what confidence and worth look like for you. Being confident is about making the choice to see and then, in turn, showing the world that confidence. You can't masterclass or 10-week course your way to confidence, unless it's a step-by-step approach to exploring your *own* confidence – the confidence that is just the clear-cut observation of all the parts that make up who you are. Confidence is being unapologetically you. It can be loud, it can be quiet, it can be hidden or in your face; it really doesn't matter. It's about you demonstrating what you have to offer every single day and it will always be different to what someone else has to offer. You don't have to do a TED talk or wear red lipstick to be confident. Confidence is in saying, 'I know who I am and this is me. Welcome.' Of course, we all have room to work on stuff and you don't get to abandon kindness when you're confident. We guide others in seeing that the world doesn't end when we stand fully in our authenticity. It's almost our duty to do so, because we all thrive when we both individually and collectively know how incredible and deserving we all are.

PAUSE, TAKE IT IN, AND . . .
Big Yourself Up

Write a heading of 'Reasons Why I'm a Whole, Damn Catch' in your journal or phone and spend some time writing out all the things you adore about yourself. Your qualities, values, traits, biggest wins, all the reasons why you're killing it, how you look and how you make other people feel. No bullet points please, full sentences only and there better be more than one paragraph. If you're really struggling, send an SOS to your group text and say you're reading this annoying book and need them to tell you their favourite things about you.

No, you really were *born with it*

It's vital that our uniqueness exists, especially when it doesn't fit into society's expectations of who is allowed to be confident and how that confidence should be conveyed. This is all well and good, but it's another story altogether when it comes to actually doing the work to get there, right. Confidence and worth aren't only things we can think about, we need to embody them to fully get them and that, my friends, takes a bit of figurative time-travelling to get started. The issue with the language of 'being more confident' and 'gaining self-worth' is that it assumes that we're trying to get something that we don't already have. We had to be confident and know our worthiness to be here, from the moment we were born. We would not have survived if we didn't. Our bodies have in-built systems and processes to ensure we survive. We had the confidence to touch everything our constantly splayed-out toddler fingers could grab. We had the confidence to try solid foods for the first time without fear of choking. We had the confidence to wave and smile at strangers from our prams. To grab a chunk of anyone's hair and pull, kick, cry and scream for as long as we wanted. What else can explain our three-year-old selves embarrassing our parents by yelling on supermarket floors because we couldn't touch the glass bottles? Even when we were born, we didn't play it cool and whisper because we didn't want to make a fuss, we didn't say, 'Oh, don't mind me, nothing to see here.'

When we hear the saying, survival of the fittest, it's actually survival of the confident. If you're too scared to ask for the free pretzel samples at the mall, then you'll remain hungry. If you don't ask for someone to give you a lift home, you'll be stranded. Being confident is not a fun tip we can learn from a magazine, it's a matter of survival and we all have it within us to be it. Especially when we look in our inner and outer stuff about why we find it hard to and have some softness for when it feels out of reach.

Newborn babies might be helpless, but they sure are confident. We had confidence because we didn't know what it was to be afraid, rejected or hurt yet, because we hadn't experienced it. The journey of incredulity and impossibility that occurred for us to be here is really something else. We arrived here with the information that not only did we survive a pregnancy, but that even further back our ancestors needed to survive through some rough times for us to be here. So much spirit, science and love had to occur for us to have a place here. You are a miracle. That's not a sweet little throwaway comment either. Dr Ali Binazir did the work that no-one else had the time or energy to do and calculated that the odds of us being alive are basically zero. It started off being 1 in 400 quadrillion, but then factor in things like your lineage remaining unbroken, the right sperm meeting the right egg, and so on, and it doesn't actually make sense that any of us are here. The odds are ridiculous. Yet here you are. Imagine thinking that despite all of that, you came here to live a life of being unimportant and ordinary. You sure didn't.

We were whole and totally merged with spirit when we were younger – we still are now – but as we got older, everything in the world moved us further away from this. We saw in the classroom that standing up to speak often led to our classmates breaking out in hysterics. We learned through countless romantic films that if we needed someone else to complete us, be our other half, and be the missing piece to our puzzle, then maybe we're not as whole as we thought. We witnessed that even when we do everything in our control to educate ourselves, be kind and work very hard, people will still only see us for our appearance. We admire the people who've 'made it' and yet there are still traits that they have to deny or quieten in order to get there. We're told that we can only be confident if we buy that new pair of jeans. That if we stop eating bread and drop a size by summer, then we'll find our self-worth. If we swap out jelly beans for supplements, then we'll be 'healthy' enough to feel worthy. No wonder we're disconnected to the confidence and worth that we were born with. The world we live in works overtime to make us feel that way. This is the stuff we carry. So, it makes complete sense that we would rather be humble and not want to own how special we are, because look what everyone else has to deal with. We're conditioned to want to fit in and if we've all been subject to being distanced from our wholeness, then no-one wants to be the only one standing on top of the cocktail bar telling everyone that they're flourishing.

This way of thinking doesn't help any of us. I've noticed that there can be an assumption that self-care, manifesting and inner work only focuses on the individual and not on the collective. I get that it can look that way, but systemic and community change requires the individuals within it to do their work and then expand that work outside of themselves. We can learn and change in groups with the support of each other, but it's disempowering to believe that we have to wait for society as a whole to change before anything internal can. When we start to apologise for our confidence and sense of worth, then who do we think we should be apologising to? This creates a pedestal where we position ourselves underneath someone because we've shrunk who we are like a tumble-dried sweatshirt, to a place which feels safer. Safer than just being exactly who we are and shining as brightly as a citrine crystal left out in the sun. Plus, why are you apologising? Being confident in who you are isn't the final destination; we get to use it to see what we want to create. It's hard work playing small, but it can feel even harder when we are courageous enough to stand in who we are, so never apologise for getting there. I know I don't. As we understand that we were whole to begin with and then a tumble-weed of life experiences that disconnected us from it swept through, our work is in examining what it was in the tumble-weed that caused us to feel unworthy and how we can sit in the director's chair and rewrite the script. Then we take the tiniest steps to connect back to it. I'm not going to lie to you, you might not fully feel it by the end of this chapter but you'll at least have the understanding of why it's so important to make it a practice that you can embody.

PAUSE, TAKE IT IN, AND . . .
Just Notice

Refer back to your answers on page 57, or do them now (no-judgement). Examine if any of your stuff links to feelings of confidence and worth. If not, write out any resistance you have to stepping into this. Did you struggle with the exercise? Find it easy? Believe what you wrote? Feel surprised? Just notice what you find out here.

What's worth got to do with it, then? In some old-school versions of spirituality, there's an idea that you receive what you think and like always attracts like. While there's truth to this, it's been simplified into complete drivel, like saying you should never watch the news or feel anything 'bad' because low vibes just create more low vibes. If you have a health problem? Well, you probably attracted that too, didn't you, you little negative Nancy? There are not even enough synonyms for problematic to describe how absolutely absurd and damaging this is. Obviously, I believe in creation otherwise we wouldn't be here now but, honestly, most of the rhetoric surrounding it needs a makeover. If it works for you, then great; if it doesn't make you feel good, then we can do much better than that.

For manifesting to be unintentional, as a result of you living a spirit-informed life and being whole, authentic and all the other superlatives, then worth has to be one of the main ingredients. When you know what you're *worthy* of, then the world gets on board with it. It can be awkward, I get it. We end up in such a state of bashfulness that even when someone gives us a compliment, we spend 30 seconds mentally scanning them to reciprocate. Lest you get accused of not being sufficiently humble and effusive. When, actually, if you own the compliment with an enthusiastic, 'That's so kind of you, thank you so much,' it has a knock-on effect of that person then owning the compliments they receive too. Your changed behaviour changes others' behaviour. Then we won't live in a world where we think being humble is a lifetime achievement. Contrary to popular belief, I think it's too much of a reach to say that when we feel unworthy, we can't manifest or call in the life that we want to step into. Also, I don't agree with the labels of low self-worth or low self-esteem. We may feel unworthy, but we don't have low self-worth because that's not who we are. Think about imposter syndrome; it's entangled with not feeling worthy, but the point of imposter syndrome is that we probably did get what we wanted, we just don't think that we should have it or we question ourselves in it. So, unworthiness being the reason why we can't manifest is often reductive. However, feeling unworthy just means that there'll be a lack of acceptance and pleasure when you do receive the stuff you're worthy of.

Think about worth this way: it's in our self-imposed limitations. When you're on a delightful holiday and put your feet in the tip of the ocean, your eyes can only see ahead and to the left and right of you. You can only feel a puddle-size amount of water under your feet as you're still stood on the sand with the water barely stroking your toes. In this moment, this is all there is of the ocean. The ocean becomes all you can see and all you can feel. If you can swim up to 100m or so, then you can expand this definition a little. That's where the sense of possibility ends. But, just because your view of the ocean right then is limited, the enormous depth of it still exists. Even if in that instance it doesn't exist in its entirety to you. You're only maybe some hours, days or months of training away from deep-sea diving to reach beyond the surface or hopping on a catamaran to go further into it. Our self-worth is related to the limits we place on what we can create. When we don't believe in our worth and lack confidence, we think that we can only achieve the puddle-size version of the ocean. You can have and are worthy of having an ocean full of blessings. Because, you got it . . . you're so blessed and so favoured. When you shift into the energy of worthiness, you can see beyond the limits, because you know that you're inherently worthy of receiving it. You won't think that you have to be humble and unnoticeable, or only take the little scraps leftover from Sunday's roast dinner. I have some beautiful humans in my life, who do this curious thing. When we're watching a show or film and they need to use the bathroom, I'll always pause it until they come back. Like clockwork, as soon as their slippered feet stand up, I hear, 'Don't pause it for me, keep watching.' That's a hard no for me, so before I hear the toilet flush, I've already asked them if they forgot they're a miracle and that they're worthy of being here. I don't need to continue watching a show for three minutes any more or less than you. We're both here, worthy of it all. You're always worth pausing the TV for. Worth and confidence can still be complicated for some of us and for various valid reasons.

In my sessions, clients bring such different stories to share and be guided through. Nadia found herself as a young widow in her thirties after her husband had passed away a few years prior. Kacey was tutoring children and knew she was choosing familiarity over wanting to step into an artistic career. Yomi really liked her job and relationship, but found it very difficult to say how she felt and share her ideas. As we uncovered more through our time together, they were all navigating these things through the lens of questioning their worth and finding it really hard to show themselves off. Nadia's came from struggling to define who she was outside of her role as a wife. Kacey had received messages from her parents when she was growing up saying that creative careers weren't an option. Yomi's originated from a fear of being rejected for being her unique self because she was laughed at for doing so when she was younger. They resulted in the same thing. A reluctance to do something or demonstrate what makes them so brilliant. We all have stuff that makes confidence and worth feel like they're somewhere on Mars. I didn't always go around telling people how much I bring to the table in relationships and how much of a catch I am. That work only happened because so many people attempted to take my power away from me. I believed I was worthless, because if I was worth something then why would I be treated that way? During the re-energising of the Black Lives Matter movement in summer 2020, I read so many stories from other Black women of the horrors they've faced in the workplace. Predicaments I've been in myself that convinced me that I was failing in my role, when I wasn't, and that I was being 'difficult' for asking for support. The kind of weathering that leads to such a devastating toll on our mental health that there's no other choice than to become self-employed. The stains of that still remain on our skin, as we shy away from wanting visibility, because we're so used to shrinking. But, no more. Goodbye to everything and everyone that's taken your power away and made it hard for you to take up the space that's rightfully yours. They can take things away from you, but they can never take away any part of your soul. They don't get to win.

PAUSE, TAKE IT IN, AND . . .
Take Back Your Power

If it feels good to do so, place a hand on your heart and repeat this, or something similar:

'I choose to take back my power and step fully into my worth, because it is my divine right to be here,' for as many times as it takes to own it.

RETHINKING POWER

You know who else doesn't get to win? Any spiritual and religious paradigms that act like wanting more and being proud isn't a good look. That you should be *grateful* for the tiny plot of land you have and not want for anything else. While there are huge power structures at play around us with a tendency of misusing that power, we have to take a step back to reflect on that. In an effort for equality and progressiveness, we've somehow ended up with an overly simplistic view of who we perceive to hold all the power in our society. We have conflated the difference between outer and personal power. Largely thanks to the role that some areas in the media play, especially when thoughts are supposed to be articulated in a minimally designed swipe-through post or, even worse, in 140 characters. This doesn't allow for either nuance or critical thinking, so explaining complex topics such as critical race theory, feminism and other social justice topics often misses the mark. Instead, we end up with cancel culture and deciding someone's worth based on how educated they are in issues and theories that often stem from academia that not everyone has access to. We *need* to discuss race, for example, but the *way* we are talking about race focuses on those who have the power and those who apparently don't. As a group of people who have had their outer power stripped away, when we hear statements such as 'White people need to do the work', 'White people need to give back to people of colour', 'White people need to lift up black people', 'Black people are not free', are we not emphasising the white superiority that we are trying to decry? Are we not highlighting a power imbalance and assuming that racialised people can only reclaim their power when it is handed back to them by the same people who may have taken it? There's plenty of work and healing to do and the onus should not be on the people who aren't perpetuating the problem, but it's important that the language we use to solve it doesn't reinforce disempowerment. From police brutality and medical bias to hair discrimination and inescapable micro-aggressions, the evidence of obvious power imbalances and blatant racism is clear to see, but we need to examine if all our language around power is actually serving us. Personal power cannot be stolen, only outer power can.

If I focused on my identity and how the world sees me, I wouldn't be where I am now. I'd still be sitting at home waiting for my burgundy nails to dry, while I waited for racism to end and women to be equal. I'd wait for safe spaces to open up, for employers to have a 'diverse' work pool and policy changes to occur. I didn't wait because I'd still be waiting. I knew that my power was personal, and I had the spirit to create, even and especially when the world said it wouldn't be possible for someone like me. We can always try. There'll be times when we're thrown into situations that we just can't see a way out of. When our only focus is on survival, so that's what we do. We absolutely *need* the world to change, but while we wait, we will always have our personal power. If you can't get there today, or even in this lifetime, that's OK. Sometimes someone's work in this lifetime is only in survival and we will hold their hands and lift them up through it. It's so easy to not be able to see our own power, we prefer to wait for others to hand it to us. You don't need anyone to see how special, smart and worthy you are; you just need them to see that you're a spiritual being, the same as them, and if they can't then they miss out on your magnificence.

Beyond this, when we look further into our collective history, we're left with power-shrinking remnants that have breadcrumbed their way into our present. We all know what happened during the witch trials. Women were killed, shunned and rejected for daring to see the world differently and recognising their potential. This is an extreme example of what happens when we are loud and unapologetic about who we are and we live in the shadows of that. In Black communities there is a reluctance to step into spirituality, often due to Christianity and the pervasive belief that spirituality is evil. That anything under the umbrella of spirituality is dark, devil worship or witchcraft, when the opposite is true. It's hard to swallow, because while in so many ways Christianity can be incredibly valuable and soothing, the relationship to slavery is tough to overlook. It was often used as a tool for compliance, or as an excuse to condone harm. At the same time, it's also a religion that fostered faith and empowerment for those who were enslaved and their descendants. It doesn't need to be labelled as good nor bad, it just is, but it can't be *all* there is. There's a theme emerging here. In order to gain compliance, a thought, campaign, or belief is planted. Christianity being used as a means to both justify slavery and ensure obedience. Physiological differences between Black and white people being invented to justify racism. Colonists using propaganda to further their bids for conquests and to rip the humanness from those whose lands they've stolen. Maeve Callan describes the slurs that 14th-century Anglo-Irish colonists used when asking Pope John XXII for a conquest, 'The Irish, a sacrilegious and ungovernable race, hostile to God and humanity.' Women, folk healers and those who dared to speak up being labelled as witches to justify a removal of their power and sometimes death. Inferiority is invented to ensure power is stolen. It is invented because it has to be, because deep down we all know who we are on a soul-level, a *heart* level. It's our nature to see each other as spiritual beings, as the *same* spiritual beings. Outer power doesn't like that, so it invents differences with made-up evidence to strip away our personal power and rationalise harm.

When all this becomes the stuff we carry, it makes us want to shut down and not step forward into our power. It doesn't allow us to see that the road to creation is possible. This is why we have outer stuff and why manifesting needs to take all this into consideration. There will be way more obstacles for some of us than others. There will be a desire to be quiet and take a step back, when we have historically seen the pain that is caused from being loud. When we have witnessed that being seen can equate to being harmed. Just know that for a lot of us, it makes so much sense to believe that if you are silent then you will be safe.

There will clearly never be enough self-worth, confidence or personal power that anyone can have that will act as a shield of protection for being murdered, abused and dismissed. Yet, it's all we have to fight with. It's all we have to hold onto alongside our rallying cries for change and action. Whatever is inflicted upon us by other people is out of our control, but we'll always have our fundamental worth within us, even if the world around us chooses not to see it. We all have personal power that fires us up to move through the world, irrespective of gender, race and socio-economic status. It doesn't serve those who attempt to take away what we have, for us to believe that we are worthy. It doesn't serve them for us to step into our power. It doesn't serve them when we do the inner work to create. We can't wait for anyone else to hand it to us, we have to remember that we have it and we'll fight damn hard before we let anyone else try to take it.

PAUSE, TAKE IT IN, AND . . .
Get Hyped

Do this quick mini ritual. Either schedule it in your diary or do it now. Put on your favourite feeling-myself-song, close your eyes and do whatever you need to hype yourself up – dance, sway, move, shake, touch yourself or smile until the song ends.

As you move through the rest of your day, weeks, months and years, let this road trip be an episodic one. There's no such thing as taking a wrong turn when we're growing and ending up where you started. You can't un-grow. You can't unknow it. There'll be days when you don't feel confident and in your worth. There'll be days when you don't want to be seen or heard. There'll be plenty of them, but we keep on keeping on. Be soft and free on those days, try to love yourself up a little bit harder. When the stuff you're carrying makes you think that you can't call in a relationship, or transition into a more favourable career, remind yourself that you're blessed and favoured just because you're alive. That even if you have to fake believe it, keep fake believing it until you start falling into its truth. Rest in the fact that you're a majestic, delicious, delightful, magnificent, incredible moonbeam of a soul, and allow it to be a practice of embodiment. Wake up to it every single day and know that you're all those things because you're you. Truly, fully, wholly you. Still not believing it? What's the worst that can happen if today you simply made the choice to? Without getting all of it, without fanfare, without even knowing what being in your worth looks like. Just making a choice to see who you are and flashing it to the world.

Work On Your Stuff

FIVE

All the Feels

Job titles don't impress me much; in fact, I'm sure the world would be a much more riveting place if we didn't have them. We wouldn't lead conversations with what we do, but with who we are. Alternatively, we'd have to use the extensive bounty of language that we have available to us, to describe who we are. From the list of titles that summarise my work, there's one that I treasure the most: being a space holder. When those words slip out of my mouth or land into text, it gives me the kind of hot-water-bottle warmth that gratitude is all about. It's also the title that feels most in misalignment with my down-to-earth approach to this work, as on first glance it doesn't make much sense, does it? It sounds like one of those terms that's as tricky to understand as figuring out what size you are in Zara. But, it isn't. There's a capsule of time in my sessions, before a card is pulled, meditation begins or akashic records are read, when my clients are sharing whatever they're going through. Real people, real-life stuff. Sometimes what they unpack is a flow of absolute elation; the love stories, healing, inventories of everything they've created and what they've overcome. Then, there are the clients who are reciting what they're in the midst of overcoming. The clients whose words become flecks between the gasping-for-breath outpouring of tears. I listen. I deeply listen, focus and hold what they're carrying with presence, letting them know that it's safe for their emotions to be there. That everything they're carrying is valid, that I believe every word, there's no judgement and no need to fix it. Nothing else exists in the capsule other than that; holding space.

The reason behind the pain, grief or heartbreak is different for each client, but in some ways it's the same. It's the ending of relationships, the conclusion of a loved one's life, the stuff that becomes overwhelming to carry, the disappointments, the loss of hope, the uncertainty of the future. The fused wiring of human experience that connects us all. Regardless of the reason and the uniqueness of the situation, when they've finished sharing, I hear a version of the same thing. Hundreds upon hundreds upon hundreds of times. The apology. The 'I'm so sorry for crying,' 'I'm sorry for unleashing all that' and 'I'm sorry for releasing that onto you.' It's what we do, right? We apologise for our feelings usually because we've been made to believe that they don't have a right to be there. As soon as our eyes get a bit damp or someone hears our breath labouring, a tissue is shoved in our face like we're auditioning for a Kleenex ad. Not only is society uneasy with emotion, we are uneasy with our own. There's always a time in our life when something is going down. Usually, something unexpected that comes out of nowhere and makes us stop. It's the not-so-friendly reminder that we have zero control over the outer world and the people within it and it feels horrendous. So, we do everything in our power to not be in it, because, yeah it feels like hell. This is similar to the diversions to avoid the inner itch and hoping the answer lies in the new city, job or person. But when we're in the visceral pain of something happening, here we enter a period of self-imposed stuck-ness that stops us from moving forward, because the healing is in the feeling of it and we don't want to feel.

SPHERE OF SUSPENSION

Look at it this way, when life throws us an obstacle – grief, pain, heartbreak or anything that doesn't feel good – we go into what I call the sphere of suspension, where we're hating every moment of it and suspended in time. A period when we're doing everything we can to not be in the emotion of the experience. There's a coffee date happening in here with **disbelief, avoidance, authentication** and **scripting**, all sipping on oat flat whites and nibbling on stale carrot cake. When disbelief comes we are trying to process the loss of control, and we're faced with such incredulity that the thing has happened. The anger or sadness hasn't even arrived yet; we're just stuck in the nerve of it all, questioning why this had to happen to us and listing all the good things we've done in our lives. Disbelief is like having an online fight with strangers on the internet, but it's you and the emotion you're in on the receiving end of it, furiously sending message after message in absolute shock that this has occurred.

The avoidance is the unwillingness to feel and we apologise because we're so used to staying away from it, that when it comes up we think we've made a mistake. The avoidance isn't always deliberate because it's happening alongside all the other stuff in the sphere. When we're in disbelief we're avoiding the emotions underneath it as we're preoccupied by thinking about what's happened, instead of *feeling* what happened. The rush to avoid looks like filling the space that hurts with busyness or playing fantasy scenarios over in our minds.

Authentication barges in when we start to run the situation through our stuff, eager to find ways to confirm that this is our fault. We write out a plot line of this episode of our lives because we must know the reason why. We rush into our minds to seek out something to authenticate the reasons why this happened to us, ready to write an episode about how awful we are and why we deserved it. I had a client who felt guilty after her dad died, so she zealously examined her stuff to authenticate it. She landed on, 'I always argued with him about small things and wasted our time together. It's my fault.' There we go, stuff authenticated, guilt co-signed. Another client got made redundant and listed all the reasons that proved she deserved it: 'I'm not good enough, I always have bad things happen to me, career stuff never works out for me.'

This obviously doesn't make anyone feel good, but that's not enough. We then start scripting. Before we even wrap up one episode of mistruths, we start scripting future plot lines based on the painful situation we're in and how this will impact our future lives. We convince ourselves that there's no more hope left for us, that we'll never get another job, good things will never happen and the rest of our lives will also be full of pain. It's a lot, being in the sphere.

I've seen the sphere of suspension play out countless times, but the most frequent is during break-ups. Hopefully, you had a reasonable, though difficult, break-up conversation rather than text message, but however it happened you're then hit with the despair of it. You can either feel the ouch, kick, scream, cry or yell, or you can go into the sphere. When you're there disbelief looks like, 'I can't believe they ended it,' 'I gave so much energy to this, this can't be happening right now,' 'This can't be over, it just can't.' It's then followed by avoidance and stalking their social media profiles, busying yourself by reading old text messages or doing the opposite and immersing yourself in work and a limitless supply of red wine. You can't get your fix of them so you go to bed earlier or find yourself napping more and daydreaming about them, spending hours thinking about memories of times shared and a future of love that will now be un-lived. You authenticate it by going into your stuff and jotting down the reasons why no-one has ever chosen you, all the exes who hurt you, listing your character and appearance flaws, which all add to the plot line of an episode called, 'I'm unlovable, clearly.' To add insult to injury, you've now scripted all future episodes to the tune of, 'I will never find love again, I better prepare for a life of solitude, because it's what I deserve.'

It's exhausting stuff and when we're in the sphere of suspension we can't see the possibility for healing. Being in the sphere isn't the problem; we'll all end up in it at some point, but when we don't want to leave, that's the issue. We often stay right there in the sphere because it feels safer. Infinitely safer than having to feel the uncertainty of emotion. We already feel out of control, so we assume that going into the emotion will exacerbate that. Feeling it all is the work here, though, and healing only comes when we can be in the rawness, sadness, fear, pain, grief and anger that wants to be felt. Or even the feeling of softness that we can give to ourselves, which is impossible when we're in the sphere. I hardly talk about having MS because it's just something that my body has, it's not who I am. Me sharing it in a public way is the same as me talking about my bra size to my optician. It's very much a 'you'll know if you need to know, I'm not ashamed but pretty relaxed about it' kind of thing. When I received the diagnosis, it was the shortest amount of time that I've hung out in the sphere of suspension. I decided to go all in on feeling how awful it was, instead of staying too long in disbelief, avoidance, authentication and scripting. I know from experience that doing the inner work makes a difference, when I'm given an obstacle and I respond to it differently than I would have before. I didn't have to force my way out of the sphere, because I knew that when I'm suspended, it's impossible to heal or step into any action that will benefit me. I'd also just been in there too many times before, especially with my career. As soon as any job I had would parachute into a field of disappointment, I'd cradle myself to sleep with the script of, 'This is ridiculous, I can't believe this, work will never go well, this always happens to me, I'll never be happy.' I'd then go back to the job and stay suspended, carrying all that stuff with me into every job I had, because I never felt what needed to be felt. The grief and anger.

PAUSE, TAKE IT IN, AND . . .
Have a Sacred Time Out

When you next find yourself fully immersed in the sphere, start a dialogue with yourself. Use the questions below as prompts so you can look at what has happened and then work out what wants to be felt. Fill in the blanks, in your mind, journal or phone:

1. What's occurring? _____

   (What exactly happened, with evidence and facts, not the emotions)

2. What I'm feeling is _____

   (Are you feeling angry, let down, sad? Write out what feeling you're finding hard to be with.)

Being in it

When you're in the sphere, you can't see beyond the resistance you're having and into the expression of what needs to be felt. One of the sneaky little tricks in our mind's toolbox is believing that there are good emotions and bad emotions; ones that we're allowed to feel and ones that we're not. That you *shouldn't* feel angry or scared, that you *should* always try to feel your best, do your best and look your best. Then the real kicker: if you leave your container of feeling good, bad things will happen. Once life has dealt us some crap to deal with, we don't want it to get any worse. So, we often feel that we have to plaster on the Barbie-like smile of optimism instead of just feeling whatever wants to be felt. The reason we want to step *into* and not out of the emotion reminds me of why I don't drink alcohol, have never been drunk and haven't done any drugs. Don't worry, it's not for any pious reasons; do your thing. I just want to feel it all. I want to see, appreciate and take in all that this planet has for me. The grief, the sad, the hurt, the ugly, the pleasure and the delicacies of it all. Without a filter. Because how else do we live if we're not present for all of it? You will never be punished for thinking about how despicable something feels. I've seen countless alleged self-help and spiritual advice that peddles this uncalled-for narrative of having to always push into positivity. Ignore it. It's never a bad thing to feel anything, otherwise why were we given all these emotions. We wouldn't have anger if we didn't know what to do with it. There's no way that we'd be able to cry if we could drown in our tears. We have the ability to feel, for exactly that reason; we're supposed to experience it. 'Time is a healer,' they say, but nah, time only heals when we take the time to feel everything that is coming up to be healed. Emotions come, they shift, move and then they leave. We don't have to fear them, we just need to feel, without labels, resistance or judgement. Without someone telling you that you shouldn't be in it. How do we get into the feels, when it doesn't feel safe or easy to? We can only leave the sphere of suspension and enter the next phase of healing when we have insurance that not only can we go into it, we'll be safe being in it and that we'll also be able to get out of it.

When I was in the throes of processing the rape I experienced at age 15, I felt the kind of grief that I didn't think was survivable. The TV version of grief that looks like uncontrollable crying on the floor and sitting in a pile of inky mascara-hued tears and worn-out tissue. The grief that made my entire body convulse in a pain so severe that I would do anything to make it stop. I wanted it all to stop. I wanted my therapy sessions to stop. I wanted my tears that seemed to be coming from an infinity pool to stop. I was desperate for it to stop hurting. This wasn't years ago; this was a few months ago. In between writing this book, selling out workshops, being fully booked with clients and surrounded by so much love. In between getting the stuff I want. There's no before and after in life. Yes, I am a space holder, spiritual guide and teacher, but I am a soul and I am human. In a constant cycle of suffering and delight, the same way that you are. What made the pain stop was my faith. This faith I have that life is impossibly rich and filled with blessings and beauty. The realisation that I can survive and thrive from a pain so severe because I have experienced joy so powerful that it stamps it out. I trusted spirit to show me how to heal and in time, to grow. I grieved, I cried, I slept, I danced to Joy Division, my mum held me, I wrote, I was supported. I survived.

BREAKDOWN INSURANCE

I later emerged from my grief into new opportunities, a new outlook, new people and a deeper respect for myself. Into the inevitable power and transformation that I trusted I'd be moved into. When I couldn't see a way, spirit showed me one; it always does. To get into that, we need to take out some breakdown insurance. The roadside assistance that we can always call on in our road trip to creation, when the car doesn't want to function. The insurance is how we can persuade ourselves to be in the emotions of it, but also the reason why we know that we'll be able to overcome it. Our insurance policy includes: **faith, realisation** and **support.** This is when spirituality becomes survival; it's the insurance to see the scope of our resilience and that we can handle it.

First up comes faith, as when we're suspended, we can't see that this precious life is made up of moments that are designed for our ultimate spiritual growth. Spirit wants us to create a life that sustains us and gives us the opportunity to have an embodied sense of the beauty that exists on this blue planet. If there's only one thing that you take from this entire book, let it be this. This is my daily intention. My eternal prayer. The only script tattoo that I'd ever risk having etched onto the surface of my skin.

Spirit, I trust you to guide me to return back to . . . *me*.

Drink that in for a moment, savour it, feel the taste of it on the tip of your tongue as you say those words. This is how we shift out of the sphere and trust that we aren't being punished, even if we think we're on the universe's shit list. That while we have free will there's something beyond us and when we have no idea what it's doing, can we trust that it's here to guide us to growth? In fact, if this was the only thing scribbled onto your manifesting list, you'll get all the blessings. This is the belief we hold that can make some of the stuff we're carrying feel a bit easier to reconcile. Our faith tells us that we wouldn't be given anything that we can't handle, so when we're sobbing for a week we know we will get through it. We always have our faith, because life is always happening *for* us, even when we're convinced it's happening *to* us.

PAUSE, TAKE IT IN, AND . . .
Trust in Spirit

Make a note or say this out loud: 'Spirit, I trust you to guide me to return back to . . . *me*' or 'I trust that all things are working to guide me to return back to . . . me.' Mix it up, freestyle, rinse and repeat if this feels good.

What comes up when you're in the energy of returning back to *you* is the realisation that you're a spiritual being. This becomes the second tier in our insurance policy because it highlights that we have this in-built tenacity to survive and thrive. When we only see ourselves as a physical, structured and logical being, we don't see that we can overcome. It took us so long to even reconcile the fact that our mental health is as important as our physical health and that the mind and body are connected, let alone that then becoming a part of our popular discourse, through the help of increasing awareness and campaigns. When that realisation hits, when you're spirit-informed, if you're in the bath, upset and confused, you don't deny yourself the release, because you know that it's part of the human experience. You know that this is part of the gift set of life, even when you want to get a refund for it. You don't resist enduring whatever wants to meet you, because you intuitively understand who you are. That's what gets me through, the strong sense that I can conquer any human experience when I tune in to my inner world and call for support. When you set an intention for spirit to guide you to return back to *you*, you're also handed the strength, resilience, vulnerability and courage to withstand anything that you have to go through or to know you can ask for help when you can't.

That's why support is the final piece to get us in and out of the depth of emotion. I get it, I know full well how terrifying it can be to surround yourself with feeling. There will never be enough faith or realisation of your strength that can go beyond the need for support. We all have varying degrees of being able to sit with things, based on what's in our stuff. Please don't berate yourself or anyone else for that matter, if you can't get there. This is not yours to experience alone. When I'm in sessions, I often ask my clients to share what's happening in their world right now. That's when the outpouring comes. It often surprises them that they had so much to say or so much emotion coming to the surface. It bubbles up so unexpectedly, because it's been waiting for the chance to. All the unexplored and unresolved feelings, longing for someone to give them permission to be there. The way we shift what feels unbearable to becoming manageable is only through support and resources. It is not only ours to carry. If we were here to do it all by ourselves, we wouldn't be surrounded by billions of people. There wouldn't be people who dedicate their lives to being in service, we wouldn't have friends, partners and family. That's why we're all here together. To not experience it alone.

One of the hardest things to do is ask for help, but it doesn't actually need to sound like that. We can book a session and just speak, we can text a friend and ask them to make us laugh, we can call someone and ask if they'll sit on the phone in silence for a bit. We can reach out to the charities, organisations, services and mental health practitioners (see page 269) that are waiting for us to engage with them. When you're in pain, the severity of it increases when you're alone with it. We can't eradicate the experience that's hurt us, but we can reduce the hurt by letting someone in. Someone to hold you while you're in it and to hold you when you're ready to get out of it. The recollection that closeness is always close by might be exactly what you need when you're in the thick of it.

PAUSE, TAKE IT IN, AND . . .
Work Out Your Breakdown Insurance

When you're next in your feels, or trying to avoid getting in them, write out your insurance policy to reassure yourself that it's OK to get in and that you'll also get out. Fill in the blanks, in your mind, journal or phone:

1. I have faith that _____

   (Explore your trust and faith in whatever you believe in)

2. I realise that I'm _____

   (Describe who you are underneath it all, your strength and resilience to overcome)

3. I can get support from _____

   (List out the services, resources, therapists, friends, family and practitioners who you can reach out to, if necessary)

OH, THE GROWTH

Once you're in the changing shape of emotions, welcome them, let them pass through, shake it out when you're ready to not be in it anymore, and let it move. This is the healing; the physical, mental, emotional and spiritual healing. Incorporated within this are the actions, the ones that are unreachable when we're stuck in the sphere. We can't act when we don't know what's prompting the action.

If you're welcoming in anger, then you can respond by finding actions to release it. Maybe you'll faceplant a linen pillow and scream, jump up and down to some funky house or write a foul expletive-filled letter to your ex that you'll never send. We have to be in the anger to know what to do with it. The actions can be small, but at least they're action. When we get out of the sphere and into the feels, it's only then that we can act. Even by saying something as seemingly straightforward as, 'What I'm going through is so rough, can I just be super-kind to myself because of that?' That's all we need sometimes and you get to decide on the action, based on how resourced you feel. Honestly, your action might be getting out of bed and going for a walk. It could be getting a Reiki treatment because you're tense. Having extra therapy sessions. There might be exercises from this book that have served you that you can bring back up or self-care practices that always comfort you. You can slowly move through the action as if you're walking through golden syrup. You can hold yourself with as much softness as you can cultivate through the action. Your action can also be as simple as setting an intention or taking a breath, as long as it's coming from a base of feeling it all instead of resisting. Spirit might offer us things that come with an all-you-can-eat buffet of heartbreak and stress, but we are always given the opportunity to grasp something that we might not have, had we not been through it. If your desire is being a poet and having an abundant, creative and free life, then spirit knows this. When anything, even the painful stuff comes your way, it's designed to propel you into that desire. The breadth of it and all the experiences and flavours that the life you want to create has to offer you. I've had clients who've been in the blur of feelings and committed to action, to then be met with an 'aha' moment and that they want their life to move in another direction. The ones who lost a parent and from the grief came decisions to adopt a child, get closer with their siblings or work through their stuff on abandonment. The ones whose break-ups have escorted them to a year of solo travel, a partner who showed them the love they never thought was possible or a period of relearning who they are at this time of their life.

PAUSE, TAKE IT IN, AND . . .
Just Notice

As you move through the rest of your day, notice what comes up. Be it an emotion, thought or sensation in your body. Before you put it in a box of being bad, good or anything in-between, spend a few moments investigating it. Focus on the felt sense of whatever is coming up for you. How does it feel in your body? What story does your mind create about this emotion? How can you get comfortable with it? Can you just notice it and learn from the noticing?

It's all here to recalibrate and get us back on the road to creation. When you free yourself from the corset of filing things as either good or bad, even if you label a situation as abhorrent, it will still guide you to return back to *you*. In due time, in spirit time, in whenever we fancy time, we'll find something there. It never has to be rushed or forced into, that's why we have to be right in the feels to see that growth is always waiting for us on the other side. We might not get it today, or even in three years' time, but we will get it. As my life is often one long-ass meditation session, I was able to see why I was offered my MS diagnosis. Some of the more judgemental wellness folks amongst us might say that I ate too many doughnuts, sniffed too much mould or had a vitamin D deficiency, and we'll just never damn well know the medical reason. Nor do I need to. What I *do* know is that it transformed my relationship with my body. It taught me how to be tender with it, a body that I had neglected and disassociated from for most of my life as a trauma response. It taught me that my body has done everything in its power to survive, to allow my soul to exist so that I can do this work and be of service. I can even sit in admiration at the fact that my baffled little immune system is destroying my myelin, because it cares so very deeply, it wants to protect me. This body that I punished so hard and resented became one that I regularly cry tears of gratitude for and touch with so much reverence. The condition? Sucks. The growth? Phenomenal.

It goes without saying that it's tremendously tedious that we often get our blessings via these nonsensical, painful occur-rences. We can hold this truth along with asking ourselves: but, how else would I see? How else would we *remember* that we're spiritual beings, but to go through the very real, human, phys-icality of it all and get through it? Forgive me for the cloying nature of what I'm about to drop here, but it needs to be said. We sometimes need to experience physical sadness to see that our souls aren't sad, to feel unlovable to see that our souls *are* love, to face illness in our bodies to know that our souls are never sick and to be in the darkness to understand that under-neath it all we are pure light. When you feel the harsh reality of all these things, and so deeply feel the *opposite* of all that you are, you can then see, recognise and feel into the capacity of who you actually are and who you could be. It's then that you grow, as you know you can.

I find out more about the meaning of life by watching David Attenborough documentaries than I do from listening to self-help podcasts. Nature teaches us that growth isn't some-thing that needs to be rushed, we just need to let it come – we can't control what occurs. If a hurricane wants to come, it'll come. If we're hiking and find ourselves stumbling into the liv-ing room of a poisonous snake, then that's what happens. We can't control when and if the rain will let up. When we get hit with harshness, we submerge ourselves in the uncertainty of being there. We don't have a timeline to feel it all, but we receive everything we need to keep going, whether it's calling in love from people, speaking to a counsellor, journalling or meditating. We don't know when the light is coming, but little glimpses shine through the dark. We can't see the growth every single day, when we're in the trenches of it, but we're still growing. Just like if you're watching your indoor mushroom kit grow, you won't notice the difference in growth from Wed-nesday morning to Wednesday evening. We don't always see the growth or feel the little by littleness of it all, we just allow the inevitability of us growing to move us forward. Then before we know it, we rise and it doesn't stop there; we take what we've cultivated into the next episode of our life and see what new levels of growth await us there.

SIX

It's Time for an Internal Promotion

D o you know how many bowls of cold, tasteless overnight oats I've consumed in this lifetime? Choking on those gelatinous tadpole eggs that they call chia seeds. I did this because every exasperatingly labelled 'clean eating' book suggested that this is the cure-all breakfast of champs. I ignored the gnawing bellyache that the oats gave me and with that I gulped down my intuition, because, well the book said so. If it's not the sad little oats, then it's the algorithms that intuit what we should see, do, read and watch. At 9pm every night, Siri aggressively suggests that I should 'send a message to Shannon', my best friend. When I put my headphones in, my iPhone doesn't even give me the chance to decide which app to open, it instead informs me that I usually open Dropbox when I'm using headphones. Basically, the world we live in is designed to keep us disconnected from our intuition. It's why our relationship to our intuition can be quite complicated, and better described as a 'situationship'.

Here's the thing – we're *all* intuitive. Even though I carry a pendulum in my purse and get called 'an intuitive' by fancy magazines, it doesn't mean that I'm more intuitive than you. We're all *plenty* intuitive; we just feel further away from it sometimes because our world doesn't really encourage us to use it. Often in our efforts to tune into our intuition, we believe that it should look and feel a certain way, but realising that everyone's intuition *will* look and feel different makes it much easier to step into. I decided to do a randomised controlled trial, just kidding, I asked my Instagram followers and clients to describe their relationship with their intuition. The answers they provided show just how varied our experiences are. See which of these responses resonates with you:

> *'It's definitely there, but I don't always trust it and I always regret it when I don't.'*
>
> *'Very up and down. When I'm not taking care of the basics like sleep, I can find it very hard to tune in.'*
>
> *'It's my superpower! I regret all the times when I didn't trust it and I feel like it's a tool for life.'*
>
> *'The thing I always ignore and then immediately I realise why I should've listened!'*
>
> *'It's like my shy fairy godmother that I want to know better — learning to hear her!'*
>
> *'I'm slowly learning how to tune in. Listening is the hard part, as with any kind of communication.'*
>
> *'It comes in waves, sometimes it's an obvious inner voice, other times it's a vague feeling.'*
>
> *'I'm working on distinguishing between intuition and anxiety.'*
>
> *'Like a reliable, all-knowing best friend, who is forgiving, even when I don't make an effort to listen.'*

'It's somatic and connected to my body. My stomach is a doorbell telling me something big is coming!'
'I know I have it, but I'm not sure how to really get into it.'

PAUSE, TAKE IT IN, AND . . .
Reflect on Your Intuition

In your journal or phone, write out how you'd describe your relationship to your intuition. Jot down any major life moments that happened when you listened to it and when you didn't and how it comes through for you now.

As you can see, your intuition is probably not going to feel exactly like someone else's and you don't need to attach any judgements to your relationship with it. When we struggle to tune in and connect to our intuition, it's often because the stuff we carry is in the way. When we listen to our intuition, we start to move into all that we are; we start to see the love, delight and beauty that we are. Our stuff convinces us that we don't want all that growth and magic. Ain't got no time for it. Our minds find all kinds of stuff and distractions to keep us away from our essence. We convince ourselves that our intuition is wrong, that we're not intuitive and that we can't trust it; all things that are designed to slow our road trip down. When it comes to our intuition, it's like peeling back the sticky label from a handwash bottle; there's always resistance, but our intuition acts to reveal and guide us on the road to creation.

When my clients ask me why they can't connect to their intuition, I ask: 'Do you have enough time and space to?' Time and space are prerequisites for intuition. We're used to things being spelled out for us – it's why people ask influencers for their outfit details when they are right there in the caption. Unfortunately, your intuition isn't going to come and scream in your face. You need to be still and pause for long enough to listen to it. Undoubtedly, it's hard to find the room for our intuition to come through, when we are so wrapped up in our thoughts and the minutiae of how to successfully stay alive and adult each day. We devour busyness and productivity and while the hustle is real, it does put our intuition on the substitute bench. This rich and wise source of all-knowingness just wants to come off the bench and play in the match of our lives. It's time we let it. There's so much commonality in when we ignore our intuition and come to later regret it. Just imagine a world where we all worked with our intuition on an even deeper level. We all knew how to connect, tune in, trust and listen to it. Do you know how much would change, how much we would question and how much we'd grow? It's pretty incredible to think about what our world would look like, if we all tuned into our intuition and tuned out of the life that we think we *should* live and where we prioritise 'being okay' instead of 'being great'.

INTUITION IS . . .

So, before we can do that, let's dissect intuition. Let's go back to our road trip. Intuition acts like the road signs – the signs that allow you to see, feel, hear and comfortably know what you need to do to create your best damn life. In each episode of life, you make decisions and work with spirit to grow and move forward. The signs are not always easy to decipher, which is why we convince ourselves that we're not all that intuitive. It's just like driving down a road in an unknown place and trying to figure out exactly what all the signs to your destination mean. You might pull over and ask a passer-by for directions, so you'll *hear* the sign when they respond. Then as you drive further you *see* an actual road sign or you might get to a crossroads and just *know* without reason if you should go left or right. The trip continues and suddenly you *feel* in your stomach that going down this small winding road without street lights is not what you want to do. Or, you might get lost but *smell* a clean, saltiness – a scent that guides you to the sea. These are all different types of signs and you might only notice one of them, a combination of them or all of them. These are the signs your intuition also uses to guide you, via your senses. If you took a nap in the passenger seat, read a book or spent the trip arguing with whoever is in the car, you'd miss it all. You'd miss the signs laid out for you. To see the signs your intuition is offering and communicating through you, you just have to be aware. Your intuition will allow you to find your way.

This is exactly why you may have believed that you weren't intuitive enough or connecting to your intuition properly. As in our road trip analogy, our intuition works with all of us in such different ways. We have the tendency to see intuition as being only at the reserve of tarot readers and spiritual practitioners; that you need to gaze into a crystal ball for hours and see visions to be intuitive. But, seeing is only one of our senses. You're probably familiar with the term clairvoyant. It always reminds me of the classified ads listing the services of local psychics – they're often called the Clair Senses. You can tell that I prefer to keep things more fluid, so instead I'll explain it through our road trip, seeing as we're all having a lovely time there, chilling in the back seat with a packet of M&Ms.

Imagine that creation is a road where your intuition will guide you, with spirit in the passenger seat helping you to notice and navigate the signs through each phase of your life. There'll be some signs that you can recognise and others that you can't, and that is perfectly fine. It's worth noting here, too, that if you have anxiety then it might take some time exploring, as well as support from a mental health practitioner, to tune into your intuition. One of my clients has social anxiety and when her mind told her to avoid going to see her friends, she believed it was her intuition. After some time, she started to journal the difference between her anxious inner voice (fear-based, obsessive, avoidant) and her intuition (calm, clear, visual). Take your time to be curious with yours and keep your resources close-by. Exploring your intuition from a calm, neutral space is beneficial, so notice if you're tired or stressed when you feel or see something.

As I mentioned, the road we travel along will have different types of signs. You'll be able to *hear* some, just *know* others, *see* the signs, *feel* them or maybe even *smell* or *taste* them. You'll drive past some of them, some will feel really spot on and others may not make much sense to you at all. These are simply the ways that our intuition communicates with each of us individually. From the age of 7 to around 13, I had all kinds of weird dreams and visions, so the signs that my intuition used to communicate with me were through *seeing* things, otherwise known as clairvoyance. I'd often find myself daydreaming in class and taken on a visual journey where I'd see people in my life doing things. Fast forward and those things would actually happen. You can imagine my horror. Bingeing on *Sabrina the Teenage Witch*, *Hocus Pocus* and *Charmed* and pretending to have superpowers is banter by the minute, until odd things *really* start happening to you and you're too young to make sense of it.

Intuition is episodic, and it's why I'm not a fan of labelling myself as clairvoyant, clairsentient, clairaudient or claircognizant. During each episode of your life, the way that your intuition will communicate with you will change and combine. There might be a particular sign that you work with the most, such as feeling things in your body. But, on some days you might hear ringing in your ears when your intuition wants your attention or just *know* exactly what you should do without any reason to. There'll be times when it'll feel very quiet and others when you feel more connected. We continue to trust through it all.

This is still true for me now. Once I got older and started heading deeper into all this and not being so afraid of it, I was still seeing things but had more control over when I wanted to receive messages and when I didn't. I took a Reiki course out of curiosity, not expecting to get a shouty call to leave my career behind. During the course, I started seeing colours. In the attunement, where my Reiki master Torsten Lange performed an energy-based ritual to awaken the life-force energy that we already have within us, all my intuitive signs became more prominent. I kept seeing purple and to this day that's what I see whenever spirit is around me; it happens during meditation, Reiki sessions and whenever I'm working with clients. I also *heard* a voice that boomed into my ears saying that this is my calling and it's time to step into it. Then came the *feeling*, which

I get the most when I'm giving Reiki, where I feel temperature changes or sensations in my hands. I've always done daily work on connecting to my physical body after the trauma it's experienced, so *feeling* things isn't one of my most dominant senses. For me, *knowing* and *hearing* are the prominent ways that my intuition speaks to me. This entire book is a result of that. So, expect your intuition to change as you do and don't second guess what comes through for you. It's always different, but it'll always be true and right for you and all we need to do is learn and feel further into it. We can't think our way into this; intuition requires embodiment.

We are well and truly spoiled and I adore that we can get Deliveroo to bring doughnuts to our doorstep in 20 minutes or we can get a same-day delivery of an outfit we need to wear that night. We like it, we want it, we can get it. While we munch our way through yuzu-scented dough and wait for the delivery driver, it gives us the illusion that spirit works with this same level of pace. It doesn't. Intuition is a slow mover. Spirit and our intuition only care about working in whichever timing will make the most sense for us to get the stuff we want in life. That's never when we want it though, is it? We usually rely on our intuition when we're being pulled into decision-making. That's often when my clients book in for a session. There's a decision afoot and they might be struggling to decide what to do and waiting for their intuition to kick in to help them with it. If you're sitting on an email that requires a response in 2–3 business days and your intuition has headed off on annual leave, then, of course, it's highly unhelpful. But, when we take the time to cultivate our connection to our intuition, if we need to use it quickly, we'll have more tools to be able to access it. Also, just as a rule: if someone needs a response from you about something that will potentially change your life and you're not ready to give one yet, tell them you need more time. Their urgency is not your urgency. They can wait. That's exactly what your intuition will tell you too.

Pausing is a must

Speeding past this step of making time for your intuition is as seductive as eating the entire box of said doughnuts, in one sitting, which I've done many times and have yet to regret. But, time is fundamental here. I can already see your calendar filled with obligations, friends to reply to and things to do that feel way more pressing than making time to listen to your intuition. I get it. What I will say, is that time spent now will lead to time saved in the future. Plus, we also have to question why we need convincing and bargaining to get us to take time out to just *be* with ourselves. When we link the dynamic between time and intuition, there's an understanding that it just takes how long it takes. It may not make rational sense in terms of conventional time as it's harder to define. We can't go into meditation for 20 minutes and expect to receive the answer to whichever question we've asked that day. We can't go into a tarot reading and expect to figure our entire life out in one go.

Most of the time we have these expectations and we push and prod our way into our intuition and expect it to respond when we ask. It *will* respond, but maybe not in the way you expected it to. If you are going into a meditation practice with the intention to connect to your intuition, in the hopes it will lead you to making a decision, it may not come up in 20 minutes. It might, instead, plant a seed of *knowing* within you that guides you to buy a cookbook. So far, so unimpressed right? Then you make one of the recipes and during this immersive experience where you're having the time of your life and completely in the present moment, it comes. While you chop up a tomato and shimmy around the kitchen, you hear an almost imperceptible voice that tells you about the career decision you need to make. It often happens that way. Was the 20-minute meditation a waste of time? Absolutely, not. It was the catalyst. When you make time to create space, you're allowing your intuition to give you the road signs to creation in whichever fashion that will make the most sense for you.

Pausing is the medicine that I prescribe in the face of uncertainty. When you're not sure how to move forward, what to do, where to go or what to say – pause. If you're struggling to connect to your intuition or spiritual practices – pause. It's like saturating your weathered hands in almond-scented hand cream after too much hand sanitiser. Such good medicine. One of my personal peculiarities happens when I'm typing on my laptop. I find a moment of tenderness at the end of each paragraph I write. I create a pause by letting my middle finger trace the length of the space bar a few times, finding slowness and presence within that simple action. Feeling the pace change between the square, hastily typed letter keys to the spaciousness of the oblong bar gives me a respite so my brain can download the next word to type. Pausing doesn't need to be a six-hour retreat; it can be as long as the space bar. It's the medicine for forming a wholesome relationship with your intuition because it allows for time to explore it. You won't be able to ascertain what signs your intuition will use to communicate with you, until you have enough time and space to sit in it. It's always there for you and just requires a pause to get curious and communicate with it.

PAUSE, TAKE IT IN, AND . . .
Explore Your Intuition

If you've got time today, then set an alarm for when it's convenient, or block off some time in the next few days to do the practices below. Allow 30 minutes minimum, but the longer you do it, the juicier it'll be. All you need is a comfortable space where you won't be distracted and a pen and journal. If you feel called to do so and want to get fancy with it, then set some crystals around you. The ones in my toolkit for this are: lapis lazuli (truth-seeking, meditation-enhancing and an aid for wisdom-seeking), amethyst (protection, intuition-boosting and the deepest sense of calm), selenite (energy-cleansing, balancing and spirit-soothing) and clear quartz (amplifying, clarity-producing and vision-defining). You can smoke-cleanse, light a candle, or do whatever feels good.

Read through the following three practices to get a sense of what to expect. If you can, try them all out in this order. Try to come into them without any expectations or judgements. If you don't get it, find it hard to stay in it, can't do it, face resistance or not a damn thing happens, that's all OK. It's an exploration – whatever you discover here is just beautiful. It is what it is.

#1

Close your eyes if that feels comfortable for you, or softly gaze at a spot around you. Take a moment to land in the space by taking a few deep, expansive breaths, or feel your feet grounded on the surface beneath you. Then bring your attention to the space in-between your eyebrows, where your brow chakra is located. Just feel into it, knowing that this is the energy centre of your intuition and perception. Feel this space expand and open up. You might visualise the colour indigo swirling around this space or you can try massaging this area with your index and middle finger. Spend some time connecting to this space and bringing your attention here. Notice and explore how this feels and what arises.

#2

As you step out of the first practice and into this one, ground yourself in the present moment and take three full breaths in your own time, in your own way. Then bring something joyful to mind – it might be a person that you love, a recent experience that made you happy or even something wonderful that you ate recently. Hold it, bring all your awareness and attention to it and then go exploring. Witness where this image is. Do you see it visually? Can you hear anything associated to it? Are there any sensations happening in your body when you bring this to mind? Can you smell or taste anything? Go on a journey with your senses and see where you travel. If you lose focus, just come back to the joyful thing. Take your time to notice what comes through and which senses resonate with you the most or if anything else happens.

#3

Shift now and move into a pause. To help you come into the present moment, find an anchor that will assist you in this moment. You can focus on your breath, breathing in and feeling your stomach rise and breathing out feeling your stomach fall. If your breath isn't feeling good to you today, then you can try focusing on the sensation of your feet on the ground beneath you or the feeling of your hand over your heart space. Then, just be. Notice. When you're faced with stillness and space, what do you notice? Are any thoughts coming in? What are they? Do you immediately start imagining scenes or scenarios? Do you listen out and find things to hear in the space? Does your body temperature change? What is your body doing? Just see what's waiting for you in the stillness and how you greet it.

Then, investigate what came up. In your journal write down what you explored during each of the practices, or whichever ones you tried. Try to write without creating a story around it. So less, 'I knew I wouldn't be able to do it,' 'Nothing came through obviously, it never does' and more just the experience and sensations. Write down if any of your senses and those intuitive road signs came through more strongly than others. See if you notice any patterns or similarities.

WHAT'S THE DEAL WITH CHAKRAS?

In the first exploration practice, above, we were paying attention to the brow (third-eye) chakra known in Sanskrit as Ājñā. Just a quick note on chakras, as nothing pains me more than someone obliviously saying on a TV show that their 'heart chakra is blocked' without any understanding of the history and various traditions that it stems from. The word chakra comes from the Sanskrit for 'disk' or 'wheel'. It's an ancient energy system that originates from over four thousand years ago in India, and was referenced in the Vedas and Upanishads, and more, before being brought to the West in the early 20th century. It is a holistic system that focuses on seven major chakras or 'spinning wheels' located in the body from the base of the spine to the crown of the head. The chakras contain life force energy (a major part of most spiritual cultures, traditions and religions) that's also called prana, ki, qi or universal energy. Each chakra corresponds to not only a physical body part, such as the eyebrow and forehead, but also works on a mental, emotional and spiritual level. The idea is to have an open flow and channel of energy passing through all the chakras for optimal balance and wellbeing. As a Reiki master teacher, I work with the chakras daily as they correspond to the hand positions we use in a treatment. You can read more on the chakra system in *Find Your Flow: Essential Chakras* by Sushma Sagar.

Chakras relate to intuition in a few ways. First, we can work directly with the brow (third-eye) chakra as we did in the practice above, as this space allows us to see and interpret both what's happening around us in the world and also what's happening in more of an intuitive space. Also, all the chakras create a pause in our thinking. We're able to use them as prompts to *feel* into the unseen and not take everything as logic and fact because we are more than just our physicality. So, in the exploration practices, if you felt something around your heart, it might be worth thinking about it as both the physical blood-pumping organ, but also as a chakra that prompts us to delve into our identity and relationship with others. Our desire to both love and be loved and how we navigate intimacy, self-love and compassion. We can use this knowledge as a tool for self-inquiry when something arises. We can see what lies beneath the sensation or thought.

That's what exploration with our intuition is about: moving away from the judgement of our experiences and being endlessly curious about them. When we know that our intuition is communicating with us through different signs, we can work out what to do with those signs. You get to ask yourself more questions, to dig a bit deeper and inquire. If you realise that your prominent sign is seeing things, then always go beyond the vision. Ask yourself how what you saw made you feel, if it connects to anything, what were you doing before or after you saw it? Use those as clues. If you noticed that you *felt* more in your body and the experience was very somatic, then maybe you can link the areas you felt something to the meaning of the chakra located in that area; could that be the message? It's all an exploration. Don't force it though; not everything means something – a rumbling tummy might just mean that you forgot to eat lunch and not that you need to step into your full expression of self. With time and practice you'll figure it out, either way. Part of this figuring out and familiarity with your intuition is spotting where you outsource it to other people.

HIRING OUT YOUR INTUITION

We like asking people for their advice or opinion and, in short, it's just another way that we give our power away and distract ourselves from our intuition. We find it easier to think that if we ask someone for permission to do or think something, then they can then deal with the regret that we ourselves get pulled into when life doesn't go the way we imagined. 'Well, everyone said this would be the best move for me, because I didn't know what to do,' aka we didn't trust ourselves enough to make the decision. Add to that the *very* human need for belonging and it's always easier to hire out our intuition and go with popular opinion than come home to the truth of what's within us.

Our intuition thrives on trust, so the more we explore and listen to it, the more we get met with what we need. It needs proof. We lose that proof when we hire out. Here's the part which deserves a highlight, in my very unhumble opinion: why are we so willing to trust someone else's stuff, instead of trusting ourselves? Because, let's face it, when we ask others to make decisions *for us*, we're often asking all their stuff. Especially, if your relationship is based on not upsetting them, rather than on growth. We want our loved ones to be happy. We want them to be OK. Sometimes, that looks like not rocking the boat, which doesn't always make sense for growth. Say you want to move to Melbourne: your best friend tells you that it's an horrific idea mainly because they don't want you to leave them, because people always leave (their stuff). A colleague tells you to go – they don't want to work alongside you anymore because they feel threatened by you (savage, I know, but their stuff). Someone else tells you it's a dumb idea because they could never imagine moving to another country themselves (their stuff). No judgement right, because we all have our stuff, but so often it's this part in people that we're asking. The ideal situation is having someone who'll just hold space, listen, ask you some more questions and help you to tease out *your* own intuition about it. For them to focus on guiding you to navigate your decision and sharing pieces that maybe you didn't think of, but only as a means to assist in *your* intuition guiding you. We tend to run information through the filter of our stuff. So, let people in, allow them to support and guide you but, ultimately, always find the route back to your own intuition. Prioritise that always, because you can always trust your truth.

Our own stuff also gets in the way. My client Sam was mad at their intuition. They said that they've trusted their intuition so many times and its always led them into some nonsense.

I guided them through a meditation to create a pause and open up their third-eye. We spoke, and when I asked them how they know that it's their intuition speaking to them, they said, 'Well, it's usually really obvious to me and says that I should do the thing, and I know deep down I should because it makes logical sense for me to.' Then we realised that it wasn't their intuition chatting to them; they were listening through the filter of their stuff, including their fears. We're so used to this shouty voice in our head that's often really mean to us, that we listen to it without investigating. When we see that our intuition works in very subtle ways, it's unlikely that the loudest blunt voice in your head is your intuition. Your intuition is probably not going to weigh up the financial repercussions of moving to a bigger house. It will most likely give you a sign for how you can make the financial pieces work because it's the best move for your family. So often, the voice we've spent a lifetime believing is our intuition, isn't. But, as we get comfortable with it and explore, explore, explore, we can cut through to see which part of us is running the show and where we need to create a pause for the whispers to come in.

Ultimately, your intuition is where it's at. When your choices and spirit-informed actions come from this space, they will always be the most aligned ones. Acknowledge that this process will always come in episodes. See your intuition as your best friend; these relationships go through many episodes. The tide comes in, the tide goes out, but the sea is always there. These relationships require maintenance; the constant pieces that enable us to always trust that our intuition is there even when it doesn't seem like it. We check in with our best friends, we inquire gently, we prompt and we have an ongoing dialogue.

We ask our dear friends to proofread text messages and co-sign outfits. How would it feel to do that with your intuition? This isn't a one-way street; how naive of us to think so. When we come into maintenance mode with this wise part of us, we ask to be shown a sign, we listen, get curious, explore, create a pause for the answers to come through in any way and in any time, listen and take inspired action. Then we return again and again. To maintain this lifelong relationship with our intuition, we just hang out with it a bit every day. You check your phone and emails constantly, so this is just like checking your email, to see if there's a new message that your intuition has for you.

PAUSE, TAKE IT IN, AND . . .
Check in With Your Intuition

Keep this in mind as you move through the rest of your life. At any point in your day, it doesn't have to be long, set an intention to receive any signs, wisdom or guidance that will guide you to return back to *you*. You can write or mentally bring a situation to mind that you're working through. Or, simply set an intention to connect to your intuition. Close your eyes, if that feels OK for you and spend some time connecting to the situation on your mind. If your main sign is to *feel*, then you might just scan your body here and see what you notice. If you *hear* things, then just create some silence to welcome any sound or voices in. If you *see* things, then you might see what images or colours come through or draw something. Work with your signs and senses as you play the situation you need some assistance with over in your mind.

When you've promoted your intuition, time and pauses take on new importance in your life, because that's what it takes to connect and then trust it more. A theme that comes up regularly with our relationship with our intuition is all the times we didn't listen to it and then regretted not doing so. I'm not into regrets, because spirit will U-turn you back on the road to creation. Don't sweat it. You were supposed to be diverted to experience or learn something. You'll return. We always do. To lessen the hold of regrets, fears or doubts about what decisions to make, we move into our intuition. If you know that you have created time and space to listen to your intuition, you've explored how it communicates through you, listened, trusted and made a decision; that's all you can do. Even if your decision ends up as an epic fail, there's no space for regret because you listened; you didn't hire out, you didn't buy into anyone else's urgency and you checked to see that it wasn't your stuff clouding the way. That's all you can do. The more you trust your truth, the more you lean in and allow it to guide you; your relationship with it will evolve. It will continue to teach you and each time you listen to it, you're saying to your intuition that you trust it. With more trust comes more availability for your intuition to be your ally through life. Always choose it.

SEVEN

Just Do You

I worked in retail alongside my fashion journalism degree to fund my 'vintage shopping for research' habit. Days I do not wish to relive, as there's only so much transferred anger one can hold when you don't have someone's shoe size in stock. On one particularly mind-numbing shift, in-between me sneaking off to the toilet to write my dissertation on post-it notes (dedication) and hauling shoe boxes onto the shop floor (hell), I overheard something. A colleague was eating her lunch and decided to season her chicken salad sandwich with some racism. She was telling someone how much she likes me and that I wasn't like 'other Black girls', wait for it, because 'she doesn't, you know, wear tracksuits, trainers or anything and she's so quiet and well-spoken'. Just to unpack this deserves a **pause, take it in, and . . .** , but, instead, we shall collectively shake our heads.

These microaggressions and stereotypes have followed me around like a pigeon chasing a chunk of leftover sourdough. I've heard how beautiful I am, educated I am, gentle I am, different I am, all followed up with, 'for a Black woman'. This particular girl had a firm vision in her head of who I *should* be and how everyone who looked like me ought to be. Now, we can get into an entire race lecture here, but I only have energy to shake my head and sigh, because this is just to demonstrate a bigger picture of how pervasive people's rules for us are. It's also at the core of any conversations around authenticity and why we often struggle with being able to define who we really are, instead of who we think we're supposed to be. It's why we spend so much energy being wrapped up in trying to be the person who we think will be liked and loved. It's why we end up trying so hard to be anyone other than our authentic selves.

We've been stepping more into defining who you're embodying as you return back to *you*, your true, soul-level, unapologetic, spirit-informed self and that's where we also find our authenticity. 'Just do you' is the standard guidance that spirit and myself give to clients in sessions. Authenticity is placed in your return back to *you* and once you've integrated this, your relationships with people and the world around you will feel a bit easier to navigate. You'll be able to create more. To get into authenticity, we need to flip through the rule book, the rules and regulations that other people and the world have for us, all based on who they want us to be. We strictly follow endless lists of the ways we are expected to be citizens of this planet. Society thinking that you need to act a certain way because of the colour of your skin, believing that you must be the cool, shiny, carefully created character that will bag a second date or choose a career that you absolutely detest because your parents said you have to follow the same path as them. We feel our way into the resistance that comes from doing the opposite of whatever we think we should be doing. We're always following a rule, contemplating a rule and living in someone else's rule-book to determine our path in life and believe that it will direct us to all the good things, but this is the equivalent of entering the wrong destination in your GPS. When we follow the rules of others, we instead end up on that country lane, driving towards who we think we *should* be, instead of who we actually are, or more accurately, who we might be too afraid to be.

IT'S TIME TO BREAK THE RULES

There are three categories in the rule book that we carry around with us and remembering this is really helpful in being able to break them: first, is some of the **Stuff** that you've been looking at. The piles of self-criticism, sabotage, beliefs, doubts and fears that we lug around daily. These individual rules are a result of what we think is possible for us. Say one of your untrue beliefs is that you're not worthy of love. This can then form a story of, 'I guess I have to stay single and not waste my time' all the way to 'I should pretend that I like this renaissance art exhibition, as this person will like me more.' Our other stuff, including the doubts and Three 'U's (see page 27) that make up our fears, can do the same thing and push us out of our authenticity. If you doubt that you're good enough, then it will always feel easier to try on the persona of someone else who you think *will be* good enough. Whether this is trying not to complain at work and stifling what you want to say, so you're not seen as a 'troublemaker', or begrudgingly holding onto a friendship that doesn't make you feel good because you want to be seen as a suitable friend. It shifts us into a role of who we think we have to be.

Then we have **Other People**, those who have certain expectations of you in their rule book. Be it a partner, friends, family, teachers, colleagues or employers. Or the people you might compare yourself to and hold yourself accountable to. This is the category of everyone's favourite ick, people-pleasing. We want to please people because we want to fit in. Because yeah, we're human and it's kind of our thing. Even when at times it feels easy to believe that we don't need each other, we do. While it seems like we're getting further away from each other by focusing more on what divides us, our work is to remember who we are underneath everything that we allow to divide us. When you recognise your wholeness, you'll start to realise that when you know who you are, you won't work like you're vying for a promotion to please people. We wait for people to define and show us who we are, so much so that who they believe we are becomes our own narrative of self. This might look like sticking with a 20-year career that you hate because a careers coach at school told you it would make sense to follow that path. One of the worst questions to ask someone who's been in an abusive relationship is why they stayed for as long as they did. While the complex reasons for my staying in such a relationship for nearly a decade could fill this book, one of them was the rules from other people. When I told people in his life about what was happening, most of them responded by saying that I should stay because of what might happen to him if I left. That I should stay because he's been the best he's ever been since he met me. That I have to continue the relationship because he'll change. That I have to keep going because he deserves another chance. That I really ought to stay because he needs help. My help. I fell asleep next to him and those were the unasked-for rules that kept me awake. Other people's rules. The rules that showed me who people expected and wanted me to be. People-pleasing in its truest form is actually a lovely thing, when it works on the principle of genuine care and love for someone else and wanting to please them because of that. All too often our version of people-pleasing looks like us prior-itising someone else's peace and happiness above our own. To listen to who they think we have to be, because it feels safer than being someone who may not be liked. But, why would you want to please other people and not please yourself? Do you know who you are? How much of an impossibly dream-like, jaw-droppingly delightful person you are? Imagine not want-ing to please that.

Lastly, is the **World**, and the stories from the world around you. We know that they're as much a story as *The Tiger Who Came to Tea*. We didn't have these stories when we came into this world. The world gave them to us and by doing so gave us even more rules to keep us away from our authenticity. Our bodies can't differentiate between when something is really life-threatening or not, so the stress response can be triggered by an email, missing a train or looking for doom online. Over time, the more the stress response gets activated, the greater the toll on the mind and body. We're so used to running on this response that we're stressed all the damn time. It's become a very normal, low-lying state for us. It's also to thank for most of the rules we have in the world. We're told that we have to be productive, that we should work within the context of an approved working week and that we must always work hard to be successful. It took a whole pandemic for employers to let people work from home, because society has this warped idea that we have to primarily work in offices. We're told that success looks like a certain salary, how much is in your current account and how impressive your LinkedIn is. We're told that we have to monetise everything that gives us even a bullet-point sized amount of joy. We should basically do whatever it takes to be booked and busy, because surely that means you've made it. We link our productivity and stress levels to our worth. We respond to 'How are you?' texts with 'I'm so busy' because we think that's how it's supposed to be. When a global crisis happens, within seconds the internet tells us how we need to respond to it. We see comments asking why someone hasn't posted about it and why they're not using their platform appropriately. They make demands about how we should be, as if they own shares in our profiles. We're told that we can't be silent, asked why we are silent and in the blink of an eye told that the post we shared was wrong. We're told that we should be angry, we should care, we should act, we should be better. We're expected to live in the rule book of everyone else but ourselves.

PAUSE, TAKE IT IN, AND . . .
Challenge Your Rules

In your mind, journal or phone, think about the rules that you've been carrying. What are the stories you have from your stuff, other people and the world that have caused you to think that you have to do or be something other than who you are?

I looked through my client notes and realised I've probably had over a hundred sessions in the past year alone where people came to me with a focus on these society-based rules. Questioning if they should leave their job or not, if it's a good idea to try something different or move into a completely new direction. Their fear? Breaking the rules. Stepping out of everything they've seen, heard or known in the world around them.

My client, Ama, grew up in the projects in Brooklyn. She never saw anyone around her who had their own business; she only saw people doing their best to get by, hustle and feed their family. Her worldview for most of her life was that she had to do her best to leave school, get any job she could, stay in it and then retire. She pushed out of this narrative and ended up becoming a lawyer, but when she found herself wanting to do something different and start her own business, these stories came back again. The new story she carried was that this wouldn't be possible for her. That she may have overcome one story, but the one where she has to stay and work for someone else remained. So, we discussed that what is true for some of the people she grew up with doesn't have to be true for her. That when we allow these rules to become true for us, we're hitchhiking in someone else's car to somewhere we don't want to go. We stop focusing on what we *know* to be true for us, but on what others want to be true for us. Also known as, Ama not starting her own business. It's always easier to listen to who we think the world would like us to be than who we know ourselves to be. Ama did eventually start her own business and moved to Portland where she is now, of course, thriving.

Does making those decisions disappoint people? Sure. Sometimes our world can't make space for those who only want to follow a path that leads to their own fulfilment, power and truth. We see too often the people who are mocked and met with incredulous stares when they share their alternative approach to life. This happens when I tell people about my issues with the institution of marriage. I'm expected to already have a spread-sheet of my imaginary guest list and to be waiting for some lad to propose to me. It bothers people that I don't, because it breaks the rules that people so rarely question. When we break the rules we may have fewer passengers to travel in the car with, but the people who are disappointed just ain't our people. Plus, they're the kind of people who sit in the backseat crunching too hard on cheese and onion crisps and asking 'Are we there yet?' Don't worry, you'll find *your* people.

These rules – your stuff, other people and the world's stuff – guide you down the road to being someone who you are not and who you don't even want to be. This isn't the route to cre-ation, but instead forcing your way into becoming someone who the world wants you to be, and you know what? That's what we're *not* going to do. This is where the difference between returning back to *you* and the idea of 'becoming' lies. There's so much pressure in thinking that you have to become some-thing more than who you are. Returning back to *you* speaks to the authentic nature that you've always been. It's about the spirit in you. It's just hard to see it sometimes. It's also covered up with all those shoulds. Like discovering the chocolate-filled Cornetto wafer cone tip after having to make your way through so much ice-cream. To reveal what was always there, waiting for you. You are already the version of yourself that you so long to step into. You're simply shedding the layers of rules and expectations that are in the way of that. Eating the ice-cream to get to the cone tip. When we think about becoming, there's an assumption that we can't connect to this authentic and whole self. That we have to become something that we don't already have. That there's conditions attached to becoming authentic. When we do this, we remain in a state of waiting to become someone else, instead of seeing that all we need to do is reveal who we've always been.

PAUSE, TAKE IT IN, AND . . .
Break the rules

Turn to this practice when you find yourself in a situation and you're not sure what to say, do or choose in order to break the rules and step into your authentic self. Then answer these questions in your mind, phone or journal. See the example at the end to see how it plays out.

1. S: Stuff

Are there any stories, swirling thoughts, beliefs, self-criticism, doubts or fears that I'm carrying about this?
If I didn't have this stuff, then what would I do?

2. O: Other People

Has anyone in my life told me what I should do here? Am I carrying any other people's stuff?
If I didn't listen to their rules, then what would I do?

3. W: World

What have I seen or heard in society that's having an impact on how I think about this?
If I released this narrative, then what would I do?

Example: You're in between date one and date two and realise that you've been trying to be someone that you're not. Trying to be who you think they'll like. You want to be authentic, but you're terrified of rejection. You grab your journal and do this practice:

1. *S: I have this belief that people will reject and leave me if I'm myself. If I didn't have this belief, I would trust that I can be exactly who I am because I can't pretend to be someone else for this entire relationship. Plus, if they do reject me then they're not for me.*

2. *O: I told my friend that this person is quite well-known and they said that established people hate when people act impressed by them, so I should play it cool. If I didn't listen to them, then I'd show more affection and tell them more about me, because that's who I am.*

3. *W: Dating advice is so confusing; I've read that I shouldn't act so interested early on and to be laidback and unbothered. If I released this, then I'd stop following a script and let the connection I have with this person determine what happens next.*

When we start to see that there's a version of us that exists beneath the rules, the shedding begins and is there a greater feeling than exfoliating and revealing skin as smooth as a panna cotta? It's when we release it all and find who we really are. Who *you* think you should be can only come from you.

In a recent session, I was working with a client who was struggling to work out what her thing is and the work she's here to do in this lifetime. I channelled this absolute gem that has stuck with me ever since, 'She is searching for who she *is not*, to be who *she is*.' It really speaks to the relationship between our stuff and ourselves and how it links to our authenticity and purpose. When we think we are only our jobs, physicality, what we do and what we look like, then we look for ourselves in those categories. When the answer isn't there. When we ask people for permission about what we ought to do, we're just finding everything that we are not. We question why things don't work out and why it feels so difficult to find our feet, when this is never the answer to who we actually are. If you keep searching for who you are *not*, to be who you are, then you won't ever return back to who you really are.

To be authentic is to be you without the rules in the way. To be authentic is to explore and create new ways of moving through the world, because you're curious about how you respond to it. It's about spending time with yourself, all four bodies of yourself (see page 133), understanding what makes your soul gasp and feels good to you. It's having a connection to your intuition and spirit, so you know that you don't have to go through life's madness unsupported. It's having enough trust and faith that you get to co-create with the universe and make cool shit happen for yourself. Creation is a process, it's this entire book, step by step, chapter by chapter, understanding, imprinting and exploring as you go. Discovering who you are and being authentic enough to stand in that and show people it.

When it comes to authenticity, it requires going inwards and inquiring, feeling and processing. Being aware of where you are in time and space and how you respond to being there. To be authentic is to be yourself, to step out of the self that's been created with other people's rules. To do that, we need to take it in and question what *we* really think and feel about absolutely everything. To be authentic is to be curious. You know when you read the latest fiction book that everyone is infatuated by and convince yourself that you like it, because you think you have to? Then, when you sit back, reflect and take it in, you realise that you hate every single page. Authenticity is owning your opinion when people ask. It's owning the fact that you and your spouse might want to be in a poly relationship and raise children with your other lovers, even when the safest option would be to silence that desire. To be authentic is to question who you are and to then own it. There isn't one definition for it, just as there isn't with worth and confidence. Your authenticity will never be someone else's. That's the point. It wipes out people-pleasing and having resistance to setting boundaries because your only work is in being your authentic self. People's reaction to you being your authentic self is irrelevant. Of course, this doesn't give you carte blanche to be a monster to people under the guise of 'But, I'm being authentic though.' But it helps to release some of the fear of how people may respond to you. You're just being asked to be yourself. Some people will adore you for being your authentic self and those are your people you get to ride through life with. Find people who just enjoy your existence, in all its messiness and delight. People who will love you when you call them panicking at 3am because you made a boo-boo. Who'll love you when you snort and choke every time you laugh. Who'll love you because you hate when people sing happy birthday in restaurants (maybe that's just me). Who'll love you when you find it hard to love yourself. Those are your people and how beautiful it is to be loved by them, just because you've dared to be your brilliant self.

PAUSE, TAKE IT IN, AND . . .
Own It

Place a hand on your heart, and repeat this or something similar in your mind or aloud:

It is safe for me to be me. It is safe for me to be here. It is safe for you to be you. It is safe for you to be here. It is safe for us to be us. It is safe for us to be here.

Inevitably, there'll be people who won't like it when you're authentic, for a variety of reasons and none of them have much to do with you. As much as it may bother you, you're not for everyone and everyone is not for you. Bring to mind one person who you no longer have in your life because you didn't want them there. It's your right to not want them there. It could be because you didn't like something they did or it could be that they treated you unfairly. It's your choice who stays in your life and it doesn't matter what someone has done to get you to that decision. The same goes for you too. I'll buy anything that has a panda on it, it doesn't really make sense for the super-curated aesthetic that I uphold, but I just love pandas and I'm not going to hide it. Someone who finds pandas creepy (imagine, that) might hate that about me. But, I've been myself and this is the only me that I can be. All you can ever do is just do you and the reaction to you being you is not yours to take on board. This work isn't a freedom pass to excuse unacceptable behaviour because someone is being themselves. What it does is foster a collective of people who care so deeply about the world around them that they bring their truest, most whole, authentic self to that world. It fosters compassion for each other because we know just how hard it is to be vulnerable and to be authentic. I know that if someone shared all parts of themselves with me and trusted me enough to witness it, that it took *work*. Even if what they share doesn't sit well with me, if it comes from a place of integrity and truth. I respect that more than anything. There's always family-style compassion to be shared amongst us all, to honour just how hard it is to shift the fear of rejection that we all have within us.

PAUSE, TAKE IT IN, AND . . .
Fill in the Blanks

In your mind, phone or journal, explore who you are and who returning back to *you* is. Don't get into your head about it, see what comes through. Write, feel, speak, dance or listen to fill in the blanks with all the adjectives, characteristics and qualities that define you:

'I am someone who is _____, I am someone who is _____, I am someone who is _____'

Rejection is a barrier to authenticity. While the rules keep us from even knowing who our authentic self is, rejection is what keeps us from stepping into it, even once we've defined it. It stops us from being authentic, bold and audacious. If we could guarantee that we'd be unquestionably adored for being ourselves, then we all would. We don't because the fear of rejection is ever-present. We don't offer our full selves to people in case we're rejected, we find it hard to express our love for the same reason and we resist telling people the truth in case they reject us for it. It always feels easier to remain silent and to pretend to be someone else. It's easier to dress up as someone who is unbothered, when in reality your authentic self is beyond bothered. When we're not being authentic, everyone loses. The world doesn't get to see your magic and the room is thrown into darkness because you switched your light off. We can't see you and you need to be seen. The world will be a second-rate version of itself if we can't see your light, because you're here, existing, for a reason. It's not a coincidence. Show people who you are. They can't love you for who you are unless they see who you are. You can still be rejected for not being yourself anyway, so you might as well be yourself, right? Regrets ain't easy to deal with, but we tend to have more of them when we know we didn't show up in ways we wanted to. I've regretted not telling someone how I felt about them and that was only because my fear of rejection made me not want to be authentic. I was too afraid to share what was in my heart, when my authentic self was desperate to.

Even in that situation if I did share and I was rejected for sharing, that's all I could do; my work is to share who I am. It's not for me to be consumed by what the response would be. It would sting, but I know that I allowed myself to be open to the possibility of love, instead of not acting out of fear of the possibility of rejection. The regrets come when we know that our fears stopped us from being ourselves. Finding ways to be at peace with rejection and to break the rules, even if it feels awful, relies on you being fiercely solid in yourself, even when the world around you is in flux. When you live fully in who you are, when you return back to *you*, give yourself permission to create and know your strength, you become the constant even in the face of change. You evolve, adapt and change yet you know exactly who you are. You don't rely on the world around you to be unmoved, because you are stable, even amongst your growth. You don't force anything that's not in your control or whether people will like you or not. Your authentic self is the constant even when everything around you doesn't make sense.

My advice? Be like your heartbeat. Your heart is a constant part of you; it's unmoved but it's responsive. Your heartbeat increases and decreases, it responds to pain, to love and to movement. It gets heightened, it regulates, it pulses through you, it does everything it can to keep you here. Its rhythm changes. It continues to beat. Even when faced with complications, it's still solid, it's strong, it's resilient. It continues to beat. It knows that we can be pushed to the limit and it'll still continue. When you are like your heartbeat, you recognise that what exists around you always changes, people will come and go, jobs will, relationships will. Everything will end and begin again. You will shed. When you step out of who you thought you have to be, you choose to rise again in a new form, maybe in new places, the debris of who you were scattering, blessing and teaching everything around you. You'll be in the air, fall onto the leaves, create new life, and it's all because you were you. The authentic you that is underneath the rules, stories, doubts and fears. The you that will always continue.

EIGHT

Access Granted to Chill

How would it feel to simply say, 'I deserve gentleness and ease' in response to having a nap, taking a day off or feasting in the decadence of doing nothing? Instead of trying to find a reason why you deserve it or ways to earn it. Instead of acting like you need to understand how to calculate price-earnings ratios in the stock market before you're allowed to just *be*. When we chase productivity, it often results in believing that we should always be 'on', and there's a familiar uneasiness that arises when we sit in empty space. We're desperate to fill it up with something, anything that feels worthwhile. We believe that we have to always be doing things to earn our place in this universe. We tell ourselves that because we've worked ourselves to burnout, we can actually take a lunch break. We act like we can only wake up later on the weekend, if we had a late night on Friday. We think that we can only book a massage as a cheeky treat, when our back has more knots than a sailing yacht. It's time to stop believing this false hype and as the familiar line that often waltzes into our awareness goes, 'We are human beings, not human doings'. Have the nap, lie-in, book a day off; just because you owe it to yourself to prioritise gentleness and ease.

Why would you not believe that your wellbeing deserves being prioritised? You never need an excuse to look after yourself. We often busy ourselves with all the things that we are *not* instead of nurturing and finding joy in who we are. We chase the work, other people and looking a certain way instead of reconnecting to ourselves, when we need to feed ourselves not only on a physical level, but a soul-level too. Yet, we want to create and we want it now. We want to grow, to find purpose and meaning here and to be energised by all that we do. But, how can you ever know what to ask for, what you want to manifest or what desires make you come alive, when you've not had time to discover it? It's why creation or manifesting practices don't always work for some people. The things you think you want are often based on who you are not. Self-care is the way that we can discover and feel into all of that, because we are spending time on and for ourselves.

Before we go any further, self-care is never, ever selfish. Alongside believing that you deserve gentleness and ease, it's also helpful to see the dual importance of helping yourself as well as helping others. Take it from someone who has slotted into the role of a nurturer since I was a child, it's just not sustainable to take care of other people and forget all about yourself. If you have a child and that child's entire survival depends on you, what happens when you can't find time for yourself? We're not talking about two hours of face masks and puzzles. This is entry-level self-care. The absolute basics. Your child needs you to be here, to have the strength and resilience to be here. It's then your duty to ask for support and find even the briefest pause to tend to yourself. This is taking three minutes to breathe while you pee to calm your nervous system or a five-minute stretch while you're waiting for the pasta to cook. This is hydrating while your kid naps and flossing your teeth. This is how your child survives, by you taking care of yourself to then take care of them. Plus, you deserve it, because you're here. This isn't a luxury, it's a requirement.

Children aside, we tend to put all kinds of people first. It makes us feel good, we love each other and we know how connected we all are, so we help each other out. There's nothing wrong with that, unless we allow our service to others to come at the detriment of our service to ourselves. We can always make space to do both. If you have a partner or loved one who you're caring for, you know how hard it felt if you were sick and couldn't do what you usually do. The realisation that someone *needs* you. Even if someone needs you right this minute and that's what's important right now, give yourself the minute later. Valuing yourself matters so much because you matter, and what you do matters to the world. Again, we can't show up and give if we haven't given to ourselves.

In the early days of my business, I'd stay up till 3am writing client notes and then I'd be too damn tired to give my clients my all in the actual sessions. Doesn't make sense does it? We can only give without feeling horrific when it comes from a space of our own enough-ness. Self-care also allows us to spend the time checking-in with ourselves on *why* we want to give to others before ourselves. Giving should feel free, loving and plentiful. You shouldn't feel depleted or resentful for giving. If you find yourself always prioritising others and neglecting yourself, check in to see what lies beneath it. Giving should always make you feel better, never worse, and as much as possible come as a result of you being full first.

It's not always the easiest thing in the world to align yourself with being worthy and deserving of taking time for yourself. To be able to throw out the belief that you need to do anything in particular, or need an excuse to take care of yourself. You're worthy because you're here, so yeah, you can't be here and live fully unless you're taking care of yourself. When we get struck down by a cold or we break a bone and can't do anything, we truly realise how much our bodies do, to keep us here. We feel it when our body is not working at full capacity. We take it for granted, so it's really the least we can do for being here, to just take care of it. We can't actually do much for other people or the world if we can't even do it for ourselves. Your body works pretty thanklessly, but it's not invincible; it needs fuel, rest, love and nurturing to be able to do things for you.

As we continue to understand that our souls continue in ways that our human, physical body doesn't, we start to see how we've got our bodies and souls confused. We believe that we are only our physical body. We believe that until we die, our body will just keep on going, that it is capable of anything, that we can push and push and it will be just fine. When, really, it's our *souls* that can do this. When we misunderstand the difference, we push the body to the point of exhaustion and illness instead of seeing that it has needs and requirements to keep going. Our soul-level self, our true selves, do have needs, but in a very different way and they will continue regardless of what we do. Our bodies won't. It's why we hate pain, sickness and death; we think that our body shouldn't experience it, that it should be resilient, but it's not, it isn't supposed to be. It can withstand a lot, but we have to do our bit to support it. Our souls will continue to exist in a way that our physical body doesn't and our role is to shepherd our soul from one lifetime to the next. One way of being to the next. One physical body to the next. But, this physical body that you have right here, in this current lifetime, that's all you got. We can't grow, learn, love and find bliss if the body through which we do all of that is not being taken care of. So, please take care.

This idea of deserving gentleness and ease and believing that you're worthy of self-care is one of the central tenets of creation. The actual practices are, of course, where the bulk of the work comes in, but how many times have you committed to doing a lavishly complex self-care routine and stuck to it for about two days? We need to believe in why we're worthy of it and why it's so important. Not because it's become a slogan-sweater-wearing, hashtag-having, commodified thing. I've always looked to Audre Lorde's definition of self-care and to where so much of the popular verbiage on the topic stems from: 'Caring for myself is not self-indulgence, it is self-preservation and that is an act of political welfare.' It allows us to see what's really underneath all the unicorn-coloured bath bombs and brands selling us the same dusty stuff, but now folding it up in self-care marketing.

I love 'treating myself' as much as the next person, but there's only so many times that I can see it shouted at me by way of some visual merchandising. But, this is what we do. We make everything a money-churner, we co-opt it and we make material goods the source of our so-called 'becoming'. We hope that they'll transform us into the version of ourselves that we would like to be. That when we buy the candle we can de-stress, when we use the crystal we can heal and when we book in for the wellness retreat we can change. It's also why people may call me a healer, but I never do. I'm not a healer. I can facilitate your own healing and, yes, there'll be shifts, but nothing that you didn't have the ability to do within you already. We already know that we aren't *becoming* these new, shiny beings. But, simply returning back to ourselves. Crystals, practitioners, oracle cards and workshops are just accessories and beautiful supports to get back to that. Now, I wholeheartedly use, swear by and recommend all those things, but on one condition. That you see them as floaties. Those inflatable armbands we used as kids when we learned how to swim. Tools and goods designed for self-care can 100 per cent help you connect deeper to yourself, to look after yourself and to create powerful changes. A huge however is that they don't do the work *for* you and they never have all the power nor the magic. You do. Your intention does. They're simply the floaties. You use them, they'll help you to reconnect, then when you don't need to rely on them anymore, you start to swim without them. You always see them as a helping hand or training wheels to your intentions, but what you can buy doesn't shape or create your practice. Only you do.

You can always take care of yourself without needing to buy anything to get there. I light relaxing candles every day, but there's no amount of de-stressing a pretty little candle can do if I'm trying to respond to my emails. It can and only will help me to chill out if that's my intention and what I prioritise. If I make enough time and space to gaze at the hypnotic flame undulating for a few moments, then yes it will help. Otherwise, it's just a candle and I'm still hella stressed. You're always the constant in your self-care practice. Self-care is an all-access pass to creation, returning back to *you* and coming into balance. It's what we need to exist. We can't create anything if all parts of us aren't up for the task. We become aware of our stuff so that we can release ourselves from the confines of only seeing ourselves as thinking and physical beings. We do that so we can see the magnificence of who we really are underneath it: spiritual, authentic, intuitive and unapologetic beings. That we are not *only* this flesh and body, but without this body we wouldn't be here. Your body allows your soul to exist, thrive and create. We explore this so we can come back here, to the basics. Just as I described this book as a cosmic soup, so are we. We are mixed up and made up of four bodies.

WAIT, THERE ARE FOUR BODIES?

We are made up of physical, mental, emotional and spiritual bodies – four bodies that merge, collide and intersect to allow us to exist. Bodies that need to be brought into balance and harmony via our self-care practices so we can create. We focus a lot on the physical, especially in the West. I mean, trust us to look within the beautiful practice of yoga and turn it into a fitness class. It's why allopathic medicine is still focused on our symptoms rather than diving into the root cause of our symptoms. It's also why I'm a Reiki master teacher. There isn't a hierarchy in Reiki. Each of the four bodies are given just as much respect as the other, because that's how healing happens. Reiki kick-starts the body's ability to heal itself. The healing that happens occurs on any or all those levels. It's why I trust the work and why it allows for non-attachment.

When a client comes in with constant migraines, they usually want a physical healing – for the headaches to go. Sometimes this happens, and they receive a very physical reduction of their pain. Other clients may get an emotional healing. They realise that the unexpressed grief from a parent passing away was expressing itself as migraines. The session brought the grief out and then the migraines eased as a result. Healing happens in and around all those four bodies, because we are all of them. Honestly, so much of being able to see our self-care practices as a way to physical, mental, emotional and spiritual balance is because it really needs to be taken care of while we're busy chatting to spirit, making moves and creating our best damn lives. We don't want to be permanently exhausted when we're living a spirit-informed life and trying to create one. We have so much more fuel to keep driving when our four bodies are being taken care of.

What are the ingredients in this cosmic soup of your being, you ask? Well, the **mental** body is one that we're finally more well-versed in, thanks to all the awareness that we've had around mental health in the past few years. The mental body tends to be spoken about in quite a matter-of-fact way, but it exists on many continuums. It's our thinking space, belief system and intellect. Where we think about ourselves and the world around us. It's where we can find so much joy when we harness a sense of presence and awareness and use our mind to create and manifest. It's also where some of our inner stuff resides, which might look like our fears, doubts, beliefs and inner critic. Our mental body, just like the other three, operates in episodes. There are days when things feel easier, and days when it feels much harder to work with. It also goes further along to diagnosed mental health problems, such as bipolar disorder, post-traumatic stress disorder, anxiety and panic attacks. It was actually the anxiety attacks that I had in the past for many years that led me to start connecting to this idea of the four bodies. I didn't know that I had anxiety as I couldn't 'find it' in my mind. My symptoms were very physical – an upset stomach, my whole body shaking for hours and my chest feeling very heavy.

PAUSE, TAKE IT IN, AND . . .
Explore the mental body

Write down the things you enjoy doing, haven't done, think you hate doing, but are open to doing again and want to try out. Then commit to exploring them to see how they make you feel.

Ideas: Journalling, meditation, mindfulness

Which leads me to the **physical** body. When I realised that my symptoms stemmed from my mental body, I saw the connection because breathwork and meditation were the only things that helped my anxiety. It blew my mind that my stabbing stomach pain could be eased by a couple of breaths and calming techniques. Our physical self is who we think we are in our entirety, but it's just the façade and there's so much that it has within and underneath it. With that said, we need to take care of it, so all parts of us can be here. There's no point doing all the inner work if your body is withering like a neglected monstera plant. You can create and grow all you want, but your body is the only way that you can experience and enjoy all the good stuff you're calling in. This body is our physical body, skin, skeletal system, organs and everything that makes up our physiology. It's our job to not neglect it, but also not to prioritise it to the point where we forget all the other bodies that exist too.

My clients who I work with on their skin know intimately how the physical relates to the emotional. The goal in these sessions is not for physical healing; it's about finding peace with a skin condition. The healing and work on the skin then lives in the emotional body. Some of my clients *have* ended up seeing physical changes with their acne after the work, but so much of that was due to the mind-skin connection, and not physically changing anything.

PAUSE, TAKE IT IN, AND . . .
Explore the physical body

Write down the things you enjoy doing, haven't done, think you hate doing but are open to doing again and want to try out. Then commit to exploring them to see how they make you feel.

Ideas: Walking, body scan meditation, massage

The **emotional** body is our feeling space. It's how we feel about ourselves, others and all the things that happen in life. It also shows how we respond to all of that and it includes our nervous system. The emotions we can feel are so varied – take a look at the wheel you searched for on page 30 to see just how many we can access. We run all the other bodies through this one too.

I see this loop play out when I'm teaching meditation. My students will meditate, then they'll have a thought, a very normal thought. We can't stop thoughts and that's not the goal in meditation either. Once the thought (mental) comes in, my students will often move into their emotional body by reacting. The reaction is usually shame that they 'Can't switch their mind off' or blame because they 'Knew they wouldn't be able to do this.' This emotional reaction can then lead to a physical response, such as the heart racing or palms sweating. We're in the soup. The emotional body also encompasses how we relate to other people and what they bring up for us based on what this body, and all the others, have been through. Depending on our spiritual body and our relationship to it, this can affect the way we feel about people and our place here. If we have a connection to something bigger than us and believe in spirit, we might have more trust in people. We might be able to shift some of the fear that we carry and feel a sense of faith instead.

PAUSE, TAKE IT IN, AND . . .
Explore the emotional body

Write down the things you enjoy doing, haven't done, think you hate doing but are open to doing again and want to try out. Then commit to exploring them to see how they make you feel.

Ideas: Emotional Freedom Technique, affirmations, self-soothing

Just like in the physical body, and even after reading an entire book on spirituality, we can't prioritise the **spiritual** body and neglect the others. Being spirit-informed comes with the recognition that we're spiritual beings at our core, but we can't just float our way around town and not feel, think or move. We're here, in human form, to experience all of it. This body is our connection to spirit, intuition and the nature around and within us. In the same way as the physical, we often have to step out of it to then come back and delve into it. Our human experiences offer us the chance to be aware of our spirit. Our spirituality also helps us to navigate and understand those human experiences. When we return back to who we really are, it feels very easy to just stay in this space. To only do inner work and spirit work 24/7, to pack a bag and move to Bali (absolutely, no shade) to avoid human interaction and stay in a bubble of positivity. Yes, it might feed your soul and allow you to then serve more, but it shouldn't feel like life is one big escape room. That's not what being human is about.

You also don't need to leave your job and become a light worker or practitioner just because you've found a connection to spirit. If you have a call, answer it, but the point of spirituality is that it's who you are and the rest still gets to remain. You can stay in your job and be spiritual. It will help you to cope and find joy in your job. We're supposed to stay in the mess of it all and apply our spiritual practices to that mess. Then we grow and find magic in the mess. We're supposed to feel uncomfortable sometimes and get angry and triggered by people doing dumb stuff. You can eat what you want, wear whatever the hell you like, stay in the same job and be spiritual. It's not either/or. It's not a personal brand. We're all spiritual beings; it doesn't need to be yet another identity for us to be consumed by. Also, never let anyone say that you're 'unconscious' or haven't 'woken up' or 'awakened' yet, just because you don't know what a complex concept, teaching or astrological transit is; or if you just enjoy watching the news and being informed. No-one is more awake than anyone else, because none of us are sleeping; we are all here having a human experience. Read newspapers, be politically active, swear and gossip if you want to, eat meat if you like it. Do whatever you want to do, it doesn't make you more or less spiritual ... because you *are* spirit. This is what it is to be spirit-informed.

PAUSE, TAKE IT IN, AND ...
Explore the spiritual body

Write down the things you enjoy doing, haven't done, think you hate doing but are open to doing again and want to try out. Then commit to exploring them to see how they make you feel.

Ideas: Prayer, connecting to spirit, rituals

The actual practices you do are not for me or anyone else to define. They should come from a place of balance, choice and exploration. We tend to do the practices for the bodies that we feel most comfortable in. I used to spend most of my self-care time in the spiritual body. Giving myself Reiki, meditating to hang out with my spirit guides, doing tarot, spells, astral projection, cord-cutting ceremonies; you name it, I've done it. When I prioritised this body, the rest of me was in an absolute shambles, especially my physical body. During therapy, I learned that due to the sexual trauma I experienced, my trauma response was to disassociate. I spent 15 years doing everything I could to not have to deal with my physical body. I neglected it, undernourished it, punished it, criticised and overfed it. I barely moved my body and couldn't really label many of the sensations I felt within it. Once my healing journey that came through yoga, therapy and other practices landed, I was able to bring my physical body back up to where my spiritual body was. Now, I can't really imagine life without meeting my body every day – talking to it, caring for it, learning how to love it. But I hear you. It's easy to want to avoid the bodies that hold most of our pain.

THE WORK IN MOTION

Finding the unique ways that your intuition communicates with you has to be through a process of exploration, seeing what comes through for you and you alone. The same is true for self-care. There isn't a right or wrong way to do it. Just get curious with your four bodies by spending time doing different things in each of them, with the sole intention of it being for you, because you deserve it. Spirit gives us signs and obstacles to grow through, but the rest of it comes through our human experiences. Self-care becomes the evidence that we're spiritual beings, because being in our four bodies is how the inner work plays out in real-time. **Self-care is the inner work in motion.** This is how the work leaves your journal and moves into the rest of your life. Existing in a human body is the greatest professor we can ever ask for.

You'll want to find some self-care practices that are for discovery and exploration, as well as ones that are for maintenance. In discovery and exploration, you might schedule in some longer self-care bits once a week, fortnightly or monthly, depending on your schedule. Do yourself a favour and put it in your Google Cal; we both know that you'll skip it or forget otherwise, because 'it's only me'. If you won't cancel on someone else, don't cancel on yourself. Hang out with yourself, learn how to love and care for yourself. Always make the date.

Within this part of your self-care practice, find things to do that will speak to your four bodies and are designed to help you discover more about who you are.

This is also where working on your stuff lives, in noticing and exploring what being in your four bodies feels like for you. How that changes and evolves, as your stuff does. This is you in motion. If your stuff includes chasing perfection, and you've been working on it and accepting that you are enough, your self-care discovery becomes an audit. You get to see if this story comes up when you're out in the world shopping. You get to see if you're being authentic when you're on dates or if you feel uncomfortable with taking a week off from exercising. You observe, respond and take it in. This is the information that guides you to create. Discovery can also be just for fun, to push you out of your comfort zone, to try new things or just to experience who you are and how life makes you feel. Within this, I'll go for a facial to care for my physical body, make friendship bracelets for my mental body as it settles my mind, and dance around my room, barefoot and naked, to see how it feels to physically release emotions. You'll notice which practices make you tingle and which really serve you and want to become a part of your life for a while.

They'll also guide you to the second part of self-care, the maintenance. This is the everyday stuff, the things that just keep you going – the basics – and I call them Daily Promises. Mine are plastered on my desktop and on a widget front and centre on my phone. That's my Virgo rising and Capricorn moon talking. The maintenance practices are almost like the rent you pay on your mind, body and soul. Again, do what feels good and, most importantly, those things that you will actually do every day across the four bodies. I have seasons with mine, as I'll check in and see which bodies are out of balance and what's happening in my life at any given time. A mix of intuition and listening to what I need is how I choose my self-care practices.

Within the structure of your Daily Promises, let there be room within each one. After a lot of self-discovery, yoga is the practice that I feel most at home in. On some days when I log in to my Sky Ting yoga membership, I'll do a very fiery flow and on others I might do something more restorative. Likewise, I do what I call a Spirit 15. This is 15 minutes of a spiritual practice each day, sometimes that's Reiki on myself, other times it's visualising or maybe journalling to spirit. Yours might include physical things you do for health reasons, meditating because it really helps with your stress levels or just drinking enough water. Expect your self-care practices to change and don't be hard on yourself. This is all an embodiment of the work.

PAUSE, TAKE IT IN, AND . . .
Note Your Promises

Remember to create a list of Daily Promises at some point, as a result of your discovery and exploration. You can also write an audit of the physical, mental, emotional and spiritual practices that you've tried and want to keep.

DOES MEDITATION *REALLY* HAVE TO BE A PART OF SELF-CARE?

As I said before, pausing is the medicine that I prescribe in the face of uncertainty. It applies here too and especially when we think about self-care. There are practices that you just won't get on with and that's OK. If you feel uncertain, do something else or work with someone who can guide and support you in doing the same thing in a different way. I'm a meditation teacher, and it's a huge part of my practice, but it isn't as easy or simple as it's often made out to be. It's not as chill as closing your eyes, breathing for a bit and blinking your eyes open to a world of enlightenment and revelations. It's also unhelpful if you're met with 'just meditate' as the response to anything you're going through.

Meditation can sometimes be activating if you've experienced trauma, which I learned from my teacher David Treleaven. According to The National Council for Mental Wellbeing, in the U.S alone 70 per cent of adults have experienced some type of traumatic event at least once in their lives. That's a lot of trauma going around and during meditation everyone's nervous system will respond differently to what's happening. During meditation, as all the attention is going inwards and being present with that, someone might experience trauma or signs of dysregulation. That's why it's so important to create space for yourself when doing this work. If you want to learn how to meditate, don't jump onto YouTube or listen to a random untrained person on Instagram live, telling you to close your eyes and visualise a forest. Find support, go to teachers – we know how to make meditation a practice that will help you and not cause any harm. With the right tools and amendments if you need them, meditation can be life-changing. It's been proven to reduce stress and pain as well as improve mood and self-compassion. Just know that it's OK if you struggle with it or if it doesn't always make you feel 'good'.

By making time to explore, you might work out that your limit for meditation is ten minutes, or you might be able to sit for an hour and have the time of your life. You might discover that focusing on your breath makes you feel anxious, but placing a hand on your heart or focusing on your feet touching the floor might be the only anchor that you need to bring you into the present moment. You might discover that walking meditations suit you best, or repeating an affirmation works. Do your thing. It doesn't need a label.

One of my much-loved self-care practices is journalling and it's the one I recommend to most people. First of all, it only requires yourself, a pen and some paper. Think of the page as a listening ear, one that won't talk back, harass or judge you; one that won't give you unsolicited advice. The page is just there for you to share, to hand over your thoughts and whatever is racing through your mind and demanding your attention. Explore set journal prompts like we've been doing in the exercises, or just allow the pen to glide over the page and dump it all there. I don't always read back through what I write, but it might work for you to. Regardless of *how* you choose to journal, it allows for self-inquiry and you'll always come to a place of truth and understanding from doing it. Whether it's meditation, journalling or the hundreds of practices out there that you discover along the way, it's all keeping you in balance as you create.

SECURE THE RING

There's something so powerful in arising each morning, bleary-eyes and all, with the willingness to show up for whichever version of you wants to exist that day. Without conditions. As a way to cement that, I want you to secure a ring for yourself. You heard that right. This isn't a promise ring – it's a ReturnRing, a remembering, a way to symbolise this continuous journey of creation. A daily commitment to returning back to yourself. To being the constant. The open space within the ring is the space for you to create, to take care of yourself and to step into yourself. The space for you to expand into who you've always been underneath it all and, most importantly, to discover who you *are* through it all.

The ring is a reminder that with each glance down, each swizzle around whichever finger you choose to wear it on, you return back to who you are. On the days when you're in the thick of your feelings, doubting yourself and don't even want to get dressed, it reminds you of who you are and what your soul is capable of. A physical knowing that it's hard as hell looking at and working on your stuff, but it is always beyond worth it. It's a sacred reminder that you can overcome obstacles and twist them into opportunities. It's something to come home to, something that lives with you. In other words, it's a Touchable Affirmation.

First things first, get yourself a ring. The rule is to work within your budget. I don't want to receive any emails saying that you couldn't pay your rent because you bought this ring. Yes, buying it might make you feel a teeny bit uncomfortable because there's always some tension in plying yourself with lovely things, but it shouldn't stretch your common sense; trust yourself. It can be anything from a ring that took you four hours to make from some embroidery floss, a £5 number from the high street to the kind of ring that requires a private appointment. Whatever you feel called to do. You already know what my choice was, because we're blessed and highly favoured aren't we?

When you've secured your ReturnRing, create your Touchable Affirmation. One line, that's all you've got. The whole affirmation on a post-it note fixed to the mirror isn't as elegant as a ring, is it? This one lives with you and is only a glance or touch away. Within your one line write an affirmation that you'll carry with you, one that you'll remember and feels strong enough to break through your stuff. One that will remind you of who you are when you forget. Choose anything that's coming up for you based on the road you've travelled so far and where you would like to go. If you're really fancy, you can get one word from your affirmation engraved in the ring; just putting it out there.

PAUSE, TAKE IT IN, AND . . .
Do a ReturnRing Ritual

Get yourself a ring and create your Touchable Affirmation. You can do a mini ritual where you:

1. Light a candle, smoke-cleanse, get dressed up, make it a thing if you like, but if you don't want to be extra, please jump ahead.

2. Repeat the affirmation out loud to yourself a few times, as you hold the ring in your hand. Really feel the words moving through you.

3. Seal the deal by saying, 'I charge this ring with these words,' and put the ring on the finger of your choice.

4. Then, of course, send me photos of you wearing it. This exercise is a non-negotiable, thank you and goodbye. Kidding, but not really.

Here's some affirmations to get you inspired, but please create your own as it's yours to define. Some of mine might feel like a reach or leap to get to (affirmations should never make you feel worse. if you struggle with them, make one that's more neutral):

I am being guided to return back to . . . me.

I am choosing myself.

I am treating myself with softness and compassion.

I give myself permission to create.

I continue to be unapologetic about who I am.

When you're in a constant state of enough-ness, you are able to give from this enough-ness, instead of your actions coming from a place of depletion. Isn't it so splendid to be able to give from a place of rest, and honouring and understanding of self? Not from any rules, excuses or guilt, but just deep awareness. To come from the space you've created just for yourself. It means that the self that you put forward is one who knows who they are and is committed to sharing it with the world.

We're well aware of how challenging it is to co-habit on this planet and all the infuriating ways that we can't control what happens around us, but we can take care of ourselves so we are better equipped at meeting those challenges and uncertainties. The best job that you'll ever have will be *you* and this work can never be selfish because it creates wider change. When we prioritise ourselves at the same time as holding others, we have the capacity to be active and give to the world around us. If we have the means to take care of ourselves properly, it's important that we do so. It not only gives us the strength to give back, but it allows us to understand just how much of a crisis food insecurity is. When we take an extra few minutes to be grateful for our food, eat mindfully and not rush, when we see just how incredible our bodies feel by eating, moving and meditating, we want that for every single person alive. We then go out into the world to share the benefits, to donate, to get active.

If we feel the benefits of working with a therapist or spiritual guide and how much it changed our lives, we tell our friends, we tell our families, we then sign petitions for everyone to have better access or we pay it forward. If we take enough time to be in the world, to read, listen and learn, we not only understand who we are, but how we view and see the rest of the world. We get to tune into the changes we want to happen and we fight to make them happen. If part of our self-care is financial wellness and reciting affirmations to imprint money beliefs, it allows us to understand money better. The same money that we can invest to create generational wealth. The same money that we'll be able to save and share with our communities.

Your relationship with yourself and the care that you give yourself *can* change the world around you. Just like a drop of rain crashing into a puddle, it reverberates out. It starts with you, then your community, then the planet. How could it ever be selfish?

Get the Stuff You Want

NINE

Riding in a Car with Spirit

There are moments in life when you look at yourself in the mirror and all you can do is proclaim, 'Why am I like this?' I had one of these moments on an early summer Friday. While my friends were counting down the hours till they could clock off and clock in to a weekend of debauchery, I was staring into the green light of my laptop camera, following my therapist's fingers as they moved from side to side like a rocking horse. We were doing some EMDR (Eye Movement Desensitization and Reprocessing) to assist in healing some of my traumatic memories – aka looking at my stuff. Then I moved into my monthly Power of Eight group call with my fellow meditation teacher, Reiki master, Human Design reader, breathwork facilitator and practitioner pals. Inspired by Lynne McTaggart's book of the same name, we meet up to set healing intentions for ourselves, community and the world – aka working on my stuff.

By the time I found myself looking at my reflection that evening, I wondered what the hell was this all for. That I choose to spend my Fridays cosied up with memories so painful they feel like internal razor burn. That I make my friends wait to hang out, because I'm sitting with my hand on my heart as seven beautiful souls spend five minutes intently focused on my healing. Why am I like this? Because, this is how I transmute the sticky stuff into the stuff I actually want. Stuff being: the still being alive despite experiencing things that would have made it easy to not be stuff. The career meets calling that makes me giddy stuff. The conscious love, friendships and connections stuff. The never-ending flow of unexpected income stuff. The there's so many damn things I've manifested that I've forgotten stuff. That's why I do it.

We all experience hard, bordering on excruciating, things. We've all experienced pain and suffering to different degrees of awfulness. There will never be any escaping that and spirituality isn't a means of avoidance. It just allows us to see that there is a life of hope after the awfulness. That we can be like those scabby plastic bottles lurking in street corners that then get recycled into a T-shirt made from plastic fibre. We can allow our spirituality to move us into what can be next. I mean, there has to be some kind of reward system for me getting you to bring up your fears, sit with fear, see where you put your worth outside of yourself, acknowledge reality and step into authenticity. Plus, all these damn exercises. This is how we get the stuff we want, by looking at and working on our stuff. This is why you do the inner work. To create. The non-negotiable? Connecting to spirit.

YEAH, BUT IT'S PRETTY SCARY, ISN'T IT?

It seems like one of those implausible things that belong in murky rooms with Ouija boards and an influx of essential oils that attack your sinuses. In our society, any kind of spirit business is either met with fear and scepticism or a creepy level of romanticising. The fear is simply of the unknown, which looks like you potentially acting as scared as if you were about to sky-dive without a harness. This plays out in quite a few of my tarot readings. The expectation that something bad will happen. That they'll pull the Death or Devil card and think they'll either literally die or find themselves in a rave with a bunch of evil spirits. Neither of which are true. I'm sure there'd be a breaking news exposé in *The Guardian* if people actually died every time the death card came up.

The fear makes sense on so many levels, though. If you've spent your entire life believing in what you can see, rationalise and understand, then your mind will have a pretty rough time shaking that up. You only need to look at the portrayal of energy workers and spiritual guides in the media to see that. I've cursed at the TV when yet another reality TV show brings in a token practitioner, just for everyone to roll their eyes and mock them. I've read so-called think pieces dissecting this work and declaring it a scam. I've done sessions in corporates and been met with people who wouldn't tell me anything, so as to not 'feed me information', before I did a reading with them. The classic test. When, really, can we expect something to work if we don't believe it will and don't do anything to assist the process? All this mocking, scepticism, testing and disbelief only happens for one reason. We want to be proven right. We want to stay within the certainty of understanding that the world and ourselves work exactly as we believe and have been told they do. Ain't no room for spirit in that. There's also some power in releasing the idea that 'evil', 'dark' or 'negative energy' exists. I've never encountered one, so I don't give it any power. I come into all my work with the assumption that only light and healing exists, so that's always what I'm met with. I don't acknowledge that anything else exists. Choose to only receive what will support you, when you work with spirit and that's what you'll receive.

To be able to connect with spirit requires the level of openness we usually see via *in vino veritas* or 'in wine, there is truth', where we suspend our fear, speak what we think and are open to whatever comes our way. Often five glasses of Lady A Rosé later. The other side of the hesitancy is often in putting people who connect to spirit on a pedestal. It happens in the sexualisation of anyone who is portrayed as witch-adjacent in films, and hiring out intuition to guides and psychics. There's a falsehood in believing that some people are gifted and born with the ability to connect and channel and everyone else are just muggles, who won't ever get close to doing the same. You have to step fully into the knowledge that you are a spiritual being to even be able to comprehend that you can connect to spirit.

Sorry, but being able to connect to spirit isn't a gift; it's not even all that special. It's your birthright and true nature. We just don't think it is, so we make the whole thing way more complex and loftier than it needs to be. We can honour and respect the work, but as soon as we start idolising, believing that it's only available to some and not others, we give our power away. Accepting that you *are* spirit, so therefore you can connect to spirit is vital. Sure, we have our physical, mental and emotional selves too and we need to acknowledge the fear that comes through those bodies, but we all have the capacity to connect.

Being spirit-informed differs from religion and old-school spirituality, in that there are no rules, no-one else involved, no gatekeepers or structure. There's no such thing as being punished if you don't act right, or need to do all kinds of things because you fear what will happen if you don't. If you mess up here, you mess up, you'll get over it and you'll be OK. My Dad was in a band and they had a song called 'Heaven and Hell is On Earth' and truer words have never been spoken. We have enough to deal with in this lifetime, so you don't need to live your life in fear of what might happen when you die, because you think you made a mistake. You'll know when you get there innit. In the meantime, live your life as you see fit.

As we get deeper into this, let's look at my definition again: *being spirit-informed is grounded in your human experience. It's the personal practices you use to connect to anything that guides you to return back to you and create.* This chapter is all about the 'anything' that you choose to connect to. You being able to define this is how you create your own personal practice and release the fear of connecting to spirit. As you know, I use the word 'spirit' as that's what resonates with me. It's a word that encompasses a sense of openness that can contain so much within it. There's an airy, mystical quality about the word, which reminds me of smoke. It can be both there and not there all at once. Hidden and seen. Able to move, shift and pass through things. Something that we see glimpses of but not always the full piece, yet we choose to believe in its existence. Calling it the universe is another common one, as it feels inclusive of everything within our world and outside of it, including the things we can touch and recognise, like nature, as well as whatever exists outside of Earth's hazy boundary. It's really an insert name kind of thing. You might already have a name or you might still be exploring one. As long as it feels good to you, that's all that matters.

The majority of my religious clients are very happy with me using the term 'spirit', while others feel more comfortable with me swapping out the word with 'God'. As long as you believe in what is said and you're happy, that's all that counts. Being spirit-informed isn't anti-religion; it can include both. I moved away from organised religion because I didn't choose to be in it. I was born into it and stayed until I realised it wasn't working for me, so I chose something else. I believe in the versions of spirit, source, God and Goddess that exist without rigidity and emphasise personal power. I believe in spiritual and religious teachers sharing what they've received and channelled as it can change lives and the world, as long as they stay in awareness with the stuff they're carrying and the impact it has. I don't believe in the outer power, control and manipulation that's enforced by humans under the reasoning of God or spirit. I don't believe in any belief system that attaches conditions to being loved by a God or spirit, especially when the essence of said God or spirit is itself unconditional love. I feel the same whether it comes from a priest, self-titled spiritual guru, cult leader or anyone who makes spirituality sound like multi-level marketing; same nonsense, just wrapped up in different names and practices. Whatever is left behind after all of that is what I'm down for. This is *yours* to define and what you believe in; it has nothing to do with anyone else. Neither does what you call it or even if you don't call it anything. You don't owe anyone a reason or explanation.

PAUSE, TAKE IT IN, AND . . .
Audit Your Beliefs

In your mind, phone or journal, answer the below questions:

1. What do I believe in?

2. What is my current relationship with spirituality?

3. What's my intention for connecting to spirit?

4. Do I have any fears, scepticism or disbelief about any areas of spirituality?

SPIRIT IS BASICALLY YOUR RIDE-OR-DIE

What keeps us going through all this self-exploration work, and also as we step into receiving all the blessings it brings, is our relationship with spirit. Just as you were driving in the car on the road to creation, and looking outside the window at the signs that your intuition was offering to help you get there, you have a passenger sat beside you. That passenger is spirit. In life, when you're riding in a car with spirit, you are in the driver's seat, as all parts of you are driving. There'll be times when it feels like the stuff you're carrying is making you hit the brakes because you're terrified of moving forward and growing. There'll be days when you feel like your authentic self and you're cruising and blasting 'You've Got The Love' (The Source & Candi Staton version) at full volume. Spirit is never driving the car because *you* have free will; you can do whatever the hell you want with your life. When you've got your hands on the wheel, there's no space for fear because spirit is right there with you; it's powerful, but so are you. There's no room to worry about 'evil' spirits in the car because you simply don't believe they exist and worst-case scenario your glove compartment is packed with black tourmaline and smoke-cleansing sticks.

Spirit is right there, beside you, through everything in life. Through all the turmoil and grief, on the days when you exercise your facial muscles by smiling so hard and pick up all the incredible people along the way. It's there if you run out of gas, need to jump out to pee or have to shovel snow to get moving. It's always there. Spirit is often described as bigger than us, and it is in so many ways as it can see above, beyond and through situations in ways that we can't. It knows what our souls are capable of in ways we can't always see. It can bring us all kinds of wild and wonderful things that we see no way of getting. It delivers. So, we respect and trust in the certainty of that. With that said, when we create too much of a hierarchy between us and spirit, we don't see that we also have spirit in us. If we don't see that, then we run the risk of ending up in the exasperating waters of bypassing and fear. Spirit doesn't have the power to go to your job for you or tell someone to stop calling you; it will be riding with you, but you'll still have to show up for life. Riding in a car with spirit requires you to have faith and trust in it. Trusting that spirit will always help you rifle through your stuff, help you to see when you can't. And when you get too tired to drive? Best believe that spirit will take the wheel (or, Jesus, if you're down with that and also love country music). Spirit is our companion through life. The ultimate ride-or-die.

It's like every other lifelong relationship. My grandparents,

Euline and Conrad, who prove to me every day that heaven is a place on Earth, have been together for 50 years. They love each other in a way that you can't even grasp unless you've experienced a love so immeasurable yourself. There are times when I'll catch them holding hands on the sofa; times when my grandpa is trying to persuade my grandma to take some herbal medicine and she has zero interest; times when they get on each other's nerves because they've been together for a bloody half-century. But, whenever I stay over I hear them falling asleep as they whisper and giggle to each other. They always have something to say. This is what our relationship with spirit is like. There'll be times when you don't want to listen to what it has to say. When you'd rather stick right there in your uneasiness, instead of doing whatever it says you should do to get out of it. At times, you'll want to push spirit out of the car door and let it fend for itself on the hard shoulder of the M25. Then you'll come back to it; you always come back and it will be there. To listen, to guide, to surrender into. I enjoy indulging in a little banter with spirit, when it pesters me to do the thing, but I'm pretending I don't know. Then the signs come in. Sometimes the signs are subtle, other times they feel like someone prodding me in the ribs over and over again. I'll play little avoidance games until the signs become too loud and I just give up and do the vulnerable or risky thing. Which, of course, always leads to me creating.

The same is true when I'm doing tarot readings; spirit can be absolutely savage. Nothing will call you out on your stuff more than spirit can. It wants you to grow, so hitting you with some home truths is necessary tough love. Often that sounds like, 'You know what you need to do, you've always known what to do, so stop playing around and do it,' or 'How will it benefit you to know what's going to happen next? What happens next is none of your business, just let it happen.' Spirit always gets us to where we need to go, in any way that will help us to get there.

When it comes to connecting with spirit, it needs to be an ongoing practice to foster trust and faith. You wouldn't just let anyone ride in a car with you forever, unless you knew them, right? Connecting to spirit need not be long or a fully immersive ritual, although it can be those things too, but to be spirit-informed you need to have a relationship with spirit that includes you connecting frequently. Spirit can't be our get out of jail card that we eagerly wait to come up in Monopoly. Like the way I'd only pray as a child when some shit went down. I'd be on my knees quicker than Concorde's maximum speed (R.I.P) to ask for help, but not pray at any other time. We need to have a consistent connection because only then can we trust that spirit is guiding us to return back to who we really are.

I was watching an Oprah documentary in 2012 and she was interviewing 50 Cent, who I was convinced was my soulmate. So much so that I would dream of nursing him and his nine gunshot wounds back to health. Don't worry, I meditated on that little whiff of co-dependency and trauma bonding. In the documentary he said, 'Either pray or worry, don't do both,' and this is applicable here. If we are connecting to spirit often, we have less space for worry, because we trust. My fruitless attempts at prayer as a child were a waste of my time because I still worried. I didn't actually believe in what I was doing, because I didn't do it often. I didn't have the relationship with God to have enough trust and faith that he would help me out.

PAUSE, TAKE IT IN, AND . . .
Get Grounded

Let's ground for a second amongst all this spirit stuff. Unclench your jaw, roll your shoulders back, do a few neck circles, swizzle your ReturnRing if you have one, shake your hands out and take three long breaths. If you're in public, do whatever you need to come into your body.

MANIFESTING AIN'T MANIFESTING WITHOUT SPIRIT

This is not only about trusting spirit to come through when life gets rough; the same is true for manifesting. You can't manifest a damn thing unless you believe, trust and have faith in spirit. If you're asking for something from spirit, then you need to get to know it first. Manifesting sometimes feels at odds with our regular lives, but in some ways it's exactly who our world pushes us to be. Making us overly reliant on outer things, being able to have things, get them and buy them immediately. Hoping that they'll make us happy or better. Then comes the sadness and disappointment when it doesn't and we go searching for another outer thing that will. We like the easy-peasy, ask, believe and receive approach to manifesting rather than one that requires some excavation and introspection, because the shortcut to creation feels infinitely easier. Which is funny, as for those who resent people looking for an easier way over 'hard work', it's still coming from society's expectations of what it *should* take for us to have meaningful lives.

Manifesting has become something it isn't; the latest thing to become commercialised and packaged up into a trend. It's a commodified good and when anything gets this treatment it needs to be sold in a formulaic way so everyone can understand it. Here's the thing – there's no formula to manifesting – no rules, no superstition and no shoulds or shouldn'ts. Right now, all you need to focus on is your connection to spirit before you think about list-writing and affirmation-repeating. Connecting to spirit allows you to see what is possible, so you can expand beyond what you thought was possible. Then there's an immersion of you doing the inner work required and welcoming spirit in to cocreate with you. People often use neuroscience or quantum physics to *prove* that manifesting works. Or that we can have an approach that only exists in our mental body and not the spiritual. I understand that this can help to contextualise it, but why are people's experiences, heritage and cultural practices not enough? Why is our one-to-one connection with spirit not enough to prove manifesting works?

All the books and evidence in the world will not help you get the stuff you want unless you connect to spirit. Because, who exactly do you think is bringing you the stuff you want? Yes, *you* are doing the inner work, but to go beyond that into a more expansive place of possibility and creation, it needs spirit. It requires taking a step back and instead of saying that you're certain you can't have a second home in Lisbon on a £25k salary, maybe you just need to include hollering at spirit in your game plan. Maybe you can examine your fears around money, release your family's rules about having to stay in the same country and learn how to say more than '*obrigada*' in Portuguese. Shift being unable to imagine how you can possibly make it happen to believing in the unseen and unknown. The thing you want and currently don't have exists somewhere where you can't see it right now. In a space where you have no idea what will happen next and how you can make stuff happen. You know what else exists in that space? Spirit. Creation is about making the unseen seen, even when you have not one fragment of proof suggesting it could be possible. So, we allow spirit to be the proof. I decided that I wanted £10k in my bank account so I could start investing and plan for my future. At a time when my net worth amounted to around £200 and I was seriously considering gluing the sole of my boot back together, I knew I'd been doing my inner work, and I knew I trusted spirit. I had no idea how it would happen, I just trusted as much as I trust that if a dessert has marzipan in it, then I'll be into it. It happened obviously, not in one lump sum, but it happened.

If I had merch, I'd probably have a tote bag that says, 'Don't fake your orgasms and don't fake your relationship with spirit.' This isn't the time for pretending. There needs to be trust and faith, so there needs to be connection, which means you should actually make time to do it. There are all kinds of ways you can connect to spirit. These are the *personal practices* from our definition of being spirit-informed (see page xi). The things that we most commonly see associated with spirit stuff. It might be meditation, akashic records, astral projection, plant medicine, spirit guides, journalling, prayer, speaking; you could fill a library with the possible ways you can connect to spirit and none of the things I've listed need to be included. Through a process of exploration and trying things out, you'll see which practices resonate the most with you. The signs you picked up from your intuition (see page 109) might also help you out here too. Just like how it doesn't matter *what* you connect to, it doesn't matter *how* you connect. It's not shrouded in mystery or anything weird, and you don't even have to burn this page after you read it.

PAUSE, TAKE IT IN, AND . . .
Connect to Spirit

Come back to these general steps whenever you're ready to connect to spirit. To connect in the easiest way possible:

1. **Create space:** Do whatever is needed to shift out of your everyday-ness by creating some time and space to connect. Spirit hangs out in a different level of consciousness, aka somewhere more chill and non-obvious. It feels like when the atmosphere gets that gentle mist across the skyline. Play around with whatever gives you the 'just taken my jeans off and put my house clothes on' energetic shift. Spirit isn't like Siri, so you can't shout 'Hey' to wake it up; it needs some slowing down and getting ready, before you can connect to it. **Ideas:** Smoke-cleanse, have a bath, do breathwork, dance, medi-tate, get still, cast a circle, listen to music.

2. **Talk it out:** Promise that you won't close the book, but speaking out loud is incredibly powerful. Our words have energetic reson-ance—Dr Masaru Emoto discovered that our words and thoughts have an impact on molecules of water, so there's evidence that it does make a difference. Talking it out is when you share what's going on with spirit, like you're perched on a therapist's couch. This is just you sharing what you're feeling, experiencing or noticing. It might be a situation you're struggling with, something that you want in your life or just going over how much someone is aggravat-ing you.

Ideas: If you can't handle the thought of speaking out loud, then try writing it out in your journal or saying it over in your mind.

3. **Get clear:** Begging isn't a good look; this is just the space when you get clear on your intention and ask for what you're hoping for. You can set an intention to receive what's in your highest and greatest good or just anything beyond – 'Come on, just help me out.' You might set an intention to receive a sign, peace or understanding in a situation. You can ask for wisdom and guidance, to be able to let go of something you're carrying, to feel a certain way or to send love and healing to someone or something happening in the world.

   Ideas: Again, you can say this out loud, journal or just sit with it. It will be fast-tracked to spirit, so don't worry about if the universe heard you or not.

4. **Go connect:** You can leave it at steps 1–3, but to feel even more of a connection, try out your own practices. You might want to self-Reiki if you're attuned, do some yoga, pull some oracle cards or do a tarot spread, place a hand on your heart and sit in silence to feel the vibes, or you might have the urge to channel or ask your guides some questions (more on that imminently). The goal here is just doing something that helps you to tune into the smoky spirit space. Experiment with what you do here; if you get stuck or nothing lands, then you can set an intention for spirit to show you how you're being asked to connect. Wrap things up by saying thank you when you're done.

   Ideas: When you're on this step, focus on being open to receiving, to see what your intuition signs are bringing up for you and just enjoy the space, trusting you're connected.

5. **Be aware:** Now get up and go live your life. You might not receive or get an answer during this; you rarely will as spirit isn't working to

your schedule. Trust that you've done the deed and just pay attention. This time of connecting to spirit is simply to create space to be, in order to receive. It's the catalyst for receiving your intention, not the end game. As you move throughout your life, you'll be met with signs, changes and new situations; you might feel different or shifts will occur. It's not our business to know how and when any of this will happen – just trust, keep your eyes and your heart open, so you can then take action.

WHERE ARE THE ANGELS AND SPIRIT GUIDES AT?

Is that it, you might be asking? When do all the juicy visions, spirit guides, angels, mediumship or pages and pages of truth bombs come in? Now it's time for the advanced class at school, so just put your rational mind on pause for a minute while we get weird. First of all the concept of channelling is when spirit communicates through you, in order to give you wisdom, knowledge or guidance. My personal spirit CV includes working with my spirit guides, channelling information in the akashic records, communicating with spirit via the steps above every day and receiving intuitive signs in my personal practices. It doesn't include working or communicating with angels or the deceased, or receiving or sharing what will happen in the future. We tend to receive what we set intentions to receive, so that's why we'll have some people who are psychics, others who are mediums and some who can connect to guides. I believe that we all have the capacity to do all these things, but it doesn't mean that you will in this lifetime. You're here to grow, learn and live in alignment with your purpose. You'll be given the *ways* to communicate with spirit that make sense for that. If being able to translate your dachshund's barks will assist in your spiritual growth, then I guess that's what you'll be able to do. If it won't, then you're never going to know what your dog Sally is yapping about. Mainly because it's not your business and your business might be in having a sixth sense for smelling where the nearest bakery is. So, leave Sally alone.

Just because we can, doesn't mean we will, so please don't put any pressure on yourself to have visions, channel or be able to hang out with your spirit guides at will. My spirit CV looks the way it does because not only would I not be who I am without it, but I wouldn't be able to do the work I do either. I'm a full-time spiritual guide, so I happen to find it effortless to communicate with spirit. It's not a gift; it's just a part of the reason why I'm here. Just like how you might need to master Excel to be able to be an accountant, I need one to do the other. For you, it might be different and please know that's OK. You can't replicate my relationship with spirit and I can't replicate yours either. It's why we're not going into the practicalities of *how* to do all this here, because we need to focus on everyday spirituality before we can hurdle beyond it. By doing so we can expand our awareness to be able to welcome in other practices. But, do experiment, see what you feel called to explore and be open to whatever wants to come through. What wants to come usually happens organically – you get to call spirit in – but when it comes to receiving wisdom, let spirit call you back. Don't double-text spirit because you did an online course on meeting your spirit guides and you're still waiting for them to show up. It might not be the time for you to meet them or you might never meet them. Spirit will have another way, a way that is better for you to receive signs and information. Trust in that.

Even when you're communicating with spirit, it's normal to doubt if spirit is actually hearing you, and if all of your messages are actually getting through. There's nothing wrong with you if you start to question your faith and want to send a series of follow-up messages to make sure you were heard. Also known as, sending someone you went on one date with a LinkedIn message if they're not responding to your calls, texts and various social media DM's. Hint: Never cute, never a good idea, just let it be. Spirit always hears you and even when it doesn't seem that way, your life is a result of spirit hearing you. It is up to us to focus more on our faith and less on the response. But, doubt is allowed in the mix too. Just know that every time we hang out with spirit, whatever we say, think or do is received. How spirit chooses to respond is not always for us to now the exact details of. Trust that spirit heard you the first time. The response may not be a stream of information, but the evidence will be in the life you've created by being spirit-informed. Some of the reassuring things that spirit does is send us signs: for me it's blue butterflies, blue doors and the colour purple. For my clients it's robins, feathers, seals, songs, dragonflies, yellow, angel numbers like 22:22, triangles, boats and more. Expect the unexpected and keep an open mind, as it's all to show you that you're never *not* connected to spirit.

When you channel and relate with spirit, it has to communicate with all parts of you. Not just the energy you embody when you return back to *you*, but all your stuff – the resistance, fears, human filter, experiences and beliefs you see the world through. It's a direct line, but one with a ton of static. Our four bodies (see page 133) are constantly changing from moment to moment. We are cyclical beings. In this moment, you might be 10 per cent irritated, 20 per cent exhausted, 30 per cent at peace and 40 per cent angry. They can all exist at the same time, because you exist. In the next ten minutes those percentages will probably change. Spirit is working with that every single day and it dictates how, when and if you channel.

I once had a client who was struggling with exactly this, after she had an intense vision during a retreat in Portugal. She hadn't had such a clear experience before and in the vision she saw her future partner and the family they'd have. Spirit gave her a name and where they would live. She was hooked on the information and booked in because she'd read every single book on clairvoyancy and how to be a psychic and she wasn't seeing anything. In most of her meditations she was 80 per cent forceful and 20 per cent pissed off, because she wasn't channelling and was desperate to. Spirit will meet you with whatever you bring; it just might not give you what you think you need, because of the percentages you're holding. We pulled some cards and the message was, as I predicted, for her to let go. To be able to find peace that her vision was a blessing and a moment in time when she needed that wisdom, so can she allow it to just be that. What also came through was that it's perfectly fine for her to come into her connection time with spirit feeling forceful and pissed off. She just needs to know that she may receive a sign or nudge to self-soothe instead of an action-packed love affair premonition, because of that. There might also be times when you lose faith or can't think of anything worse than connecting to spirit. This might happen after you experience a loss, grief or something happens to you. The things in life that make you question everything. When this happens, be with it, don't judge it. You can be in a season of not communicating and instead simply say, 'Spirit, please hold me through this' and soothe yourself for as long as it takes to come back.

PAUSE, TAKE IT IN, AND . . .
Affirm This

I am exploring and releasing any beliefs, stories, judgements, doubts and fears that I'm carrying about my ability to connect with spirit.

Focus on connecting and spirit will decide how to give you information and what to give you, based on how you're feeling and what you're bringing. You don't need to be at peace to connect to spirit, but being more at peace might mean that spirit will share messages with you via writing, for example. You can be as angry as hell, and it might mean that spirit will choose to guide you to a life-changing Instagram account instead of being able to connect to your late grandmother like you've asked for. In a day or year later, that could all shift; you might receive wisdom in totally new ways. Why? Because you've changed. Spirit adapts to you because it's here for you.

You also probably won't even realise or believe you're channelling most of the time anyway. What you receive from spirit is different to your active, human mind and we can tell this by asking the same question. Say, you want some clarity on moving forward, ask yourself this in your journal without connecting. See what comes through. Then, follow your steps to connect to spirit (see page 164), and ask the same question in step 2. See what comes through this time. Do you receive the information in a different way? Does it feel the same? If it does, keep at it, your mind might just not be into it today. Be open, release your expectations, focus only on the connection and if you feel the urge to start writing, speaking, listening deeper, close your eyes or search for something; then do it, you're channelling.

PRAYER NEEDS A NEW PR

While the five steps to connect to spirit (see page 164) can be as simple and short as you like, we can make it even more bite-sized. I'd recommend committing to the process for a while, to really foster a connection and give yourself the pause you need. With all this work, we take it in to then look beyond it. We step into full discovery mode with our self-care practices, so we can then chill and focus on maintaining them. We get so familiar with our inner critic and that pesky self-sabotaging voice, to then be able to have compassion and non-judgement for it. Owning that our stuff is a part of who we are. Once you're feeling at home in your spiritual practice, and regularly connect to spirit, you might want to have a daily constant that only takes a handful of minutes. This is what I do every morning before I get out of bed, and it's a prayer.

Prayer is a big word isn't it. Depending on your experiences with religion, you might have felt a shift in your body as you read it. I get that. Feel whatever it is that this word brings up for you; be it confronting, neutral, curious or anything in-between. When I think about praying, I can almost feel the indents on my secondary school-weathered knees. The marks that were a symbol of hours spent kneeling on wooden pews with the tiniest slither of pleather laid over them. Praying confused me because I wasn't sure if I believed in the figure whom I was supposed to be praying to. To pray meant to believe, trust and have faith in a God who I didn't feel belonged to me. That I didn't have access to unless I followed certain rules, went to church, and didn't roll up my school skirt above my knees. Praying felt like an act of duty instead of agency. Fun fact: my party trick is reciting the prayer I said before each class in my Catholic school, in both French and Spanish. I remembered a few years ago, when I launched into 'Au nom du Père et du Fils et du Saint-Esprit, Amen' and was struck by how much meaning the words lost because I didn't have a relationship with God or spirit. As I *did* enjoy the daily repetition of it, I wondered if I reclaimed prayer, by making it feel like an empowered choice and more like having spirit on speed-dial, if things would change. It did.

I had a chat with spirit, I asked about prayer, my resistance to it and how I could reclaim it. Spirit has always got me covered, so I channelled a prayer. A prayer that was the missing piece to my morning, regardless of anything else I do in my practice, I say it. On the days when I have ten deadlines and find myself browsing dresses I'm not going to buy on Reformation instead, it's there. When I'm crying in bed because I told all my clients to believe in love and now that I'm being called to do the same thing it feels like hell, it's there. So, plastered on the front of my phone is the prayer, it goes like this:

Spirit, I ask you to bear witness to all the stuff I'm carrying. I ask you to show me where I can grow and where I can heal. I ask you to take my place in areas of my life that I feel unable to move through. I ask that you listen to what is in my heart and mind and provide answers and possibilities where I am unable to see them. I ask that you take my hand and give me what I need to pass through this moment of time. I ask that you allow me to surrender into your hands, that which I am no longer able to see clearly, understand or to carry within me. Allow me to be at peace with myself, to know myself as you see me and to understand where I am and what I am placed to do in this lifetime. And so it is.

If this wasn't channelled and I wrote it myself, it would have probably been more like 'Erm hey, show me what you got, peace out,' but here we are. Reclaiming prayer is pretty wonderful and bloody powerful. It's a shortcut to connecting to spirit in more of a brushing your teeth and flossing way. It's maintenance. It's what it is to be spirit-informed and there's something really beautiful that happens when I wake up to the security of these words each morning, no matter what the day itself has to offer me. This is where spirituality becomes who we are and how we move through the world; a state of being instead of constant doing.

My great-grandmother Sylvie told my grandma, 'If you can go dancing, you can go to church' and that's pretty much how prayer slots into all the hot gal activities I like to partake in. I wake up, say a prayer and let all that happens in life happen, knowing I've put my faith in something, anything. If you feel called to, create your own, something that feels familiar, empowering and birthed from a place of choice. It might be words that come through when you next connect to spirit; see what happens. If you really can't get past the word prayer, then change that and make it your own; it can be called a note to spirit, spirit comms, whatever you fancy. Once you have it, you can recite it in the morning and afterwards trust that you're riding in the car with spirit. Creating is (un)intentional to some degree, because spirit is guiding you to where you need to be. It's helping you to filter through the crap standing in the way of your desires, while holding you through life's peaks and pits. This is all you're doing in this prayer – creating connection and welcoming in trust. A daily practice of peace. You can spend longer moments with spirit, you can do as many rituals as you want, you can have super-intense manifesting activities, but know that even in this minute or two of praying, you are doing profound work. Riding in a car with spirit is grounded in having a personal prayer and following steps to connect, so when shit *really* goes down, like it always does, you know spirit, so you trust spirit. When you want to get very intentional about getting the stuff you want, you already intimately know who you're asking for it from. It just becomes easier. If it's not your vibe then come back to, 'Spirit, I trust you to guide me to return back to me,' or just spend some time with your ReturnRing (see page 144).

PAUSE, TAKE IT IN, AND . . .
Ask

Get your journal or laptop out and follow the steps to connect to spirit (see page 164). Ask to receive a personal prayer for you to recite and just be available for what you receive. It may not feel like it's being delivered from spirit; just feel the vibe, be inspired, trust and write what feels good.

This work is not docile work; just think about all the stories and fears you have to bust through to even be able to believe in something, let alone believe you can communicate and receive wisdom from it. This isn't about uncovering all the secrets to life; I mean you may well do, but spirit will simply show you where to go next and where your growth lies. It's in the car right there next to you and even if you end up in a ditch, it will always pull you out. Even when you're not intentionally connecting to spirit, it's always around, in the air, just like smoke, moving in and out, in-between. Holding you, supporting you in the crevices that we can't see, rooting for you and cheering you on, something we can always come back to and how comforting is that?

TEN

Becoming a Lover of 'Now'

I used to catch an attitude as soon as me and an impractical heel embarked on the London underground or even worse New York's subway system. I found the entire experience to be an act of violence on my senses. From the carpet seats soaked in unknown excretions to the air flow that diminished with every stop; the whole thing was offensive. I armed myself with distractions to enhance my brief time there, until I realised that my offence wasn't even caused by what was happening in the present moment. My disgust stemmed from all the past experiences I had of getting on the train and being held captive at the juncture of door meets pole by my fellow commuters. The times when I'd have to listen to people screaming at one another to move down, as if the carriage would suddenly expand into a Versailles-length hallway. So, I decided to actually look around. For the first time, I took out my earphones, stopped looking for things to be upset about and just allowed myself to be there.

What I found was the shared humanity that can only come from locking eyes with a stranger, even if just for the briefest moment, when you both mutually acknowledge the rising temperature that you're about to succumb to. I saw a poem sleeping beneath the train map, which contained the words I needed to hear in that exact moment. I noticed that despite my fear of all the human juices the fabric seats had drank up, the seats were actually super-comfortable. I went on like this for 10, 15, 20 stops. Just watching and noticing. Being curious about everything I witnessed and there I found the beauty in the present moment, or should I say, what I thought was a hopeless place.

'Presence' has 1.2 million hashtags on Instagram and that's an indication of just how important it is, but also the number of eyes glazing over after hearing about it yet again. It's like grati-tude. Spiritual buzzwords that are repeated over and over again until they lose meaning, when in actuality their repetition is just proof that they work. Being reminded of the importance of presence is somewhat annoying, because for the most part we don't actually like the present moment very much.

You're going to hear about it again, because the present moment is where it's at. It's the strike of the match, buttoning of the jeans, the gate at the station opening when you wave your Apple Pay. It's the beginning, the emerging and the offer-ing of creation. The present moment is the opportunity to return back to *you* and how you get the stuff you want. It's all there is. We often prioritise the future as we believe that what it has to offer is bigger, bolder and better than what's available right now. When really, what's here is all there is, but we often hate being inside of what's here. It's easy to believe that we will be better or different at some point in the future or that life will be. We might not be able to touch that future life right now, but we *can* touch it today as it's all that we have available for us. In the present, we get to caress, live in and wear the fabric of who we are. We can't get to tomorrow and be who we want to be or get the stuff we want, if we can't hold what's already here.

LIVING IN THE THREE

Relationships are like a crime scene where we unpack our stuff and wait for our date to collect it all up into evidence bags. Most of my clients are working through things in this area, and whether they're choosing to be single, in the dating pool or in long-term relationships, there's a tendency to live in the three, being in the past, present and future at the same time. As I just found my vintage Spice Girls lollipop tin, what we actually want is for three to become one. We want to live primarily in the present. We want to be able to respect, honour and learn from the past and work towards the growth of the future. But our life must mainly be in the one. In the present. When you arrive in the future, you will call it the present and you would have created it from this moment.

When it comes to dating, living in the three is so common. Rae booked in for a session with me for exactly this reason. Whilst on a date, the woman opposite her would be having a wonderful time, inside a newly opened restaurant, while Rae would be inside her own head. She'd be living in the **past** and remembering what her mum told her when she was aged six. That she should get married when she's older to a nice, successful man who lives within a three-mile radius of her. She'd then aerial cartwheel into the **future** by imagining her and her first date (now wife, obviously) picking out mid-century dining tables from West Elm, even though she didn't even know yet if said date had any siblings. She was everywhere other than being in the **present** moment and getting to know the person in front of her. Rae had no idea if her date was someone she could be with or, in fact, anything about her. So, I asked her what she was missing when she had one foot in the past and one in the future. Her reply? 'I miss everything.'

From dating to a train ride, we miss out on so much. When your mind is filled with things that don't allow you to see today, you miss the preciousness of life. Sure, your past can shape your present and your present shapes your future, but the one that matters the most right now is the present. It matters because we're in it. When you begin to see each day, circumstance, and yourself in the story of the past or the story of the future, you are missing out on what today is here to show you. I was able to see the value of this through Reiki, as it is a spiritual path as well as an energy healing modality. Included in the system of Reiki, alongside palm healing, are the Reiki principles, created by the founder, Mikao Usui. They're often used in meditation and practitioners sometimes recite them as part of their practice. They go as follows:

Just for today
Do not anger
Do not worry
Be grateful
Work with diligence
Be kind to yourself and others

PAUSE, TAKE IT IN, AND . . .
Recite the Reiki Principles

Repeat them to yourself for around 5–10 times. Just fall into the page, see each word, feel it within you and see what arises, without trying to be any-where other than here. If your mind pulls you into a thought or story, just come back to the words.

The first line, 'just for today', is such a powerful way to guide us into the present moment. It's hard to make sweeping prom-ises and commitments to ourselves. How many times have you said that you'll start eating differently or run every single day until you retire? Then, when tomorrow comes and you're too tired or want a fruit-sized bowl of *cacio e pepe* you move into self-criticism. When we say, 'just for today', it's really *just* for today, because today is all that exists. We focus on doing the thing today, because tomorrow will be different; we will be dif-ferent. It gives us permission to start again. In the same way that 'do not anger' and 'do not worry' are not these shouty demands, but rather opportunities for us to not hold and stay in the emotions that so often reside outside of the present. If I'm angry, I'm probably angry at something that infuriated me ear-lier that morning or further in the past. If I'm worried, I'm probably feeling it about something that I have no idea will even happen in the future. When we release the worry or anger, by giving them permission to be seen, we can be present. We can begin again. Even if for a transitory flash of time. We can't be in a state of beginning when our thoughts of the past or wor-ries about the future are making us stop.

When I teach Reiki and go through the Reiki principles, I get my students to meditate on them. They repeat the phrases to themselves and come back into the space sharing just how much anger and worry came up. That's the point. Allowing the anger and worry that's in the other tenses to come up for air in the present. When they arrive, we explore them, get curious, see what they want to teach us and if in that moment we can release them, we come back to what's here. A new beginning.

CHECK YOUR CONTACT LENSES

When the past and future make us stop, it's often because we feed on the past like a mosquito on human blood. When you explore the past, you witness and produce evidence of why the present moment looks the way it does. We often see the present in the same way that the lifecycle of contact lenses changes. When you get a fresh-out-of-the-blister-pack pair, you're in the present. Everything looks vibrant, realistic and almost as it was always supposed to be. You're in awe that you can read the bus number before it comes close to stopping, without even using the blink-created lubrication of your eyes to help you make it out. As the days go on and the contact lenses get dirty from the microscopic pollen particles that always magnetise towards you, this is what it's like to see life through the past. The optical muffling that means that you can't see what's being offered to you in the present moment.

I don't always buy into coincidences in life – there's not always a reason why – but I do believe that if you were supposed to see something you will. Don't get me wrong, this isn't the same as believing that awfully dismissive 'everything happens for a reason' sentiment. Which, funnily enough, only seems to be said when you're going through hell and people want you to feel better and quickly, mainly because they're queasy with your emotional display. If you are on board with there not being any coincidences, it's actually quite useful. It can help you to see.

When you're living in the three, you miss out on what spirit is showing you. It might want to show you the toddler planting their sticky fingers on their dad's face. It might want you to see an advert for the running shoes on the taxi speeding past you. It might want you to see the sun leaping through the edge of a building. Seeing all that might shift something, spark something, make you want to write or just to *feel* something. When your contacts are dusty, you're not seeing the potential for growth laid out in front of you. As expected, we sometimes prefer to hang out in the future. This is when your lenses prescription changes and life looks like the equivalent of putting 3D glasses on for the first time. Everything around you has a technicolour coating of distortion on it and you can't really work out if things have increased in size and lucidity. This is what being in the future looks like. When everything is polished in aspiration and expectation. It causes you to focus on what *isn't* here and how much you wished it was. But, really, why do we put the future on such a hard-to-reach platform? Why do we waste the *now* to get to the next? What do we think will happen when we get to it? We'll just want to get to the next version of what's next. You've made the life you have right now and there was a time when you were eager for it and wanted it more than anything. At least some aspects of it. All the jobs that, to put it bluntly, I detested, I really wanted. I'd be sat in one white-walled office thinking about just how great the next job would be. When I got the next job, I'd love it for a minute until I started to daydream about what was next. I couldn't see that I had spent most of the past trying to get to the future and now the future was here, I wanted another one. I conveniently skipped the present moment in each situation. If I'd made space for three to become one, I would have noticed that there were so many wonderful moments within the madness. I would have seen how I was responding to the present and allowing that to be my guide.

The question my friends, is this: do you allow yourself to be fully present and be with the stuff you've got and wanted or are you more focused on what's coming next? Didn't like that did you? Yeah, me neither. When I was in my London to New York days, I would have a countdown on my phone of when I was next travelling. I'd run around town telling anyone who'd listen about how spectacular my trip would be. Yet, when I actually got to New York, I'd find myself two days in, living all the way in the future and being upset at how little time I had left. I'd already be thinking about how sad I'd be in a week's time when I had to go home. I missed out on being in the whole damn city because I was concerned about how I'd feel when I wasn't there anymore. What kind of foolishness. Luckily, I've stopped wasting airfare because I gave myself permission to let three become one. I shifted from trying to hold the past and future with a tiny peek of the present, to just being in the present only. I did this when one day I caught myself and decided to check in. I was walking through Central Park, balancing an oversized salad, and found myself doing everything other than seeing the park. I did some self-inquiry – one quick question to myself: 'Wait, where am I right now?' and with that question

I came out of living in the three and crashed into the present. I saw where I was: I was entertaining a **past** story about how much I didn't want this salad, but I *had* to eat it because I thought my thighs were too big. I was wrapped up in the **future** and thinking about how much better my life would be if I just lived here permanently. I was even planning my forced sadness on my return flight and all the miserable films I'd watch to feel even more sorry for myself. When I saw that I wasn't 'here', I decided to get into it. I found an anchor, any anchor that would get me there. Be it my breath or using my senses to see, hear or touch something in the park. Then I was back.

PAUSE, TAKE IT IN, AND . . .
Let Three Become One

When you're in any situation and feel that you're 'in your head' or living in the three, say to yourself, 'Wait, where am I right now?' Then tune in, see if you're in the past or future, mind or body, physical, mental, emotional or spiritual. See where you are, what's coming up and if you're not here, then use your breath, senses, or whatever anchor you like to get back here.

Anchors will get you into the present moment quicker than your phone seems to malfunction as soon as there's a new model available. It's also at the core of what meditation is all about. Meditation is ultimately a practice of presence and stillness, where we witness thoughts and feelings as they enter the mind and body, then shift the focus to an anchor. I even have an anchor tattooed on my wrist because they represent such a potent tool; well, that's the lie I tell myself, to cover up the fact that it's a matching tattoo I got with an ex.

You can pick 'n' mix your anchors, which are the practices to help you to come into the present moment. Whether it's breathwork, grounding, finding an object to place your awareness or even saying, 'Yo, come back' to yourself, this isn't the reserve of traditional meditation practice, where you sit on a meditation cushion, inhaling incense and exhaling impatience. You can allow your life to be a moving, continuous, ever-evolving, constant meditation. Your life becomes a meditation when you see just how divine it is to come home to the present when you're elsewhere. It's quite spectacular, even when we have past, tired eyes. To be able to create, you have to feel everything that comes from being human. When you look at your stuff, you're connecting to the human experiences that you encounter and the human filter through which you feel and see things. When you work on your stuff, you're being in the humanness of it all – the uncertainty, suffering and confusion – and moving through it all in an intuitive and authentic way. The present moment shows us who we are and the greatest example of that is when you love someone, as doesn't everything come alive? They're the people who feel like home, who you're so wrapped up in and delighted by that they lead you into a room of presence. Where everything you do with them feels new, like everything you've already seen before is now ripe for exploration. The people who make the mundane feel so supercharged, like your skin is wrapped in layers of sparks. The loves who make mindless walks in familiar cities feel like visiting unknown lands. The people that remind you of how connected and similar we all are. The one whose face, smile and laugh become places you never want to leave. The love you hold that makes the past and future become so irrelevant, because you just want to witness them existing, right here, right now.

My mum, Lystra, taught me unconditional love by way of presence. When I was aged eight she walked out the front door with a hospital bag in one hand and hopes that she'd be back in a few days in the other. She wasn't. The next time she walked through our front door was three months, eight operations, five litres of blood lost, a disability and unparalleled strength later. I struggled to not live in the three when I was with her. I was hit by **past** flashbacks of my feet running out of hospital rooms after seeing parasitic tubes and drips invading her body. The same body that I dwelt in for nine months. Before the flashbacks had a chance to end, I was straight in the **future** and convinced that our life together was a decreasing timer. With each minute passing, I was sure that she'd be back in hospital. There was no way that spirit was going to give out two miracle passes; I didn't think she'd make it. As I got older and leaned into my spiritual practices, I recognised what I was missing in the **present** when I was with her. I realised that she's the woman who brings out the Baileys when I have the bare minimum of good news (which I dilute 1 tbsp with 500ml of coconut milk). She holds me when I feel like I'm about to drown in my hurt. She's a teacher of presence because she allows me to show her who I am. She doesn't see me with past, tired eyes, she doesn't love me with conditions or assumptions, she just sees me for who I am today. Tomorrow may well be different. So, I started doing the same. We lost three months of togetherness and I refuse to miss anymore by living in the three when I'm with her. Yes, I still want to call the ambulance when she gets a minor headache sometimes, but the work continues. For the most part, I treat her like a mesmerising, one-time-only experience. If we're picking out avocados in Marks & Spencer or laughing at *90 Day Fiancé*; we're just in it. All the way in.

It's so charming to meet each day like you haven't met it before. To wake up, let go of yesterday and make no assumptions about this new day. How many times have you seen a friend, partner or family member through dirty contact lenses? We say, 'They're always a nightmare in the mornings' so assume they'll be a nightmare today. We tiptoe around and avoid them. Maybe they're a nightmare in the mornings because you've been avoiding them in anticipation of a bad mood that might not even be there. Maybe today will be different for them because they've slept better. Allow people to show you who they are. We enter into new relationships carrying stories about who we think the person will be, based on our past experiences. We turn our dates into genetically engineered people made up of exes and who we think they'll be based on societal norms. We don't allow them to show us who they are, as we're too busy assuming who they'll be or who we want them to be. When we make the decision to act like tourists in our lives, every moment becomes one of pure information; information that we take in, allow to move through us and respond to. Without judgement, without interpretation from the past, without rushing through it. It makes us remember what we're doing all this for.

LET IT COME

It's almost counterintuitive isn't it. Getting the stuff you want is in the future, yet it requires being present, letting life come to you and not being consumed by anything that's not here yet. Your relationship with spirit will guide you into this way of thinking by creating the trust and faith required to chill a bit. Back in 2010, when I was a fashion intern at *Tatler* magazine, packing suitcases for shoots and eating popcorn from Pret, if you told me I'd be doing what I do now, I would have fought you. At the time, my worldview only had time for Gucci loafers and walking past street-style photographers at London Fashion Week, to get on the blogs. I would have told you that I didn't go to fashion school and work for free for years to be a bloody spiritual guide. No thank you ma'am. It would have never helped me to know what would happen when I grew up. You do not need to know, because you'll know when you get there.

We don't know what will best support the version of us that doesn't even exist yet and, believe it or not, it might not give you as much relief as you think, to know it. You'll reach the future whenever you arrive there and it's honestly OK just to hang out here in the present for a little while; it can be *very* nice here. You had no idea that your life would look exactly how it does now. Even if you did create it, you still didn't create the *how* of it. Letting life come requires a cocktail of trust, faith and creation. When you trust that spirit is showing you what you need to see and bringing you whatever will guide you to return back to *you*, you're not being a bystander. You're using that information to create and you create by greeting the day, seeing what is has to offer and then taking action. This action springs from today and allows tomorrow, and the next day and the next, to come. Without needing to know what's coming or what the road looks like, because you trust. It's a blessing when you can surrender and not feel the need to hold on so tight. To have so much faith that you're not manipulating things into happening, but instead being inquisitive and open to what *could* happen.

I'm not at all into the idea that tarot is about fortune-telling and future predictions. I did past, present, future spreads when I was starting out and always felt odd asking about the future. Maybe, because I thought all the tantalising stuff was happening right now. I wanted to pull a card circa now and know what to do to get me out of the mess I'd found myself in; I couldn't care less about what my career was doing in ten years' time. I didn't know who I'd be by lunchtime, let alone in an entire decade. It was so refreshing to further this by learning from Lindsay Mack who believes that 'tarot truly exists only in the present moment'. I've lost count of the incredible clients who've told me that a tarot reader guaranteed some rubbish like they'll get married within the year. Then they come to me on December 31 and tell me they're still waiting outside Cartier for both a ring and a fiancé. Needless to say, I'm not telling you any of that if you book in for a session with me. You grow from today and the cards that come through are here to guide you to keep growing into what's next. If not, they'll show you how to deal with and make sense of what's coming up today. That's where the truth is. If we pull a card that speaks to abundance, success and purpose, it might well be what's available in the future, if you continue to show up for yourself and sit with the stuff that's convincing you it's not possible. It's not a promise. The rest of the cards in the spread will guide you to the areas of inner work for you to consider and help you on your way.

For me, tarot is an intuitive route. The cards don't have all the magic; the pack is just a tool to help you investigate what the stuff you're carrying often makes really hard to find, as it wants to stop you from making shit happen. After the reading, you're armed with the wisdom to get to where you want to be, if you choose to take it. My clients who apply the cards' teachings come back and tell me how they've created so many remarkable things. But, it wasn't promised just because a card said so; they had to show up for it because it's a co-creation. For the duration of the session, I try to get my clients to be in the present moment with me. Being there makes space in their mind to dedicate to creating their best life. When you're focused solely on the worry or fear that exists in past or future, we lose the space to make the opposite happen.

THE PERIOD OF MATURATION

When it feels super-unsettling to be in the present because you just want the future to arrive already, getting familiar with the period of maturation will help. Imagine wanting to rush the maturation of Grana Padano cheese by forcing it to be ready to eat at two months instead of 20. You know what you'll get? Cheese that no-one wants. The future needs time to mature too; we release urgency and ask spirit to bring it to us at whichever time will benefit us to receive it. We easily forget that we're all connected, which means we all have a role to play here. Life is like a synchronised swim; if one swimmer is out of sync or stays under water for one second too long, the whole thing gets thrown off.

When I can't sleep and the memes aren't doing what they're supposed to, I read about phenology. It's the study of timing in

regards to life cycles and periodic events of living organ-
isms. Basically, how plants and animals do all kinds of crazy
things based on seasonal and climate changes. Wait till you hear
about this – blackbirds always and only build their first nests in
February and, while weather affects the timings and subsequent
breeding season, it has to happen at this time because everything in the universe is perfectly synchronised. A blackbird
can't decide to create a nest in July instead. If it did, then it
would not only have an impact on the broods, but on the lifecycle of everything it eats. It would probably somehow, in
some weird way, have an impact on us too. Most living things
have insane, strict schedules like this, because we all impact
each other. There'll be times when I'm going through something and I'll be called to watch a show that's been on my list
for years. There'll be something, a line, plot or character who'll
bring me something that I need in that moment. Something that
acts like a catalyst for me to grow or understand something in a
different way. What I learn from this TV show might be exactly
what I need to share with someone else. I didn't watch the show
last month, or the year before, it had to be now because sometimes life has to mature.

You might be riding in a car with spirit and driving it, but
you can't control what happens outside the car and the speed at
which life is moving you along. You can only control how you
respond to it. Wanting life to happen at a certain time is like
expecting the Earth to go from spinning at 1,000 to 10,000 miles
per hour. You can't do that. Instead, you let life come by focusing, enjoying and being with what's here. Plus, we'd miss so
much if the Earth was spinning so damn fast. We wouldn't see
the sunsets and gooey, slow Sunday mornings – poof, gone, all

because of our urgency. You don't need to know why the stuff you want is taking so long to come, or how your story winds up, but I get that the waiting is difficult. Feeling the resistance to the present moment, and hoping that what's to come will rescue you from whatever you're feeling, is real. The present is quite literally a present because it's a space to prepare for what's to come. We don't yet have the stuff we want because we're not done with what's available for us *now*. There's more to see, take in and acknowledge, before the stuff comes in. Treating the present like the gift it is, makes what's to come even juicier.

PAUSE, TAKE IT IN, AND . . .
Do the 5.1

Use this popular grounding technique, to come into the present moment whenever you find yourself living in the three. Find 5 things around you that you can see, 4 things that you can touch, 3 things that you can hear, 2 things that you can smell and 1 thing that you can taste. Or in any order and amount that you remember. If any of your senses aren't available to you, find 5 things in any of the senses that you have access to.

The main way that I can bribe you into enjoying present-moment awareness is not an all-expenses paid trip to Dubrovnik, but because it shapes your future. I know how much you want to be in the future, so if being in the present is your ticket outta here, then maybe you'll reconsider? When you touch the present moment, you're responding to it and learning more about who you are and what gives you a little jolt. You're defining what you want to receive more and less of, based on what you see. When you ask spirit to help you to create, you often discover it in the present moment. Here, is the only place where we can experience delight, serenity, love and abundance. You can move into the future in a more grounded way, when you let yourself experience previews of the joy of it now.

During the COVID-19 lockdown, I wanted to travel outside of the UK but instead embodied the feeling of travel by staying right where I was. In my grandparents' garden in Bedfordshire, I laid on my Lululemon yoga mat that's as thick as it is expensive. I did the 5.1 exercise (see above) and started to gaze at the cushion-filler clouds. In less than a minute, I was in a self-created paradise. All I could see were clouds and the trees dancing in the wind. I wasn't living in the three; I had no idea what time it was or where I had to be. I could have been anywhere in the world and I no longer cared to be sipping on a non-alcoholic pina colada in Santorini, because I was here. With the same earth beneath me and the same sky above me. If you're counting down for something, find the adventure where you live; close your eyes and feel the sun on your skin, go look at some clouds or something. If you're waiting for your ideal partner to arrive, start seeing the spirit in everyone, by seeing them with fresh contact lenses. Treat everyone you meet as these just-landed-on-Earth, wonderful mortals that you get to spend time with. If you want to feel prosperous, then fondle a luxurious fabric and recite everything you're grateful for. When you respond to the present moment, you get to see how you want the next moment to feel for you.

Even when the present moment feels painful, we let ourselves be in it, instead of trying to assert ourselves into the future where we might feel better. We'll get there when we need to get there. While you're in the pain, give yourself over to the present moment. It's too heavy to also carry the past story of, 'This always happens,' 'I deserve this' or 'I could have done something differently.' None of that needs to live amongst the hurt you're already in. Neither does being in the future and saying, 'I'll never be happy' or 'I bet this will happen again.' Just let yourself be in the emotion of the present moment, give yourself to it until it shifts and you offer yourself an opening into healing, whenever that wants to come. It would be a very grim world to live in if we believed that what we're going through was a result of us thinking a 'bad' thought 5–10 years ago. Don't even entertain that idea. If you feel like you're not 'handling' the present moment in a way that you would like to, don't even think about blaming yourself and saying that this is why the future might not work out. It's all superstition; thoughts are just thoughts. They pass and they move through. A spirit-informed life of action is how we create what's next, not a passing thought or emotion. Again, it's too heavy to believe that every single thing is cause and effect, especially because we'll never know the cause, so why waste our time hunting it down. You do your best today and what arises will come. Doing your best is reclaiming your power and seeing that you have the ability to create, but you don't need to weigh yourself down with the fear of creating 'bad' things. Spirit will guide you back, as life is not out to get you.

By the nature of you just existing in the present, you're creating the future. It sounds like a greeting card, but each day really is a blessing, because we get to start over again. We think enlightenment comes at some unreachable point in time, but in fact enlightenment is only available in the present. I don't enjoy the gravity of the word, but enlightenment comes when you're in flow, laughing for no reason or loving someone up and you notice yourself out of thought for the briefest second. That delicious pause. You're not thinking of anything, you're just in it. Existing. The pause that lasts for as long as it takes you to think that you're enjoying being out of thought. Which makes you then go back to thought. This is only available in the present moment and it's quite exquisite to get lost in. It reminds us why life is worth living and why we want to get the stuff we want. It's how our senses simultaneously connect us to what's outside of us, but also to guide us to go deeper inside of us. What you want doesn't really exist in the future, it exists now. You may not have all of it, but you can start experiencing it. You may not have a romantic relationship right now, but you probably experience love in so many forms, every single day, because you are love. You'd miss that if you only believed it looked a certain way and could only come through in the future from a very specific person. The most beautiful moments in your life existed in the present moment – the hugs, the laughs, the fun, the vibes. If you ever missed the wonder of them, it wasn't because you weren't there; you were just living in the three.

Your authentic, confident and worthy self only exists within the scope of presence. It's available when you slip out of everything and into what's left. Returning back to *you* is when you are just being and not having to do anything or be anyone else. Not trying to be free from thought, but letting the thought transition and pass through you, until you return again. Within the present you take what you need to continue, to keep moving forward. You stop fighting with and trying to reconcile the past and attaching yourself to future uncertainty. There's a reason why the last line of *The Great Gatsby* is one of the most well-known in literature: 'So we beat on, boats against the current, borne back ceaselessly into the past.' Our work is to stop pushing, pushing, pushing against the current of life and instead choose to see each day with fresh contact lenses, for all it has to offer. We let, 'Wait, where am I?' become the score to the movie of our life, prompting us to return. Welcome back, love.

ELEVEN

Permission to Create

Something that displeases me to no end is hustle culture. Even worse, the narrative that success should be lovingly sat on the lap of hard work. We praise the stories of 4am wake-up calls, 80-hour weeks and a lifetime of tough, thankless graft. The journey to my writing this book isn't one of those stories. It isn't the podcast-worthy grind story that the world would love it to be. What people would queue up for to hear is me sharing the JK Rowling-esque number of rejections my book proposal had. How much I struggled with writer's block and the calluses caused by typing so hard. They'd want me to over-share details of all the baked beans I ate and the calls I'd made to every publisher to see if they were interested. I'd wrap up this fantastical tale by giving top tips on why you should never give up and that hard work wins the day. That's *not* what went down here though and you know it. All I did to get a book deal was look at my stuff, work on my stuff and give myself permission to create. Not one early morning in sight, no years of manual labour and no trail of proposals behind me (but there were a lot of jacket potatoes with beans and cheddar cheese).

Some of the elements of my fable *are* true. I did staple bunches of A4 pages together when I was child, and wrote my own short stories, complete with my mum's illustrations of the characters. Ever the delegator. I studied fashion journalism, worked as a writer and there's a bunch of friends out there with CVs, text messages, emails and job applications that I've anonymously helped them to pen. Writing has always been a huge part of my life, so I knew I'd probably write a book one day. I trusted it would happen if it was aligned with my path, but I wasn't attached to it.

One day, I was in-between clients and I got an email asking if I'd like to write a book; my now publisher had found me through some press features. I wrote a proposal in about a week, knowing that if it wasn't this exact book you're reading now, then I wasn't writing one. I believed I'd write a book on spirituality at some point but I wasn't in a rush, because it meant so much to me. It needed to be right and it was. The entire process was more chill than the days I'd skive off in retail jobs. It was filled with ease, grace and cosmic connections, just because I showed up in my life in general.

Looking at and working on my stuff is how I live my life. So, while the journey to my book deal was pretty (un)intentional, it has been in process unbeknownst to me for years. I had to explore my stuff to check in and see the areas where I didn't want to be seen and to stand in who I was. I had to sit with the ick of choosing to own and step into my spiritual beliefs and to do that in a very public and blunt way. I moved through life believing that I was blessed and favoured, so I said no to opportunities that didn't feel good and went for the ones that did. When things didn't work out, I said 'It is what it is,' because I knew that I was being authentic and I trusted my intuition. I didn't chase, seek and *need* to write a book to be publicly affirmed, because I know how to do that for myself. I sat with my fears and doubts about what people would think by handing it over to spirit. After all that, I got the stuff I want; in its physical form, it's the book. More importantly, beyond that, it's being able to share this message so everyone can be spirit-informed and create their life. That's what I want and I got it by giving myself permission to create it. I showed everyone who I was, I allowed myself to get out there, to take risks, to be seen. To have the confidence to reach out to the newspapers and not be humble about what I do. To trust so much in spirit and my work that they'd feature me again in the future, which they did and that's how my publisher found me. Doing the inner work has to come with giving yourself permission, because how else can you bring forth the opportunities, experiences and people that you deserve?

PAUSE, TAKE IT IN, AND . . .
Let Go

Give yourself permission to be as loud, wide, bold and audacious as you want to be. If you're in a private space, or if you're in a public space, and couldn't care less, do whatever you need to embody that. It might be moving your body in the widest stance you can. Stretching yourself out like a starfish. Jumping up and down. Using your voice to scream or taking the longest exhale of the day.

IT'S NOT ONLY ABOUT YOU

You creating your life is wonderful. The impact that it has on the world is even better, as it can be life-changing for all the lives you'll touch. You were born for a reason. You chose your parents for a reason, although in some cases it might feel hard to understand why. So did everyone else that you have met and are yet to meet. You're connected to every person on this planet, just by virtue of you being here, but you're incredibly connected to all the people whose lives you'll collide into. Even if it's only the briefest oops of an interaction.

Think about the person you love most outside of your family. Don't you think it's wild that you were born during the same lifetime? Not a century ago, not 500 years ago, but right now. Even more wild is that you found each other during this lifetime. We are energetically connected to each other, from the great loves to the barista you smile at every day through the café window. My hyperbolic language is necessary, because you are vital, we all are. We are all Lego pieces and you can't make a 1,426-piece Medieval Lego Castle, if one piece is missing, can you? When you're bold enough to create your life, you're also a part of making that happen for at least one person in the world, if not many. You're the missing Lego piece for someone getting the stuff *they* want.

Let's say that you're afraid of telling someone you love them, but your expression of love will be the catalyst for their spiritual growth, healing or even career goals. Let alone, the greater intimacy you'll receive by doing so. What if by wearing a pair of glitter trousers that you adore, but feel nervous to go out in, you inspire a young child passing by to be expressive. Not to mention that you'll look absolutely magnificent in them. What if I didn't have the confidence to leave my career behind, step into this way of teaching about spirituality and trust that my voice should be heard? I wouldn't be able to answer my publishers' prayers of someone writing a book like this. I wouldn't have felt the absolute elation of writing every line. What if all of us stopped, didn't act, didn't show the world who we were, didn't have hard conversations or wear what the hell we wanted? What if we were all too afraid to create? It's our duty to do so, yes, for ourselves, but nothing in the world will be the same if we don't do it. So many people become inspired when one of us gives ourselves permission, as it gives them permission to do the same. The collective needs you and everyone's waiting. No pressure, though.

PAUSE, TAKE IT IN, AND . . .
Reflect on 'Permission'

What does the word 'permission' bring up for you? Are there areas of your life that you can step more fully into? Where do you often wait for permission from other people before you can do something?

Giving yourself permission to create is a total, unapologetic, full-throttle reclamation of you recognising that when you know who you really are and aren't afraid to show the world that, you can make things happen. That you have it *within* you to make it happen. Some people call it magic; others call it manifesting, but it's essentially . . . creation. Permission looks like not asking or waiting. It's when your biggest desire is to invent a no-chip nail-polish that lasts for a month and works with your nail growth. Most of us would give up because we'll jump straight to how impossible this sounds, how much money it requires, and the fact that we don't have a cosmetic science degree. If that's your intention, if that's what you're asking spirit to help you with, then nothing happens unless you give yourself permission to go after it. When you do that you're saying, 'I don't need to know the how right now, but between my brilliance, connection to spirit, and belief that I am powerful enough to create, I'm going to make it happen.' The next day, you write up your vision, make a presentation, ask spirit to guide you and get out there. You sit with all your stuff that makes you think it's not possible and you get to it. To keep driving on the road to creation, we have to allow ourselves to see that we have the power to get there. The work in itself is transformational, but you having the awareness that you can *create* from this space, is where the up-level happens.

We lose our power when we see ourselves *only* as our physicality – what we do and what we look like. When we see ourselves as authentic, intuitive, whole beings, who are both spirit and can connect to spirit, navigating a human experience, we can then see our game-changing ability to create. When we're spirit-informed and doing the inner work, we see that we have the power to create what's here on Earth, from our inner reality. When we do life in this way, we see that whatever is going down on a spirit-level can manifest itself on a human, everyday level. Embodying this is how we manage to get a walk-in only table at the restaurant called **Creation**. The inner work that you're doing and will continue to do is opening up space within you, to welcome in the best kinds of stuff. We welcome it in when we see ourselves as being the same as what we're trying to receive. It's how energy works, it's what the roots of the law of attraction is about, it's what spirituality focuses on. You are love, so you can get love; you are abundance, so you can get it; especially when we look at and work on the stuff that's in the way of us seeing it. While I do believe that so much of creating is (un)intentional, when we go back to our definition, it's important that we look some more at our personal practices:

Being spirit-informed is grounded in your human experience. It's the personal practices you use to connect to anything that guides you to return back to you and create.

These are the things we do to remind us of our closeness to spirit. The practices that get all the air-time in spirituality and manifesting, but are only a small part of the puzzle. When we use nature and other tools to help us create, it's vital that giving ourselves permission doesn't come at the cost of anyone else because, as we know, what *we* do also impacts the collective *us*.

HOW DOES CULTURAL APPROPRIATION FIT IN TO ALL THIS?

There have been so many interesting and necessary conversations surrounding cultural appropriation within wellness and spirituality. Unfortunately, appropriation has become more pervasive as these practices are gaining in awareness and therefore popularity. This work is important. This work is sacred and it should be treated as such. When we treat wellness and spiritual practices as commodified goods and turn things into 'trends' or focus on how much money we can make from them, appropriation is inevitable. When our practices become things that we consume rather than something we believe, live and stand in, we end up here. Here being endless overpriced wellness shops selling products without any reverence for where they're from or what they do. Ceremonial White Sage being used as glorified airfreshener. Gimmicks on TV shows. Yoga teacher training courses removing Sanskrit from their programmes. People saying they're Shamans after completing a two-hour online training course by someone who certainly wasn't a Shaman. Unethically sourced crystals sold for hundreds of pounds by fashion retailers, with no guidance on how to use them. Not to mention the mainstream acceptance and usage of practices within Ayurveda, African spirituality and Native cultures. The same traditional practices that were often banned, made illegal and stripped from the people whose culture they came from during colonial rule and slavery. Yet they've now found their way onto the high street with no honouring of their heritage. It's upsetting and it's a problem that needs to be solved; so I find it incredibly disappointing that the solutions in discussion seem to be creating more harm and division than intended. Such proof of this time of increasing polarity and decreasing critical thinking.

If we focus on the reasons behind why we're doing these practices, and have a firmer grasp of the heritage, lineage and teachings behind them, then things can change. They need to change because right now we're forgetting what spirituality and wellness actually *is*. In this social-media fuelled, incredibly performative, fear of being cancelled age we live in, we have lost the art of nuance and the willingness to spend some time in the grey area. Cultural appropriation is more complex than trying to create a spreadsheet formula for your taxes. So, we need to acknowledge that it's impossible to find a one-dress-size-fits-all solution to remedying it. The clue to there not being a succinct swipe-through Instagram post on this lies in the word 'cultural', itself. We are talking about the unique, wildly different, free-thinking people within any one culture. We might be the same on a collective soul-level, but on a human one, we are not. If we're saying that a practice is appropriative, it's important for us to appreciate that we can't assume the beliefs and views of the entirety of said cultural group. One of the suggested solutions for appropriation (and a reason for cancelling people who don't do this, apparently) is to gain permission before using or doing a practice from another culture. Pray tell, who exactly are you supposed to get permission from? This assumes that each culture, religion or group has one united voice. A spokesperson who speaks for an entire group of people. There isn't a spokesperson because that's not how life outside of the internet works. There's also so much bias within that, as if you really want to do something, you will just ask everyone you can find, until at least one person gives you permission. It's the same as when we look for scientific 'research' to back something up. You can find research to prove or disprove whichever hypothesis you have. If you want to drink red wine every night, you will find studies that say it's great for your health and ignore the ones that say it's not.

Another solution for cultural appropriation is often about giving back to the community that the practice originated from. On the surface, this seems logical and thoughtful, but again we need to think critically here. COVID-19 exacerbated and illuminated the various injustices and inequalities that are still present within our society. From Black Lives Matter to Stop AAPI Hate. From the increase in domestic violence during lockdown to the COVID crisis in India. These are all causes that needed awareness and, more importantly, action, yet amongst the posts, stories and articles circulating were ones that linked wellness practices to what was happening. 'If you have done yoga or meditation, you need to give money to support India' or 'If you have ever had Traditional Chinese Medicine, you need to help.' Why do we need to shame and guilt-trip people into donating money or giving their time? Why are we assuming that the people using these practices are 'better off' than the people they're being asked to help? Why do we then continue to shame people for being silent about any issue? Doing all of this doesn't create any real or sustainable change.

People sent me money during the re-energising of BLM because they read somewhere that they should 'give back' to the community. I didn't need the money. I personally felt disempowered and I know that it was only done to assuage the guilt that the populace had imposed on them. When we shame and scare people into action, they might share a donation receipt or a non-committal post, but only because they were too afraid of what would happen if they didn't. Change doesn't happen when we only act because we're scared of being called out. Change happens when we take the time to research the practices we're using. Change happens when we take the time to look at the grassroot services that are working tirelessly to support people, and us choosing to help, only because we want to, not because we meditated one time and feel guilty.

We have cultivated a culture of fear and shame that expands

into all pockets of our society. What we don't need to feel is fear and shame within the spiritual and wellness practices that function as remedies for fear elsewhere. Yes, we need to look at everything critically and within that criticism we must remember why we're doing all this. For some people, it will just be to follow trends, but I know that just by you reading this book it is beyond that for you. We can all work to not cause any harm to anyone in our practices, but we must also refuse to be shamed and scared into not using these practices. They weren't created for some and not all. We credit, we honour, we educate, but we don't dictate who should and shouldn't use them. There's so much beauty in our differences; we have so many cultures so we can learn and share from them. We can work towards ending injustice without creating more division in the process. There's so much infighting happening and the people who are often called out the most are not the ones we need to be fighting with. We should be coming together and putting pressure on unscrupulous corporations, retailers, training courses, governments and those who are *still* stealing land, opportunities and diminishing people. We don't need to only be arguing amongst ourselves on Twitter.

PAUSE, TAKE IT IN, AND . . .
Reflect

Take a moment to sit with whatever is coming up for you right now. Come into a space of non-judgement and just reflect on how you're feeling or if it sparked any unexpected emotions. It's a meaty topic, so spend a few minutes here self-soothing. You can do The 5.1 exercise (see page 192), take a few restorative breaths or grab any resources, be it a blanket or hot drink. Be gentle with yourself.

Then, what do you do with all this? You keep figuring it out and you definitely don't have to agree with anything I've just said. The point is exactly that. There will be a bunch of people who look like me, believe in most of the same things as me and will disagree with all the above – and isn't that just beautiful? We don't have to agree or only have one solution that we should all stick to or else we'll be punished. I will share what has worked for me and my clients. It might resonate, it might not, but it might assist as we go into creating your own personal practices. It's not a bunch of questions that need to be written down, it's not prescriptive, exhaustive and it definitely isn't a *should*. A few questions might be helpful and the rest might not. They're just mere suggestions of things to consider if you've been questioning using or buying something. What's been particularly helpful for me is using *both* my **insight** and **integrity**. So, here's some guidance, and the point is that whatever conclusion you come to is yours and rightfully yours:

- **Integrity:** Have you researched what it's all about? Looked into where it came from and the views, beliefs and thinking behind it? Have you thought about if there's any relationship to colonialism or any systemic abuses enforced on the culture these practices came from? Have you read or heard the differing views of multiple voices on the use of the practice? Are there any sustainability, sourcing or overharvesting concerns? Have you looked into who you're purchasing from and the supply chain?
- **Insight:** Have you asked yourself why you want to do it? What's your intention? How all the integrity pieces above sit with you? Have you looked into how powerful

the practice can be and how it might change your life in some way? Have you explored how it fits in with your own personal belief system? Do you already have some knowledge of the practice that you can draw on? Is it already part of your own lineage or heritage? Is there anyone you might be knowingly causing upset to? If you saw everyone in the world as a spiritual being, what would you do?

If all else fails, just question doing anything unless it makes sense for how you live the rest of your life. You don't need to smoke-cleanse your apartment or use crystals if you have no understanding of what energy is or how to connect to spirit. Blunt but true. It will just be a waste of your time, resources and money. The work only works when you know what you're working with. Of course, we have collective trauma that we need to unpack and heal as it relates to colonialism, religion, race and, well, everything that our fellow humans did to create the world as we know it. As we move through all that, we can give each other the grace of getting things wrong and offending each other. We can examine who we are punishing and cancelling and check we're looking at our own stuff before we come to any conclusions. We can question who gets to judge and who is judged. We must remember that we can't make any assumptions about anyone's personal practices, knowledge, lineage or heritage. You don't know if someone has studied the *Yoga Sutras of Patañjali* and *The Bhagavad Gita* before stepping onto the mat. You don't know if someone uses white sage in their practice because everyone in their family line has. Just in the same way that we don't know if someone selling facial Gua Sha has copied and pasted an entire Wikipedia article into their 'about us' page, to avoid being called out. We question and we can have compassion.

IT MIGHT BE IN THE BLOOD

As you dive into your personal practices, take a look inwards and closer to home for inspiration. Do some degree-level research — actually, maybe more like a 20-minute internet browse into your own lineage and heritage. There might be some really good stuff there and you might be surprised by what you uncover. It's totally fine if you don't find any spiritual practices there; just know that it's quite spectacular that you're the first in your line to step into this. It's also perfect if you just don't vibe with the beliefs or practices within your family or your country of origin, or wherever you live now. Give yourself permission to create your own, but let's explore if there's anything there too.

It's sometimes hard to see or believe, but we also chose where we'd be born in order to assist in our spiritual growth. Yes, even if you think the town you grew up in is the most grotesque place to reside in, it had something to teach you, even if it was to listen to your intuition and get the hell out of there. My lineage means absolutely everything to me and it showed me how subconscious so much of this work is. That we'll always be guided into it if we need it. It gave me further evidence that I could create, because it's part of my heritage. When people ask me how I know what I know, I always say spirit. The other is through my lineage and that answer is Mammy Sylvie. My maternal great-grandmother, born in Grenada in 1906, who spent her life in Trinidad, gave birth to ten children, including my grandma, and died in 1989, four months before I was born. An incredible woman who I never got to meet and didn't even know the depth of her work till a while after I started mine, but her story lives on through me and I hope will inspire you too.

Mammy Sylvie's children and her faith were her two greatest loves. They prompted the action she took and the words she spoke and the reason why she was always working. She was a healer, medicine woman and doula; a spirit-informed one at that. In this work, she practised the ancient therapy of cupping, which she might have learned how to do in Grenada or, well, in a dream. Whether it was the local football team, one of her children, grandchildren or someone in the area who hurt themselves, the cups would come out. As soon as someone said they were in pain, she went straight into prayer, reached for some herbs and made a concoction to either massage them with or for them to drink. In her healing arsenal, she used anti-inflammatory poultices (herbal pastes applied to a cloth) and knew exactly which herbs to use or 'bush', as they say in Trinidad, for absolutely anything. In her apothecary, you'd find vervain, fevergrass, black sage, St John's (justicia secunda), and more. My family may have been poor, but they were very self-sufficient. The herbs and flowers were planted alongside cassava and corn, to feed the family. As a proponent of humoral medicine, she would use certain herbs to cool the body and bring it back into balance, aka a black sage tincture she'd give to the family during school holidays before purging them with senna leaves to clear out all the sugary mangoes they'd been eating. Mammy Sylvie also delivered babies and helped many women to become pregnant. She was giving post-birth yoni-steams before the media started calling it a celebrity trend and passing judgement that no-one asked for on its efficacy. When she wasn't doing *all* that, she would dance the cocoa (polish beans with her feet) and pick coffee for agriculture companies. All this on top of washing and ironing for wealthier people and bachelors. Honestly, it's equal measures tiring and admirable just hearing her packed schedule.

She was a Spiritual Baptist, a Christian religion that was brought to Trinidad by former American slaves and emphasises the Holy Spirit. She didn't mess around with her faith. She had a prayer room outside and a bowl called a calabash, made and dried from a gourd, filled with water, ixora flowers and a candle she'd light at 6pm every day. There'd often be mysterious symbols written on the wall, which remind me of the sigils I use in manifesting workshops. I didn't know any of this by the way; I only heard about her practices when my grandma saw me smoke-cleansing and told me all about it. She remembered Mammy would smoke the room with incense, asafoetida or orange peel, going into the four corners as I always do. While I use Lanman & Kemp's Agua de Florida for cleansing before sessions, unbeknownst to me Mammy used Agua de Kananga available from the same brand. The similarities don't end there either. She prayed so much that she would receive spiritual guidance on which practices and herbs to use on people and she trusted in her work because of the strength of her faith. A lot of this happened in the Baptist practice of mourning. During a period of 3–7 days or more, members would fast, pray and meditate. They would be isolated from everyone, lie on the floor, eyes covered and be taken care of by nurses of the faith. They'd receive spiritual gifts during this time and Mammy would go on these intense spiritual journeys, praying constantly before sharing with the congregation what came through in dreams or visions. During this time, she'd speak in tongues, and reveal what she'd seen. Sometimes she would have visioned going to India, China or countries in Africa; she'd then channel the native languages and also explain the wisdom she'd receive from these cultures. Wild, I know. But, makes all the sense in the world that she engaged in Traditional Chinese Medicine and Ayurvedic practices, a process so similar to the channelling I've done and still do. Whether I'm working in the akashic records or astral projecting, I just assumed that everyone was receiving encyclopaedic length pieces of wisdom or able to leave their bodies, as it felt so normal and intuitive for me. Apparently not. Like my great-granny, I am also told what oils, herbs or tools to share with my clients or myself, when I'm vibing with spirit.

Clearly, her work and faith live on in me, but her energy does too and that's what's so fascinating about lineages. Parts of our ancestors live on through us, including their hopes and dreams that weren't able to be expressed. Not all our ancestors had permission to create and the ones that did have so much to offer us. My family didn't have any money, but Mammy would always tell her children, 'We might be poor, but when you step out of this house, you're rich.' She spoke of the importance of dressing properly and always having clean clothes. She'd switch up her walk (and her wigs) whenever she left the house. Oh hello, manifesting 101. This is exactly why I will always fight for the importance of everyone having access to these practices. There's been a backlash to manifesting, with people saying that it's privilege-based and not everyone can do it. I get it, but we can't disempower people who aren't financially secure by saying that they only need resources and not naïve optimism. Yes, we need physical resources and community support, but we also need hope. We just need to change *how* we talk about manifesting. We also need to see that it is possible for us all to create, especially when we consider the stuff we're carrying that impacts our ability to believe we can do so. We can have both. Mammy Sylvie worked hard to feed her family, but that was coupled up with her intense faith. That's why she always believed in possibility.

There is, of course, undeniable privilege in wellness and spirituality. Insidiously divided up in what feels like 'the haves and the have nots'. This work is for everyone, it's ancient, it's ancestral, it lives in so many of us. In the commodification of wellness and spirituality, we have made it feel exclusive when it isn't. We have enabled a culture of, 'I manifested this' when it probably just means, 'I bought this', as a way to sell courses teaching you how to do the same. This isn't just about optimisation – it's survival; and the tools and concepts we can carry with us to just make it through life and to enjoy the ride. This is what spirit-informed living is about. We have priced people out of these practices and made it feel like it isn't for everyone, but it is. It always has been and I'm so proud that my great-grandmother is evidence of that.

PAUSE, TAKE IT IN, AND . . .
Reflect on Your Past

Think about what you know about your lineage, heritage or the land you were born in. Are there any practices or teachings that originate there that you want to know more about? Are you carrying any beliefs or resistance to it? What new traditions and practices would you like to create?

CREATING FROM NATURE

Your lineage, heritage and awareness of appropriation are all great pieces of information to keep in mind as you create your own practices. When you give yourself permission to create, it's quite special to bring nature and spirit along for the ride to assist in you seeing the possibility. This is why those wellness shops are like Noah's Ark, packed with tools that can assist in your practices. The rituals, spells, crystals and all the other fun stuff come so late in this book because without the principles behind using them, you're just not going to get as much from them. When we use nature to guide us into creation, we're paying attention to what exists in the world around us and that we're a crucial part of that world too. I've been doing rituals for such a long time, with a box under my bed filled with melting candles, every essential oil you can imagine and so many small little pots. It can get complicated and expensive, but the formula I use for everything I do now, is **The 5.2** (see page 216).

You were introduced to **The 5.1** on page 192 to help you move into the present via your senses; The 5.2 version is when you want to up the dial on your spiritual practices, but still keep things grounded. These five elements of nature have been referred to in Ayurvedic teachings, ancient Greece, Wicca, Neo-Paganism and various spiritual traditions. You'll recognise them as your zodiac sign will fall into one of them, so you might be a fire sign, earth sign or so on. The suits of the tarot cards are based on the elements, and crystals are often grouped in this way too. The way we use them is by seeing them as helpers to push the car that you and spirit are riding in, when it is moving real slow or just needs a boost to travel to creation and get the stuff you want. You don't *need* any of them to get you there, but yeah, they're fun, pretty, celebrate nature, call spirit in and add some ritual to your practices. Within the context of **The 5.2**, work with your integrity and insight (as above), trust what you're drawn to and what you're curious about.

PAUSE, TAKE IT IN, AND . . .
Do The 5.2

Jot down some ideas for each of the 5 elements, that you'd like to try or add to your practices. There are some ideas below, so see what feels good to you and read more into them, if you fancy.

AIR

It's all around us as this gorgeous reminder of the potential that's in the unseen. Not only can air move carefully straightened hair out of place, but it can blow even sturdy structures around. This force of nature has the ability to transform and change pace and is associated with communication and our mental body. In your practice, you can use it to restore, cleanse, shift and move energy. Consider it a fresh start.

IDEAS

- **Breathe:** Find a breathing pattern that works for you and take a moment to reconnect to your breath, when you're doing your practice. If you're OK with breath holds, then try breathing in for four counts, holding the breath for four counts, breathing out for four and holding for four. Repeat this a few times.
- **Smoke-cleanse:** You can purchase sustainably sourced smoke-cleansing bundles or, better yet, make your own using herbs such

as mugwort, rosemary, thyme, lavender or basil. You can even light a cinnamon stick, orange peel or incense. Be sure to open all the windows and doors to allow any stagnant energy to clear. Move the smoke into all four corners of the room, and the rest of the space. As always, your intention is important. As you waft the smoke around your body or space, you can say something like, 'I cleanse and release any energies that are no longer benefitting me and welcome in only the energies that are.' Then spend some time visualising this happening.

- **Feel the wind:** You can open your windows or doors to get some airflow going or, if you're able to, move your practice outside and feel the breeze on your skin.

EARTH

This is everything we stand on that reminds us of our foundation and need for support. This element is what we need to feel grounded when everything else feels out of balance. It's particularly useful when you're freaking out about your earthly possessions, such as money. Use the earthiness for when you want to feel a sense of calm and security.

IDEAS

- **Walk it out:** Walk around your house barefoot, go to a botanical garden or local garden centre or have one of those long walks in the park where time feels endless.
- **Mini bowls:** Add some Himalayan pink sea salt to a bowl, to have with you during your ritual. Or, you can add some soil to a mini pot to keep things nice and simple.
- **Crystals:** Intuitively select the crystals to use, or use some that match what you're doing. For example, Pyrite if you're doing some inner work around believing you're worthy of accumulating wealth.

Remember to cleanse (with a natural source of running water or smoke), charge (under the sun for at least four hours at its brightest or overnight on full or waxing moon) and connect (hold the crystal, notice what it brings up, how it makes you feel and visualise its energy moving through you). Before you use it, set an intention by holding the crystal and saying something like, 'I charge this crystal with the intention to _____.'

WATER

If we're not trying to remember to drink enough of it, then we're craving being surrounded by it, whether that comes in the form of an ocean or just a bath. We can't survive without water and this element corresponds to our emotional body, the moon, intuition and our dreams. We can call this in when we need to soothe, but to also feel a sense of emotional release like when we cry. Don't forget the force of the rain and waters' ability to put out fires too.

IDEAS

- **Infused water:** Water is sacred as it is, so you can just have a small bowl with water around you. I was told that Mammy Sylvie would pour three drops of water on the ground before she practised, to invite in spirits, so that's what I've been doing. You might be called to use Florida or Kananga water after doing some further investigation, or make your own moonwater elixir. For this, you just need to fill a jar with water, add a crystal of your choice (moonstone or selenite are great), place your hands around the jar to set an intention, place the jar under the light of the moon to charge it with the moon's energy, then collect it the next morning. You can add some of this to a bath, cleanse crystals in it, put in a bowl during your practice, or do whatever you fancy.

- **Drink up:** Use your taste buds and incorporate a beverage of your choice, during your practice. You might want to savour a herbal tea, cacao, delicious mocktail or go all out and wine it up. Do your thing.

FIRE

Incredibly intoxicating to look at, but also rather mind-blowing is fire's ability to shift into what it is, all from some friction or a spark. Fire can be something we cook with, be relaxed by, but there's also an underlying promise of danger within it. This element is about passion, creative energy, the sun, alchemy and strength. It prompts us to see that we are always able to create.

IDEAS

- **Light a candle:** Before you even get near to fire, please practise fire safety and if you think you're being careful, be even more careful. Light a candle and spend some time with it, whether that means seeing the flame move, taking in the scent or choosing a candle colour based on what you're working through. I tend to use red for love, green for career and money, black for releasing, white for cleansing and purple for spirit stuff. You can hold the candle to infuse your energy, visualise your intention and let it go.
- **No-fire fire:** If fire feels triggering for you, you're avoiding smoke for health reasons, or it just feels terrifying, then here's some other options. Utilise fiery crystals like red jasper, garnet or carnelian for energy and motivation. You can also place some red or orange items around you or if you have a tarot deck, then take out the Queen of Wands or any of the Wands suit that resonates. If you're a fire sign (Sagittarius, Aries and Leo), then you, my friend, are more than enough.

SPIRIT

The last, but never the least, and, honestly, if everything else doesn't work for you, let this be your focus. You are spirit. So, when you gather up the other elements, bring yourself into all of it. Use this time to connect to spirit and bring your intentions, desire and energy to the table. Whether you assemble The 5.2 on a decadent modern altar, or laid out on a tray in your bed, spend some time with them, return back to *you* and connect to spirit.

We are nature, we are in it and we are surrounded by it. What's possible on a spirit-level is possible on an earth-level. Even when we have no idea how we'll get the stuff we want or we need support and resources from the world around us, we can always give ourselves permission. When we feel the life-changing benefits of doing the inner work, we can take that to the next level by seeing that we can transmute and shift it into creating possibility and potential. This is why we have our inner power; it's because we can do something with it. This is the work that goes beyond these pages. We don't ask and we don't wait; we use our audaciousness to make things happen, which in turn makes things happen for others. A lot of the changes in your life begin by you giving yourself permission. When you believe in your power to make shit happen, when you believe in spirit, yourself and other people, that's how you create.

TWELVE

In the Traffic of Life

What superpower would you want, if you could have any? The question asked during conversations that are staler than a biscuit that's been left in an open tin. Well, I'm asking it now, because I bet you'd pick something that would result in you having some kind of control over the world. It would solve everything wouldn't it, if we had both the knowing of what would happen, but also could control it. We've been duped into thinking that we have to wait for the world to do things, before we can. That the only way to experience Hollywood levels of happiness is when the outer world changes. When there's no more illness, anger, racism, poverty, global warming, rude people, homophobia, bullying, abuse – and the list goes on and on and on. If all else fails, we at least want to have control over our own worlds, with better jobs, partners who adore us and more money in the bank. That's just not how the custard cream crumbles though. We can't control the outer world, because it's simply impossible, even if superpowers are being handed out on a Monday morning. We can fight for change in the world, but we can't wait for change. So much of the annoyances and pains of life are symptoms of the human condition, that to some degree will always be here. It's our job to see that our control lies within our inner shifts. When we believe that the outer reality of life is all there is, we can't find growth or true decadent bliss here.

Rightly so, we push for research to cure cancer and diseases, but who are we pushing? We're pushing the same systems that don't even recognise that we are more than physical or that we have four bodies. The same systems that don't tell us how to incorporate joy and hope alongside treatments, or feed our bodies in a nutritionally beneficial way. We assume that we can rid ourselves of stress by just removing ourselves from external stressful situations, rather than looking at our inner ability to down-regulate, soothe and find coping mechanisms. Yes, we can and should do all those things, but there needs to be an 'and'. We take action to create real, long-lasting change in the outer world, but while we do that, we can use our power to change our inner world.

In tarot sessions, I've had countless clients ask me if their job would improve, if the house they've bought was the right one or if their partner will propose. Questions I never answer. Instead, I might ask the cards about the doubts they're having in their relationship, what's at the core of their uncertainty in their career or where is the resistance to trusting their decisions. Questions that get us to the good stuff because the questions are about *them*. Their inner world. Your partner might never propose, your job might be a nightmare for the foreseeable future and your new house might have five-figures worth of structural issues. We can't control or see if any of that will happen, but we can control how you respond and show up for all of it.

TAKE THE DAMN FILTER OFF

I'll break it down for you another way. There's no greater shock to the system than opening your front-facing camera, seeing your face in an Instagram filter, then going back to the unfiltered version. Also known as your real face. There was a time in my youth, well, a few years ago, when it became the norm to post a photo of my face with a filter on it. Everyone I followed used filters, whether they admitted it or not, and it almost became a habitual rite of posting passage. There's a creepy sense of contentment and safety in being able to see everything in this glossy, unrealistic way. Almost like we can't stand to face the real and therefore sometimes messy parts of human existence.

I realised that it's exactly why the new wave of manifesting feels so at odds with what I believe in. It's why living a spirit-informed life to return back to *you* and create your best damn life is what I believe in. When you work on and look at your stuff, you're removing the filter that you had on the world, so you can see and respond to life in a different way. The stuff we carry around with us is like the social media filter that we view the world through. When you look at and work on it, you can slowly remove the filter to get the stuff you want. You see the world in direct correlation to what your stuff is. If you don't believe you're worthy, that's what you'll be met with. If you fear being unhappy, you'll spend a lifetime avoiding it. If you believe that everyone of the gender you're attracted to will hurt you, that will be the fear you carry into every date or relationship. Depending on your stuff, you might see the world as a place that just feels grim to be in, with not a millimetre of potential. Makes you think about all those big eyes, big lips, small nose filters in a new way, right? This was such an epiphany for me when I was trying to perfect my last selfie. When you are willing to look at and work on all that arises within your inner self, the outer world shifts and appears in ways that benefit you. Needless to say, I don't use filters anymore.

We've been driving down the road to creation, so you can *Get the Stuff You Want*, but how has stuff changed from what you work on and carry to what you want? Through the inner work we are almost metamorphosing our stuff. Death and rebirth baby. What you create is the world around you, the unfiltered world, and how you see, respond and place yourself within it. That's what manifesting is really about, well according to me anyway. Filters don't actually make the world look prettier. We see filters as being able to transform faces to fit into society's ideals, but all filters do is mask reality when reality is already perfect, because it exists. We control how we see and respond to everything. We label things as imperfect, usually because of our own stuff. When we put a filter on pain and hard things by pretending that everything's all good or distracting ourselves, we are not available for life, which means we aren't available for growth. What does this mean for the Balenciaga trainers, £5,000 bank transfer and Samsung Frame TV you've been trying to manifest? You can have as much material stuff as you want, but without the inner work it won't make you feel better, you won't trust that you'll receive it and, quicker than it comes, you'll be asking for something else. You'll be met with all the things you need to have a fruitful, purposeful and joyful life, if you see the world in a way where that will be possible for you.

At this point, you already know that you have the inner power to create, but we have to integrate this first. Getting the stuff you want comes from a state of being and existing; it's a more fluid and less tangible place. From here, you can choose what you want to fill that purposeful life with because you know who you are. When you have that approach to life, you can Balenciaga it up all you want, and all the fun stuff, the lavish stuff, will require minimal effort to call in, because it's not hard to create. Trust and believe.

PAUSE, TAKE IT, AND . . .
Reflect on your journey

Pretend that you've just downloaded a filter removal app on your phone. How are you already seeing and responding to the world in a different way and how do you want to feel next? Have you discovered anything new or interesting about yourself through this work so far?

In my 17 years of manifesting, I called in all that stuff. Most of my material possessions are a result of manifesting and they felt rather spectacular to receive. Yet, I'd trade it all, well maybe not my luxury bags, for how I see and respond to the world around me, because of all the inner work I've done. I adore my life, I love being a citizen in this world and even though this planet can be ghetto as hell at times, I'm a big fan of it. The way I live my life, the way I guide my clients to live theirs, and my biggest intention for you, is to move through the world being present, audacious, purposeful and as a powerful creator. To be spirit-informed. We aren't spirit-led, we are informed. We are all spiritual beings, whether you know what your human design or rising sign is or not. To be spiritual is to be alive, because spirituality isn't a verb. Spirituality isn't something that we are doing, it's a state of being, because it's who we are. We get to be everything that we envision and get all the stuff we want because of that. When we have purpose, the game not only changes, we create entirely new games. Living in purpose is the greatest 'stuff' we can have and it's one of those things where we will never stop seeing tips and tricks on how to find it.

CHASING YOUR PURPOSE AIN'T IT

In one of my online monthly workshops, I led a class called 'Newsflash: Finding Your Purpose Is a Myth'. As you've gathered by now, I'm like the person in the film who knocks everything off the carefully curated dinner table in one swipe. Glasses, cutlery, plates and all. I like to knock down the things we're told, so we can investigate if they actually make any sense.

We're always told that we're here to find our purpose. If you search for that phrase, you'll find a million articles, books, talks and blogs on how to supposedly do just that. Talk about pressure. That pressure rubs off on my clients who come to work with me after really struggling with not having 'found' their purpose yet. Feeling this sense that life isn't quite right, that something is missing. That they haven't found their 'thing' yet. Wondering what the hell they're supposed to be doing on this planet, not feeling lit up by life and waiting for the aha moment.

Believing that we have a purpose we are yet to find brings

with it so much seeking, chasing and questioning. As if your purpose will arrive with all the force of your glycolic cleanser getting in your eye. That there's an end point and when you arrive there you'll have total clarity. It's a bit like chasing shadows. We can have some level of certainty with our desires, but clarity is always evolving and ever-changing because so are we. How would it feel if we defined clarity as only a step to take before we take the next one? Just one foot in front of the other. No stress, no pressure. There's a lot of emphasis placed on needing clarity to be able to manifest. That you have to be very specific and clear on what you want before you can get it. That clarity must also come for you to find your purpose. I believed this too.

Then, I thought. Actually, the only thing you need to have clarity on is who you are. When you return back to *you* (which is continual, lifelong work), you know who you are, so everything you do from this knowing will be based on that clarity. Your 'dream' job will never be what you want it to be until you know who you are. If you are someone who is authentically outspoken, but has been shutting that down out of fear of being 'too much', that will determine the workplaces you feel at home in. If you've spent so long trying to be someone that fits in, you won't know which people are *for* you. It's even true for that pair of jeans on your manifesting list – until you've explored your personal style, honoured your unique body type and navigated your fear of being seen and being different, is it really those exact jeans you want or the jeans you think you *should* want? When you know who you are, you have the clarity you need to create and you only need enough clarity to take the next step. As Martin Luther King Jr said, 'Faith is taking the first step even when you don't see the whole staircase.' Apply that to clarity and release the pressure of needing to have it all figured out.

PAUSE, TAKE IT IN, AND . . .
Reflect on 'Purpose'

In your mind, journal or phone, reflect on what purpose means to you. What's your relationship with it? Is it something you feel like you have, are waiting for, chasing, or at peace with?

The staircase reveals itself to us step by step. The way that I channelled the concept of purpose from spirit feels a bit like a children's book, but we trust. Keep in mind, that you don't have to actually believe this – it can be a metaphor – but I'll share what I received and what makes the most sense for me. It's very similar to what happens in the Disney movie *Soul*, which had me crying at the TV like a fool and saying, 'See they know too, they know.' Before we incarnated into these bodies, in this particular lifetime, there's a waiting room. Like when you're at a spa, waiting to be called for a massage. You're sat and hanging out with the other souls who are waiting to be incarnated, as well as some spirit guides who aren't going to be incarnating into a human body. Maybe they're just spirit, maybe they were humans before, we're not nosey so we don't need to ask any questions. When you're called in, you're given your next assignment on Earth. You're given everything you need to grow, the personality you'll have and, if you believe in astrology, the time, date and place you'll be born into to help you with your assignment or what we call your purpose. You choose all those things before you head into the University of Human-ness. You learn everything through your human experiences, you live in purpose, you die and you take those lessons into your next human assignment. Or, so at least we think or some of us were told. It's cool if you believe and think in something completely different. But, this does help us to see that we already have our purpose; we've been living in it since we got here.

The next step in the University of Humanness is when we're born as these whole, authentic, confident, spirit-informed, adorable little creatures. We subsequently leave this energy, because the rest of the world and our life experiences step in to convince us we're not any of those things. So, we walk into the closet. This part was not given to me by spirit, but from the depths of my own colourful imagination. I like to see this closet as one of those really obscene, marbled, big enough to be a one-bedroom apartment types that you see in *Selling Sunset*. When you're inside, there are outfits upon outfits on rose gold hangers. They're not the spring/summer collections from New York Fashion Week though. Each outfit represents an element of your human identity. You have your wardrobe staples, so the gender outfit, one for race, one for age and one for name, then as you get older you accumulate more outfits. What you do for school, your job title, your relationship or marital status, your sexuality, if you're a parent, your net worth and so on. We get so attached to these outfits, because we believe that these labels are all we are, so we keep wanting more and more. We crave changing our relationship status and getting a better job title and believe that our purpose is within those. Your purpose is not in the outfits you identify with – yet we spend a lifetime looking for it in the closet.

The outfits are designed that way. They fit real nice for some time, we love how they look and then they suddenly look tired, so we buy more. It's the same for fast fashion and it's the same for our lives. Career is the best example of this and what I find most people I work with are navigating. When you think that what you do is who you are, your purpose becomes what you do for work. When we see purpose as one of these identity outfits, it's the outfit that's all the way on the top shelf that no ladder can reach. We keep trying on more things, hoping it will help us to climb to the top. Job after job after job. And for relationships, swiping every single night on dating apps; all to find purpose and getting stuck in the same loop of seeking and chasing. It's like we just can't handle not knowing why we are here, so we live in the three (see page 178). We chase the purpose that we hope to find in the future and resent the lack of purpose that we didn't have in the past. Surprise, surprise, purpose can only live in the present. It can't only be something outside of us, nor can it be fleeting. If it is, then it means that we can find it, get attached to it and when the external thing like the job changes or ends, then we no longer have purpose. If you believe that your purpose is to be a spouse, and your partner leaves, then are you saying you no longer have purpose? If you believe that your purpose is to be a parent, and your children grow up and want nothing to do with you, do you not have purpose? If you believe that your job is who you are, then you get made redundant, then who are you? All very real things that my clients have been through. That's why our purpose and getting the stuff we want can't be based in the outer world or things out of control that are subject to change. We continue because we are souls; our outfits we use, try on and borrow in this lifetime don't. Makes sense then that our purpose has to be within and that maybe we've always had it and don't need to find it.

WHAT'S YOUR SUNROOF?

Doing the inner work guides you into a life of purpose, which is another reason why I have an (un)intentional approach to manifesting. If you mind your business and live your life, you will fall into it. If you're focusing on the life you could be living, you aren't seeing the life you currently have because purpose is created in the present moment. We have to be available to see what's here, so we can create where we'd like to go next. A way to take the pressure off is to see your purpose less as this one thing, and more of a multi-purpose purpose. A purpose that is expansive, multi-faceted and subject to change.

I'm about to throw another car metaphor your way. I had to book in for my first driving lesson because of all this, because it's not lost on me that for someone who can't drive (yet) I speak about driving a lot. There's a sunroof in some cars and it's always present in the car. But, the amount of light that it allows in shifts. When you're driving in the dark, you might see some stars coming through or you might not see anything at all. There'll be days when the sun's brightness fills up the entire car. When we have a multi-purpose purpose, all we need is enough clarity, the first step, to find our sunroof. One word that guides us.

Your sunroof might be creativity like it is for my client

Rebecca. She's had several businesses and creativity has been the constant between all of them. When she's not working, she's just a creative spirit. It's what brings her joy and makes her soul jump up and down. There are times when she isn't in love with *how* she's being creative; she feels disconnected to her purpose and the sunroof just isn't letting light in, but it's there. Even in the darkness, it's there. So, when it's dark in the car, she releases her attachment to how she is being creative and tries something else, then the sunroof can again create more light. You can be creative in so many ways when it's who you are. When Rebecca wasn't attached to how she was creative, she got to have a multi-purpose purpose. How your purpose takes shape changes over time, as you outgrow pieces of it and try on new ones. Your sunroof will reveal itself to you because it's always riding in the car with spirit and you. It's just that sometimes we can't always see the light.

We've been building on this road trip to creation idea – this evolving journey where you're driving in the car with spirit in the passenger seat. The road signs guiding you to get the stuff you want are your intuition; all the different ways that your intuition communicates with you. All parts of you exist in that car, all your stuff and everything underneath it. During some seasons of life, it feels like your stuff is slowing the car down and at other times it isn't. We have the sunroof in there, our purpose, which cycles through pulling the car into darkness and uncertainty, and then light when we feel truly aligned. The way you discover your exact purpose is to allow it to greet you. The sunroof gets brighter and brighter when you step out of the car and into the traffic of life. It's pretty easy staying within the safety of the car, hanging out with spirit, reading endless books on how to live life and only ever doing the inner work without embodying it. You have to get out of the car and see where you can explore and feel into your purpose, instead of expecting it to smash through the window.

I believe that I've found my multi-purpose purpose. My guidance word, my sunroof, is expression. Many people believe it is to be of service, but being of service is simply one of the ways that my expression manifests, because what I do isn't who I am and what I do is service work. When I'm writing, I'm expressing; when I'm giving a talk, I'm expressing; when I'm in sessions, I'm expressing. When I have aggy opinions about things and don't hesitate in sharing them, I'm expressing. When I wear a ton of make-up, eyelashes and vintage-inspired clothing, which isn't dependent on trends, I'm expressing. I channel what I express and that is my sunroof. How did I realise this? It didn't come through in a vision or dream. Imagine, I speak to spirit every damn day and not a clue was given. I stepped into my work I do now through being in the traffic of life. The first step in clarity that I took was going on a perfume workshop.

I didn't see the staircase, I just knew that I loved perfume, so I did a workshop. I had five weeks off between leaving one job in beauty to starting another – plenty of time to be in the traffic of life. When I sat in a workshop by the Experimental Perfume Club, geeking out and making my own fragrance, the founder Emmanuelle Moeglin said that I had a great nose and maybe looking into essential oils could be a fun hobby. So, I did. I researched everything there was to know about essential oils and started making blends to use in my rituals, to scent my space with and to help family and friends sleep and relax. I didn't sell them; I was just thrilled by expressing what was in my heart in a physical way. I read in one of the essential oil books about chakra blends, which led me to reading about chakras, which led me to taking a Reiki 1 course. A course that obviously changed my entire life. A course that helped me to see my sunroof and one of the ways I wanted to express myself in this lifetime. If I had just sat with my knowing these jobs weren't for me and not acted. If I had kept believing that it was fine for my mental, physical and emotional bodies to take a beating in every job I had. If I had kept waiting for my purpose to find me . . . I would not be here doing what I do. My clarity took me one step at a time, from a perfume workshop to making oils to leaving my job. One step at a time. I discovered my sunroof, but there are still seasons of my life when not one drop of light is coming in. When I'm so overwhelmed by my past trauma, that I don't know how to express what I need in a relationship. When one way of expressing myself no longer works for me and I don't know what it will be. But, I trust that my sunroof is always in that car with me, guiding me, even when I can't see.

Being in the traffic of life is just like an actual traffic light. It might be the next step or already where you're at in your solo dates and self-discovery that we explored in Chapter 8. It's when you get out of the car, step out of uneasiness, walk down new streets, read different books, say yes to things and no to others, meet new people and live life. Then you check in to see if it's a **red, amber** or **green** for you; whether the things you discover about yourself make you feel a sense of flow or an ick.

The **reds** are the absolutely nots and your 'No' might change in the future, but it's a 'No' from you right now. It doesn't feel good and that's OK. When we feel like we're in a red, we also sit with it for a bit and do some inner work around it. A red for you might be cycling – you've tried, you worked through the resistance and it's still a 'No'. You take what you learned from the experience and move on. A red for me is working in a company with structure and hierarchy, where my ideas are contingent on someone else agreeing with them or having enough budget to execute them. Even if the company is lovely, it's not for me. It took me so many years to see that it was fine for this to be my 'No'.

The **ambers** are the things you try that are cool and somewhat enjoyable, but that are not the most thrilling thing for you. For me making essential oils is an amber. I still make them for myself and to gift friends and family, but I've worked in product development and doing it professionally is a big red. Ambers are such powerful teachers. Even when dating or in friendships, there might be someone who isn't a red or a green. They're just absolutely delightful and a beautiful human, but just not for you. They can teach you about what you do and don't want.

Then the **greens**, the sweetest possible spot. These are the things that make you feel beyond grateful to be alive. We're not productivity chasing here, so this is just you in all areas of life. It might be snoozing in the park, morning breathwork, interior design shows or painting watercolours. It might not even be activity based or in things that you 'do', but the things that allow you to see and respond to the world around you in a different way. You're able to fully immerse yourself in life without attachment because you're focused on the doing and not the destination.

PAUSE, TAKE IT IN, AND . . .
Reflect on Joy and Pleasure

In your mind, journal or phone, reflect on what brings you joy and pleasure that's just for the sake of it? Connect to the feeling it gives you. As you do so, explore if you have any beliefs around things you think that you *should* find joyful or ways in which joy should be meaningful or productive.

There are times when we just have to be in the human experience of it. If you're in a job that you hate more than when fabric gets stuck in a zip, it might be a red, and there might need to be some acknowledgement of that. Not everyone has the ability to leave red situations and move closer to greens. There are bills to pay, families to feed, and physical, mental, emotional and spiritual bodies to keep in balance. It's not always doable to leave a red, which can be hard to face. But, because it's an outer world piece, we can always work on our inner reality around it. If you have to stay in a work situation for survival and to pay rent, but it doesn't feel good or light you up, the Reiki principles are good to keep in mind. I did not care for the line, 'Work with diligence' when I first heard it. I didn't want to be in a job that filled me with dread walking into the office, let alone to be working with diligence there. Yet, it's often our only way to regain some control over the situation we've been handed.

You can apply **The Sacred Time Out** (see page 80) by sitting with what's occurring, what you're feeling, choosing what to do with what's occurring and finally saying, 'I will allow myself to feel that, and I can get through this.' You're not trying to pretend that the job is great – you're letting yourself feel horrific about it – but you know that you need to stay in it to pay your bills. You can then work with diligence by trying to make work as pleasurable as you can, so you feel like a **green** when you're in it. Can you listen to a podcast while you work? Can you make yourself the most delicious lunch to have there? If working from home a few days a week is an option, can you bring that up with your employer? Are there affirmations you can repeat to yourself when you're in the middle of a boring task? Can you go to the bathroom and take five minutes to breathe or watch videos of animals doing useless things just because they're the best? Can you ask a friend or partner to send you a text every day at 3:30pm to give you a boost? Might there be tasks that you're doing that are teaching you wonderful skills to take with you into your next opportunity?

I absolutely detested doing my tax returns and bookkeeping when I started my business. I now have an accountant, but at the time I couldn't afford to have anyone do them for me. I would put them off, resent the entire process and want to cry through it, because my stuff told me that I wasn't good with numbers. I doubted that I'd be able to do my accounts correctly and had this huge fear that HMRC would be coming to arrest me because my books were woefully incorrect. I worked through all this, because I reminded myself that I can figure out most things with the assistance of a search engine, books and YouTube videos. I then made my red a green by listening to music while I did my calculations and seeing it less as a chore, and more as a way for me to be able to contribute to the economy (a reach I know, but it helped), and I said a little thank you for every single penny that I was paid from people who trusted me with their lives.

Until we can shift or move past the red, we all have the capacity to shift how we show up to it. If you really can't get there, you honestly don't have to, but you can try to make the rest of your life outside it green. How do you give yourself the pleasure fix you need by making the time outside of work glorious? Remember, your sunroof is never just one area of your life; it's all parts of your life. If your sunroof is to design, it's not about only designing in your work, it's about designing a life of magic in every single aspect and giving yourself the permission to see your life as one that you are consciously designing, shaping and creating.

Focusing on the doing and not the destination is how we get to the destination. Being in the traffic of life is all the evidence you need to figure out what you desire and the authenticity of your desires. You may never figure out anything beyond, 'Yes, this just feels so damn good' – things are allowed to feel good without knowing if or what you should do with them. If your life is full of greens, then that's a pretty spectacular life; you don't need to label your sunroof or question if you've found purpose. A life of a mismatch of random things that don't really make sense, but feel downright marvellous, is a remarkable life – don't question it. As we spend more time out of the car and into life, we get closer to understanding our desires. This is the tangible stuff that's linked to the inner feelings. The stuff that aligns with how we move through the world, see and respond to it. The human experiences that assist in our spiritual growth and match our purpose. We often find clarity hard to reach or feel unsure about how to even see if something is a red, amber or green, because we're always in a dance with our desires.

PAUSE, TAKE IT IN, AND . . .
Do Something Different

Schedule in some time this week – yes, this week – to do something different, unexpected or interesting, just for the sake of it. Do the thing and check
in to see if it was a red, green or amber for you.

DANCING WITH DESIRE

It's lucky l like dancing, because we're always dancing with our
desires. Depending on the stuff you're carrying, you might
need to explore if your desires are really what you want and
why you're going after them. You have the desires that you
believe are possible for you according to your stuff. Those are
the ones that feel safe and achievable.

One of my greatest desires is to have children, but based on
my past experiences, I struggled to believe that this would be
possible for me within the context of a loving, stable and secure
partnership. So, I started to research all the ways to have a child
outside of a relationship. Now, this is both sensible and empowering, but when I dug deeper I realised that it was actually the
stuff I carried about not being able to have a wonderful partner
that was governing my intention. I *want* love and a partner, I
want a family, but my stuff convinced me to choose a lesser
desire because I didn't believe what I truly desired would be
possible for me.

Another example is if you love travelling – it thrills you and
you can afford it, but you're terrified of going for the desire that

looks like travelling the world in a really big way. So, you play it safe and shut that down by going for a safer option of one mini trip a year. We also have desires that are based on validation. Sometimes we choose the things that we believe will be admired by others. Do you really want that promotion and shiny job title, or do you want the love and congratulations you'll receive from other people by getting it? Do you really crave remote working in one gorgeous location to the next or are you craving the inevitable likes and wows you'll receive by having that lifestyle? The apartment that you think you want in an area that doesn't really feel good, is it just to say that you live in that postcode?

In a macadamia nutshell, we can use the **Break the Rules** exercise (see page 119) here as well. See if you are choosing desires based on your own stuff, other people's or the world's rules; desires that aren't authentic. This isn't to say that it's not possible to have desires that come from here. Spirit really can't tell the difference between one thing to the next; energy is just energy. Spirit isn't looking to see what's on the brand directory at Harvey Nichols, nor is it scouting Rightmove. Energetically, there's no difference between an expensive leather belt and a one-bedroom studio in Manchester. If wanting the belt is based on your stuff, it might not come through because there'll be a gap in belief, trust and faith to receive it. Or, the belt might come in and you have a lovely time wearing it, but end up going straight to the next fancy thing on your list, without the validation pieces being navigated. Sometimes, you get the belt and somewhere along the line spirit brings up whatever inner work will help you to receive the growth.

This is all awareness. You can still want or get the thing,

even if it's in this category. Don't judge yourself. But, through self-inquiry if you discover it isn't something that you really want, it's just a sign to dig deeper. To get to the core of what within you is asking for assistance. This is how creation occurs. It gets us to the desires that make us shine, to make us receive love and opportunities; not the quick fixes. It's all information and you always have the agency to decide what to do with it. The desires that benefit us are the experiences and things that come from being in flow, when you know it's all good, because it feels good. Even if you end up living in the three (see page 178) or a fear pops up, on a soul-level you just know that there's some goodness here. This is when you're fired up, moving forward from passion and are just happy to be in it. This is how I feel even if I'm on my seventh client of the day. A huge reason why I do what I do is to be of service, but it becomes an authentic desire because of the way I do it. There's no part of me that desires being a nurse or being a facialist for example, yet those are both beautiful expressions of service work. I do what I do because it lights people up, but also because it lights me up. It wouldn't be an authentic desire if only my clients were loving it, but I was exhausted, depleted and resentful. That's not enough. I'd be doing it for other reasons. Pleasure is a requirement here.

When my client Natasha was trying to figure out where she should live with her family, she craved community, open space for her children to play in and street parking. She wanted to feel safe and secure. Based on the stuff she's carrying, she feared leaving London and being out of the buzz; she feared what her friends who had pleaded with her to stay nearby would say. When she started looking at houses that made her feel safe and secure (with street parking), she was able to connect to what she really wanted and not what she thought she *should* want. These desires are pleasure for the sake of pleasure, even when it comes in material things.

I'm anti the version of self-righteous spirituality that says you shouldn't want the clothes, the make-up, the sports cars, the private memberships or the season tickets. If you want the luxury of flying first class, just because it feels wonderful, then go get it. If you want to wear lipstick because you like playing with colour, you don't need a reason beyond that. We're here to experience pleasure and beauty, to feel the ease and gentleness of it all. If you're supposed to learn or grow through something, you will. If all that make-up is here to teach you about a bigger beauty standard thing, it will reach you whether you buy the lipstick or not. You're aware, you inquire, you focus on what feels good and you make the choices based on what will assist in your growth. If you just want the cute thing, the world won't implode.

PAUSE, TAKE IT IN, AND . . .
Be Enough

Close your eyes if that feels comfortable and safe to do so, or gaze at a spot on the ground. Take some deep breaths. Call in spirit. Then repeat 'I am' to yourself for as long as it feels good. You don't have to fill in the blanks or wait for an answer. You being here is enough.

This is why I will continue to scream into the void that creation and getting the stuff you want isn't lazy, easy or passive. Doing the inner work can be a *lot*, because all four bodies are involved in the process, let alone the trust that's required. But, most of all, understanding what our desires are, feeling into the sunroof, getting out of the car and living life, all lead us to inspired action. Action that is all about living and embodying the work. The work that exists in motion, in real life, in the traffic. There are endless pressures in life, trying to mould, bend and shape yourself into who the world might like. Chasing what's next, wanting to do anything to be better or different. It's enough as it is, without feeling the need to also be spending sleepless nights waiting to wake up lying next to your purpose. All the clarity you need to get the stuff you want in this moment, or to step into purpose, is to see what the next step is. It doesn't matter what the step looks like, how big it is or how high you have to climb. Simply one step to get you out of the car and into life; a life that will always be yours to create, design, adjust and check in with.

THIRTEEN

Tracking the Universe Ain't Cute

There's a part of my personality that's allergic to things becoming a *thing*. As soon as something reaches the tipping point of being littered into every conversation and your mum's WhatsApp group, I refuse to be involved. I read *Harry Potter* for the first time about five years ago because I didn't enjoy the hype. I still haven't watched *Game of Thrones* because y'all went absolutely overboard with it. It's too much. I don't even want to drink matcha anymore, so thanks for that too. Manifesting is about to embark on the same boat of being a *thing*. This one, I am more than down for, as I want every single human being on the planet to have access to it. Yet, as predicted, with more eyes becomes more garbage. In an attempt to force it into a trend box, when it is most certainly not one and definitely not new, we've managed to dilute what it is. Practices change and evolve, because we do. Yes, preserving original teachings is important, but all the origins of manifesting came through a human being. Channelled from spirit sure, but passed through someone's humanness. People with different experiences, stuff, motives, hopes and ways of expressing themselves. People who lived during certain points of time. In the same way, I under-stand the nutritional hysteria around Paleo diets, but does it make sense to eat in the same way our ancestors did, when they just didn't have to live through the exact same craziness that we do? Manifesting *has* to change for us, because we have changed. That's why I've expanded manifesting into creation and why living a spirit-informed life is the only way to get to creation. Manifesting is a side effect of doing the inner work.

It can't be passive and rely on us sitting by the window and waiting desperately for all the stuff we just visualised to come to us. It can't be that way because our belief system just isn't fit for purpose. We have been hardened by how brutal life can be. It's hard to believe that a job can fulfil and sustain you if you're still processing the trauma caused by every job on your CV. It's hard to believe in love if you're 65 dates in on Bumble and have been ghosted so much that you're sure people are mistaking you for an extra in *Casper*. It's hard to believe in the good of humanity when billionaires literally flee to space during some of the roughest years in our collective lifetime. It's hard to believe in kindness when we cancel people and make them feel irredeemable because they said something problematic when they were 12 or because we just don't agree with them. It's hard to believe in our inner power when the entire world convinces so many of us that we don't have it. It's hard to believe that we're spiritual beings when too many industries and systems thrive on us thinking that we're only physical. We ain't mani-festing a damn thing, if we think that belief is all it takes to receive.

With that said, as manifesting becomes more practised, we can't go too far in the other direction either. You don't need a

PhD to manifest and at times it feels that way. My clients are stressed. Very stressed. They come into sessions saying that they've been prompting, analysing, visualising, repeating affirmations, doing hypnotherapy and writing list after list and getting nowhere. They want to know precisely how much clarity they need, if they should do it on the new moon and whether the money will still come in if they didn't charge their abundance crystal. They want to know if they've done something wrong or not done enough inner work to get the stuff they want. That maybe they've been too low or that there's just something wrong with them. They want to know how long they should be visualising for and why a manifesting meditation didn't work. Or why a coach promised to teach them how to manifest six figures and they're still waiting on a bank deposit from spirit. I'll tell you this for free: it's not that deep.

CREATION IS (UN)INTENTIONAL AND INTENTIONAL MANIFESTING

If your manifesting practice isn't giving you as much as the very thing you're asking for will, then you need to change it. For me, creation includes both (un)intentional and intentional manifesting, with the former being the most important. When you have clarity and you're being in the traffic of life to figure out your desires, you're being intentional. You're creating the world around you because you know yourself enough to know what brings you pleasure and feels purposeful. Whereas (un) intentional manifesting is really about existing in an unfiltered world, being spirit-informed and letting the inner work shape how you see and respond to the world around you. The type of manifesting that's ultimately just a way of joyful living. A life that is created and received as a side effect of looking at and working on your stuff. Many manifesting practices don't take this into account, but how amazing is it to just be able to find luxury in the present moment, to feel resilient and know how to cultivate mini bites of peace when the world is going to shit? To be delighted by yourself and life and have the willingness to shift obstacles into opportunities and take pauses to be with what hurts. Your life will be bloody amazing, so why is that not what we all prioritise? The way you see the world, and the way you feel in it, is what creation is about.

This always has to come before you start getting super-specific and focusing on the material stuff, because who needs a Range Rover if you feel awful about yourself and the world when you're driving in it? You just wasted £103,000 on a chunk of metal and, yes, I know the exact price because I frequent the website often. Here's the thing; I know myself, I continue to do the inner work and I know that I'd probably be quite delighted by this car. It's not for other people; I've worked through my money stuff and it's very on brand for me to drive a car that's obnoxiously unexpected, because I'm a frolicking contradiction. I trust spirit enough to know that if I really want to drive one, then I probably will at some point if it will benefit me to receive it. If it's another car, then I trust it will be another one as long as it gives me freedom and has a heated leather steering wheel. I also know that the car will not make me feel any desired emotion unless I already know how to feel it, because I'll still be whatever version of me that exists when I'm in those sweet front massage seats. I'm not writing it on a list, I've just felt into how splendid it will be to drive it. I'm not waiting for it and I don't need it; I'm just going about my day. Because of all that unintentionality, I can now be intentional about wanting that car or any car, just because it's a pleasurable and fun addition to my human experience.

PAUSE, TAKE IT IN, AND . . .
Sit with this

(Un)intentional manifesting occurs as a side effect of doing the inner work. It's where you change how you see and respond to the outer world and receive the opportunities that will most benefit you; almost without asking for it. The manifestation isn't always a tangible thing, but life feels limitless, rich with potential, where you can move through whatever you're going through. From here, you can be intentional about your human experiences, as you have power and agency to create. Intentional manifesting is when you define the tangible stuff that affords you pleasure, ease and purpose.

That's why we've spent the majority of our time together focusing on the (un)intentional, because that alone is revolutionary. When we start to get more intentional, some of the superstition and old-school spiritual stuff comes in. This is where some of the questions, doubts, rules and formulas take place. We can make it simple, though, because again, manifesting has to change, because we've changed. Making time for yourself is important, but, seriously, who has the time to add in a long-ass manifesting practice to an already hectic agenda. It needs to be able to slot in and not feel overwhelming to do so. Which is why I'm an advocate for having a listless list approach to manifesting. We're often told to be very specific about what we want, because how else will the universe know what to give us. A valid point, but a point that doesn't consider that we are evolving, episodic, seasonal, confused, indecisive beings. I mean, I cried once because I couldn't decide what to eat for dinner. You might want a two-bedroom apartment, with a stained-glass window in your bedroom, double sinks and a hammock on the balcony as of now, but what about the next day? What if when you go inwards, it's not that list of characteristics you really want, but rather a home with enough space for you to work in, so you're saying no to all other kinds of homes that would be perfect for you?

My client Maddie had a list the length of The Shard building in London. It was 87 floors deep with bullet points of her ideal man. She had his physical attributes, his qualities and the things he'd like doing. A sprinkle of thoughtfulness with a dash of banter and a ladle of business acumen. Manifesting can't be the equivalent of a build-a-bear workshop, because life doesn't work that way and neither do real people. One of Maddie's bullet points said, 'He likes to travel' and it's a wonderful example of why strict and very specific lists aren't always helpful. A lot of people like to travel; it's as common an occurrence on dating apps as seeing a shampoo ad on TV. There are different ways to like travel, though. I might be a travel-seeking Sagittarius, but I only enjoy luxurious travelling. If I was given the option to backpack and hostel my way around the world or never leave this country again, looks like I'll be making my way around the United Kingdom for eternity, then. I am Maddie's worst nightmare and hellish travel companion, so technically I won't match up to her list, even though I like to travel. Meaning, she might walk away, when instead we could have showed each other something. With a listless list we are focusing more on feelings rather than what we can quantify or qualify.

Creating intentions from curiosity opens manifesting up to a juicier place that feels slower, more roomy, less rigid and way more fun. Getting the stuff you want should never feel like a chore or that you're creating from fear, lack or worry. Or should I say, the feeling like you're on your knees and desperately hoping for something to happen and not believing it will. With all the power you're cultivating, choose to create a life on the basis of how you want it to feel. If writing a long specific list feels draining and unrealistic, then switch it up to something different. When (un)intentional manifesting is a part of your life, it feels easier to connect to the idea that everything can show, teach or guide you into something. We might be tempted to ignore a person who doesn't match exactly what is on our list, but if we focus on how we want our partner to make us *feel*, we can see what's available for us in people that we may have overlooked. Who knows, if you go outside of your list and have a beautiful and brief relationship with someone, they might share something with you that will help you to grow into the partnership you do desire. If you focus on how you want to feel, you'll always be met with what you need to receive. I asked Maddie to experiment with releasing her list and to pretend that she was a guest on a podcast, sharing the life she desired, as if it had already happened. A practice that has helped me and some of my clients to get really enthused about what creating a damn good life can look like. I've been doing this since I was a child. When my dolls were boring me, I'd pretend I was a on a chat show being interviewed. I'd carefully detail how brilliant I was and all of the brilliant things I did. Drama Queen Extraordinaire. Here we're only focusing on telling the story of a feeling and it helps us to get intentional.

PAUSE, TAKE IT IN, AND . . .
Be a Guest

Pretend that you're a guest on a podcast, sharing details about the life you are creating as if it's happening or has already happened. Record yourself (don't worry, you don't have to listen to it back) or mumble it to yourself when you're in the shower or going for a walk. If this gives you the ick, then you can write or dream it up, but saying it out loud makes it more real.

1. **Call spirit (optional):** This is an optional extra. You can connect to spirit if you want to and let this be your personal practice in the steps to connect. You can do either version of The 5 rituals (see pages 192 and 216) to get you in the mood. If this is one of the only intentional manifesting practices you do, then feel free to make it more special.

2. **Theme it up:** Work with these themes – love and relationships, career and money, then, self and lifestyle. Let these be the things you're asked about on the imaginary podcast. You might look at one at a time through several voice recordings. See what works for you.

3. **Do the thing:** Now, get to speaking. Say it in the present tense as it will feel more real – we always create from the energy of it already happening. Pretend that someone is asking you about how you live your life and what's happening in your relationships, your career and with yourself. Say how it all feels to you and bring up the emotions of it already happening, without fear and without limiting yourself. Allow yourself to push past what you think is possible. This is dreaming big x1,000.

Here's an example:

Life feels blissful right now. I just got back from a trip to Paris with my best friends and that made me feel so energised about potentially moving there. Work is going so well as I had the confidence to leave my job and to set up my own consultancy practice, which feels so huge and I'm proud of myself for doing it. I have an incredibly loving partner who I live with and one of my favourite things about them is that they bring me back a bottle of kombucha every evening as it's my favourite thing and that makes me feel like such a thought-of part of their life.

If today you can only get to one piece of clarity, then that's all you need. You can keep adding to your podcast stories, you can amend them, remove some, tweak things. It's your life. It's your story to create. I have a series of voice notes in my phone; I never listen back because I trust that what I've said is coming. When I want to go bigger or amend, I just start a new recording. If you've ever seen me walking around and talking into my phone, this is what I was doing. For everything I say, I always include how the action or tangible thing will make me feel, because we're only using the experience to get us closer to how we want to feel. It's not about the bottle of kombucha, it's about feeling considered. So, you're telling spirit that's what you want in your life, be it via kombucha or words of affirmation.

Being a guest also provides clues if you're struggling with your sunroof. If you're playing with purpose, you might learn something here. As you speak, you might find yourself endlessly detailing that you enjoy playing the violin, the same violin you have no idea how to play now. You might not know why you wrote that and it might not mean that's even what you want to create; it might just be a sign that you're in need of a hobby and to learn something new in the present moment. When you have your podcast story in mind, you can work towards it little by little. If you said that you're an international speaker and that feels very far off, you can start now by practising in the mirror or just watching TED talks on repeat. Combine the physical with the spiritual by also connecting to spirit and asking for what you need to help you on your way. Live in an (un)intentional way and show up to life and whatever opportunities come to you. The being a guest practice releases control and structure of *how* you need to manifest and it becomes the onion that you get to peel back and find different layers of.

Once you've connected to a looser vision of what you want to create, then you can work with certain pieces of it one step at a time. While I like to keep things practical, working with astrological seasons or the phases of the moon is helpful here. Not only for the spiritual connection and as an intuitive prompt to go deeper into yourself, but it makes logistical sense. I have my daily practices of connecting to spirit and I just see spirituality as me living my life and doing the work, so the main ritual time I have is on the new or full moon. These are my monthly check-in points.

As we head into a new zodiac sign each month, you can also use the themes of the sign to help you choose what to work on that month. If we're in Leo season, for example, and in the podcast exercise you said that you had your own business, but right now you struggle with wanting to be seen, use the astrological energy to your advantage. During Leo season, you might want to take a few steps back from your bigger intention and focus on going out to meet new people and seeing where you find it hard to be in the spotlight. The same is true for the moon cycle; for each new moon, you can work with bite-size intentions that are on the road to the bigger ones, again choosing the areas that make the most sense for you. For all things moon, my girl Tamara Driessen, author of *Luna*, has got your back and has a handy low-down on everything you need to know.

Then whenever you're setting intentions, in whichever way you want to, you take it through the work. You're already living in alignment with an (un)intentional way of manifesting, so you're doing the inner work anyway. Consider the intention-specific ones more of a speedy tune-up. Let's say that you're working with the full moon in Capricorn and you're setting an intention for financial stability, so you want to call in £3,000 to invest and create passive income. This feels like a true desire, because in the podcast practice you wrote that you only work two days a week and supplement your income in other ways. Starting with investments is a great step on the way to this. Then you Run It Through (see below) the work. You'll look at your intention and see what comes up for you. If your first thought was wondering *how* it will come or that there's no way that you can make it work with your salary, then that's great information. If some old beliefs about not being worthy of money or being smart with money come up, again, great information. You're checking in to see what you're carrying and what needs a tune-up. Then you might want to run the intention through some of the exercises you've already done in this book. The work pushes you further into receiving your intentions. Here's some that might help:

PAUSE, TAKE IT IN, AND . . .
Run It Through

1 **Answer these questions:** Are you carrying any inner and outer stuff around this intention? If so, where did this come from, what receipts do you have to prove that the opposite is true and what might it be here to teach you?

2 Use the **Break the Rules** exercise (see page 119) around your intention to see if it relates to you being authentic or listening to others' expectations.

3 Follow the steps to **Connect to Spirit** (see page 164) or do the **Check in With Your Intuition** exercise (see page 109) if you want to ask for guidance on next steps, if you're struggling to believe or doubting if it's possible.

4 If in doubt, say this or similar: 'Spirit, I trust you to guide me to return back to . . . *me*,' or spend some time with your **ReturnRing** (see page 144) and Touchable Affirmation.

BRING BACK THE FLOATIES

This grounded approach to manifesting doesn't mean that you can't get in on everyone else's fun. This is a FOMO-free zone, but we're not entertaining the idea of superstition. Superstition in manifesting looks like all the fears my clients have, and making yourself a manifesting dictator. Feeling the need to control every single aspect of your being to be in the best possible position to get the stuff you want. Choosing not to bother with your intentions if you're three days past the new moon. Not allowing yourself to feel absolutely horrendous for as long as you need to feel horrendous, because you're convinced it'll delay all the goods from getting to you. Believing that you need to be an energetic match and be in the same frequency of what you're calling in, that you're now just faking your way to feeling good. All the 'rules' and practices make sense, but we as a people have changed, so how we use the practices needs to change. When we feel like we need to buy spirituality, instead of being spiritual, there's just more stuff to consume to get us there. We delegate our healing journey to the next book, deck, coach or course for our answers. As this work gains in prominence and accessibility, we can't afford to believe that our power and ability to create can only come through the material goods that prompt our inner abilities.

This is why we can apply the idea of floaties, which I introduced to you before, to creation as well. Floaties here are the moon rituals, crystals, spells, affirmations and meditations. When you have your intention ready to go, if you feel called to, you can pick some floaties. With the understanding that floaties help you to swim to what you want to create, but you're doing most of the work alongside spirit. You might want to use some of the elements in **The 5.2** exercise (see page 216) or you might want to add in some other tools.

If I have some extra time and I'm setting an intention for, say, greater acceptance and compassion with myself, then I might write my intention on pink paper, or say it out loud in **Be a Guest** (see page 251), while surrounding myself with rose quartz and malachite crystals, dried rose petals, and patchouli and ylang ylang essential oils. All the floaties that align with my specific intention.

You can also play graphic designer and make some images and resources or beg a friend who's nifty with design to do it for you. The web design tool Canva is fabulous for this, if you can't navigate Photoshop. I screenshot my bank balance and erased the number, then input the amount of money I wanted to have in there in its place. Seeing my name and exactly how it would be to see that number helped me to believe way more than those fake cheques from the bank of the universe circulating online. Two years later and I opened my account to the same number. You can fake anything – an inbox filled with opportunities, an email you send to yourself with a job offer. Manifesting floaties are whatever it takes to help you believe, knowing that it's not your design skills that are making it possible, you are. You don't need all these things to be able to manifest; see it instead as using whatever tools and practices you need, to trust and believe that it will happen for you.

Then comes the real-world practices that will float you right to where you want to be. Say your intention is to become debt-free. You've run it through the work and examined the areas to investigate, you have a chunk of pyrite under your credit card and faked an email notification from your bank saying that your balance is now £0. You're not focused on how it'll happen; you're living life, minding your business and trusting that spirit will give you the financial freedom you deserve. Now what? Add some practical steps. Read all the free tips you can find online about managing debt, see what transferring your debt to a 0 per cent interest card is actually about, all that jazz. Ask people for their debt freedom stories. Do all the money management things and anything physical that assists the spiritual. It shifts something, but also you're gently tapping spirit on the shoulder and saying that you're ready for it to come through, so even if it feels like it's happening at a glacial pace, you're prepared to get it.

What comes next is where we sometimes end up in a bit of a faff and have a crisis of faith. It's also one of those areas where we really have to squat our way into strengthening our trust muscle. When you're adding intentional manifesting or even living in a way that's open to possibility, being able to let go and release it is Big Spirit Energy. Client after client tell me that they've done all the things and now they're just waiting; they want to know where the hell their stuff is. When you order something you really want online, you might compulsively track where the delivery is every five minutes, repeatedly hitting refresh to get an ETA on when your package is arriving. The excitement of opening it, the anxiety of not being sure if it'll work out, all combine to make for thrilling stuff. It's cute. What's not cute is tracking the universe. Spirit, doesn't act like your go-to courier. You might be refreshing the tracker for those new shoes, but you *do* know they're coming. You don't message the driver and ask which route they're taking to your house. You don't send a message to check in. You trust it's arriving, so why don't we trust spirit to deliver?

All we need to do is ask for what we want, intentionally or not. Once we do so, we trust that the story is being written. We keep doing whatever we need to do while we wait for it to be delivered, but when we start doubting, asking why it's taking so long or even if, it will happen, we're not trusting. We all know what happens on *The Great British Bake Off*, when they sit nervously on the floor, peering into the oven. They don't believe that the cake will rise or they got the ingredients right, so they keep opening the oven. My grandma used to work as a pastry chef and she told me at the tender and curious age of four, under no uncertain terms, to never open the oven during baking or you'll ruin the cake. No-one wants a ruined cake, just because we couldn't wait or didn't trust it would bake.

Spirit heard you the first time and when you change your mind about the stuff you want, need to add or edit anything, spirit heard you then too. You don't need to send any imaginary follow-up emails to spirit to check in and ask, 'Hey sweetie, did you get my last message about that thing I asked for? It's still not here yet. Did you forget where I live?' We're not doing that, we trust in the maturation period, we go out into the world and slather ourselves in the face mask that is the present moment. We see what wants to come through and we trust that if not this, then better. We don't rush or force, we simply allow.

Not tracking the universe and sitting on your doorstep waiting for the stuff you asked for will feel easier once you see that so much of creation is about changing how you see and respond to the world. When we expand the definition of manifesting to being the way you move through the world, intentionally calling things in always feels like a want, instead of a *need*. There isn't so much obsessive and frantic energy around it, because you know that doing the inner work is how you get to where you want to be. When you have a passive approach to manifesting, without understanding that looking at and working on your stuff is a huge element, it's easy to be waiting at desperation station. When we're in a passive place, we write down that we want the money to pay for rent, get super-stressed, keep tracking and can't let go because we *need* that money. You don't need that stress, though. We set intentions for our wants, desires and what would be pleasurable. We ask spirit to support us with our human needs, but we do the inner work required to meet those needs. Spirit will be right there with you on that journey, if you let it.

TRUST, TRUST, TRUST

Let spirit in, so you can let go. Letting go of anything in our lives is never easy or fun, even the painful things, because on some level we believed it was keeping us safe or at least serving us in some way, to have it in our lives. When we *do* let go, we are declaring to spirit that we trust in what's coming in. We trust in the space that becomes available when we let go. To start to believe in the certainty that you will get the stuff you want, let your breath be a reminder. As long as you are alive, you will be breathing. Some of us may struggle to breathe or have machines that breathe for us, but we are all breathing. When you breathe in, you have complete, unspoken trust that you will breathe out. You can control how long, how deep, how slow the next breath will be, but you know there will be one. You are living proof of certainty. Outer certainty we can never have, but inner certainty we always have access to.

You are spirit, so see your intentions as an exemplification of the fact that you can create and bring things into existence. Breathe in your intentions and desires. Pause to let go, surrender and trust. Then breathe out into the knowing that you will receive it and that you also have non-attachment to the exact form it will take. If it is not this, then it is always, always better.

To surrender requires you to leave the *how* behind by breaking up with needing to know, see or understand *how* you'll get the stuff you want. The *how* is none of your damn business, because it is quite literally above you now. Spirit is working behind the scenes to deliver it all to you; it's not your concern what spirit is doing to bring it to you. Your concern is doing the inner work to believe it's possible for you, trust in timing and carry on with your life. You don't need to know the route that the delivery driver will take to your house, because it'll probably be the route you never thought it would take. It might be long, weird and confusing, but it will come. When you put what you want out there, it's already yours.

Think about when you booked a holiday and the level of faith you had. You paid for your flights and accommodation, asked for time off work, prepared a braggy out-of-office email, and maybe even had the audacity to book a restaurant three months ahead of time. I say audacity, because you don't have the holiday yet. It's in process but it hasn't arrived. Yet, you took all the actions of someone who has complete certainty that it will arrive and happen exactly as you hoped. You had giddy heart palpitations when you got your flight confirmation, told your friends, daydreamed about outfits, maybe even made a list of things to do. You did all of that because you trusted. You felt it because you had it; you just weren't in the motion of it yet.

The harshest lesson has been learned during COVID-19 – that there is no certainty. That same holiday could have been cancelled; it wasn't certain but you acted as if it was. There's no difference with your intentions. You wouldn't book a holiday if you didn't think it would happen, so we call in our desires because, what's the point in asking if you don't think it will happen? This is what it means to surrender. Surrendering is the biggest fight, the boldest action and the fiercest move we can make. Surrendering isn't about giving up, but saying you have so much trust even when you can't see a way or a how. Surrendering isn't an act of weakness or despondency; it's choosing unwavering faith to direct you into growth. Surrendering is when we allow spirit to show us when we can't see. All we can do is go with what we have to hand, to allow our faith to be our certainty when the outer world can't show us it.

PAUSE, TAKE IT IN, AND . . .
Forgive

Take a moment to forgive and thank yourself. Forgive yourself for when you resented all the stuff you're carrying or judged yourself for carrying it. Forgive yourself for being unsure or uncertain. Forgive yourself for all of it. Then, thank yourself for being here, showing up and for having the willingness to do the inner work and create.

Getting the stuff you want is dependent on having trust and faith, and doing the inner work can be your evidence of that. As you work through your stuff, listen and act from an intuitive place and don't shy away from things not feeling good – life changes. It changes in a way that's more than setting intentions for the pleasurable additions to your life. Don't get me wrong, doing the inner work can feel like a chore at times, when you're hyperaware of everything and prepared to investigate, it can feel like a lot. I've definitely complained and wanted a regular life, when my eyelash extensions are crispy with tears because I chose to sit with my fears. Then I realise, that this is what we're here for; to grow. The more proof we have of how rich life is when we do the work, the greater we can trust that it's worth it and trust that the stuff we want is coming.

You are the ultimate manifestation of the work, because you have changed and so has your view of the world. There's no greater evidence than that, so let that be the faith you need to convince you of what is possible. That everything you asked for is possible, because you are here. You were created, in a very biological way, but in a way that doesn't actually make much sense when you really think about it. You are a creation. We are *all* manifestations. We search for the reasons why we are here and there are many, but we will never fully understand the why of it all. We know how we are born, but why in this specific way? Why can we do so many things and not do others? Why do we feel, see and experience things in the way we do? We spend lifetimes of research, thinking and analysing to answer these questions; it's remarkable to explore, but we won't always find the answers. What we do know is that we're here and we trust in that, even if the how is too complex to compre-hend. When we hold on to welcoming in what most benefits us, we can fill up our jugs with trust because it just may not look the way we wanted it to.

If you've been calling in partnership, meet someone spec-tacular and it ends, it can feel brutal, but when we know that it's all leading to creation, we can see some hope through our grief. We know that we've set our intention, so if it is not this person right now, they are steering us to the next person, a more aligned person. When we don't cling on to the exact, line by line specificity of what we asked for, we're allowing life to surprise and entice us, with what could be.

That's what keeps us out of the classic blame game. The game we sometimes play with ourselves when we don't get the stuff we want. That *we* must have messed up, that there's more work to do, more things to 'heal'. Let's draw a line in the perfectly golden sand here. Just because doing the inner work is a route to creating your best damn life, if life doesn't look the way you hoped it would, or one of your intentions didn't come through, the answer is not in doing more work, digging up old trauma or avoiding living and choosing to read instead. Manifesting might be a side effect of the work, but the relationship isn't co-dependent. This isn't a results-based approach; we don't consume ourselves in the work only to get the stuff. If we do that then we are chasing.

We do the work to exist in the world in a different way and that's why my definition of manifesting is a broad one. Doing the inner work is a way of doing life, but never equate something not working out to your lack of doing it or going 'deep enough'. We trust that spirit is always guiding you to return back to *you*. That also means that maybe now is just not the time for the stuff you want to come through. It could be that what you hoped for isn't what will benefit you, so something else is making its way to you. You can feel the very real sense of loss and disappointment and you don't have to jump into seeing what's next. It will reveal itself whenever it needs to. You get to reflect, reassess and leave the space of blaming. Doing the inner work isn't just the inquiry and emotional stuff; it's also being soft and free with yourself. That's the work you can make sure you do, when things don't work out. Hold yourself.

WHY WE SHOULD ALL BE SPIRIT-INFORMED

When you look at and work on your stuff to get the stuff you want, what do you do once you've got it? You carry on living. That's what. In its most basic form, being spirit-informed is a way of living. You live within the context of doing the inner work because you are the constant. It is not a series of practices that you only do at home and becomes a solitary routine; it's how you show up, see and respond to life too. It's how you see the same situations in completely different ways, because how you see them has shifted.

Being spirit-informed is not only having a continuing relationship with spirit, but seeing spirit within yourself and outside of yourself. It's choosing to constantly return back to *you*, without feeling the pressure of self-optimisation. You are enough. We should all be spirit-informed, because we're able to harness our power and agency with the certainty that spirit is there riding beside us and, wow, what we can do with that faith is beyond our scope of possibility. When we ourselves see the world in this way, we touch other people with it, who then touch even more people. That's how the world changes. One person, one belief, one thought at a time. This is our comeback when people just don't understand all the 'spirit stuff' we do or get why we like to spend so much time within ourselves. It's our response when this work is labelled as self-indulgent, individualistic and narcissistic. We're taking it in, so we can take it out, because the work *really* becomes the work when it lives outside of us. The work starts within you, then into the street, the eyes you meet, the hearts you love, the humans you breathe life into, the ideas that you craft, the fingertips your hands graze and the words that move from deep inside of you into someone else. The impact of you doing this work exists so far beyond you. Leaving a trail of hope, love, optimism, wisdom and pure delight. All waiting for someone else to step into that trail and pick up what you left for them to discover.

When you live in a way where you are rifling through your stuff, feeling into fear, meeting your own needs before expecting the world to, know that you're so blessed and favoured, promoting your intuition, doing you, prioritising self-care, connecting with spirit, being in the present moment, giving yourself permission, living with purpose and trusting spirit to bring you all of it; both your inner and outer worlds shift. We take it in but we never stay there, because what you can create from the work is why we do the work. We create the opportunities to redefine who we are as citizens, lovers, children, parents, siblings, partners, employees and employers. We can redefine who we are as humans. A definition that continues to evolve as we all do, as right now our collective problems feel like ones that we can't see a way out of. Which means that we need to shift our approach to how we're seeing them.

We have tried fixing things with systems, laws, structures, road maps and plans. Many of them have worked, but within what has worked and what is yet to, we rarely emphasise one piece. Seeing our difficulties, pain and injustices through a spirit-informed lens. We are missing the ability to see our shared compassion, love and common humanity. We are missing our sameness and the power that every single one of us has inside of us. We are missing our spirituality. What would life look like if we all shared the same vision; we may never agree on the ways we get to that vision, but what if we had the same one? A shared goal, a joy, something to delight in and pray for. Imagine the world we could collectively create, because we would all know that we can create our own inner worlds.

We speak about the pain of climate change, racism, misogyny, abuse and poverty. We sit at dinner tables and unite on Twitter threads about the cascade of hurt that comes with being human. Why do we not share with *equal* velocity the connections and rich experiences that come from being here? Why do we never have a vision or story to tell about the beauty and healing that could exist here? When there's a movie or book about the future, the dystopian ones are what sells, keeps us invested, page-turning and eyes fixated.

When we take this work outside of ourselves, we can come together and define what world we want to create. Doing this work gives us the evidence of our ability to. We are the proof. We are shown every day that by doing the inner work we're able to navigate and move through whatever arises, before the world itself changes. For us to be able to see what could change on a grander level, we need to be able to access that within us first. That's what the work does. It facilitates the move from introspection to community, individual to collective. We will get to the solutions and the '*hows*' of it all, but our shared vision is how we create what comes next for humanity. Look at the life you're creating for yourself, look at how differently the same world you've known can be, just because you have returned back to *you*. Imagine if we all did that. Imagine if we multiplied everything that you and I are doing by the 7,800,000,000 people that exist here alongside us. Imagine if everyone knew we had the power to create a future that serves and benefits all of us.

What a world we could create. What a world I trust we will create, because this is exactly how we get there. One of us at a time. Looking at our stuff, working on our stuff and getting the stuff we want. And you. You being here, doing the damn thing, continuing to show up and allowing all parts of you to exist. That's how.

SO, PAUSE, TAKE IT IN, CLOSE THIS BOOK AND . . .
Go and Take It All

. . . the way out into your community, the world and whatever lies beyond it.

RESOURCES

MENTAL HEALTH AND EMOTIONAL SUPPORT

If looking at and working on your stuff feels overwhelming or you'd like some extra support, then working with a therapist, counsellor or mental health practitioner is always recommended. If you are looking for mental health services, contact your GP or healthcare provider in the first instance.

While therapy is helpful and beneficial to many people, it's also OK if it's not for you. Mental health services can be free and available via the NHS or charities, but there is often a waiting list. Private therapists are another option, but may not be financially do-able for everyone, so do take your personal situation into consideration and know that your choices are always valid. There will always be support available for you.

Below I have listed some resources where you can get more information, reach support services and receive guidance, including in an emergency:

Mind www.mind.org.uk

Samaritans www.samaritans.org or call 116 123

Shout Crisis Textline Text SHOUT to 85258

Campaign Against Living Miserably (CALM)
www.thecalmzone.net

Hub of Hope hubofhope.co.uk

Anxiety UK www.anxietyuk.org.uk

Improving Access to Psychological Therapies
www.nhs.uk/service-search/find-a-psychological-
therapies-service

British Association for Counselling and Psychotherapy
www.bacp.co.uk

Counselling Directory www.counselling-directory.org.uk

Cruse Bereavement Support www.cruse.org.uk

Stonewall (LGBT support) www.stonewall.org.uk

Rape Crisis rapecrisis.org.uk

PERSONAL TOOLKIT

As you work through this book at your own pace, you can
gather your own resources to support you. It might be practices
like The 5.1 (see page 192), The 5.2 (see page 216) or any of the
exercises throughout the book. Reach out to loved ones, friends
and family, and any peers who can hold you through this, support you and make you laugh. Spend some time in nature, get
enough sleep and have some fun!

You can create a mini toolkit and have it near you at any
time. This might be some soothing essential oils, a warm blanket, an affirmation written on a piece of paper, cuddly toys,

crystals, photos of loved ones, objects that make you happy or a mental memory of a safe and happy place that you can come back to. The below might also serve you:

Grounding Meditation www.gisellelpm.com/
    book-resources
Self-Compassion Exercises (Dr. Kristin Neff)
    self-compassion.org

COMPLEMENTARY AND ALTERNATIVE THERAPIES

Below is a list of suggested therapies that might also serve you. Some practitioners are registered with a professional body such as the Complementary and Natural Healthcare Council (www.cnhc.org.uk) or one for their own industry. If they are not, always try to work with practitioners that come highly recommended, reviewed or through word of mouth. They should be able to share any of their qualifications and lineages with you upon request.

Aromatherapy
Emotional Freedom Technique
Herbal Medicine
Massage
Meditation and Mindfulness
Nutrition
Reiki
Yoga

You can find ways to work with me one-to-one or in group classes at www.gisellelpm.com

FURTHER READING

Gary Chapman, *The 5 Love Languages: The Secret to Love that Lasts* (Northfield Publishing, 2014).

Tamara Driessen, *Luna: Harness the Power of the Moon to Live Your Best Life* (Penguin Life, 2020).

Silvia Federici, *Caliban and the Witch: Women, the Body and Primitive Accumulation* (Penguin Classics, 2021).

Hazel Ann Gibbs De Peza, *My Faith: Spiritual Baptist Christian* (Xulon Press, 2007).

Thich Nhat Hanh, *Peace Is Every Step: The Path of Mindfulness In Everyday Life* (Rider, 1991).

Jasmin Harsono, *Self Reiki: Tune in to Your Life Force to Achieve Harmony and Balance (A Little Book of Self Care)* (DK, 2019).

Linda Howe, *How to Read the Akashic Records: Accessing the Archive of the Soul and Its Journey* (Sounds True Inc., 2010).

Wim Hof, *The Wim Hof Method: Activate Your Potential, Transcend Your Limits* (Rider, 2020).

Jon Kabat-Zinn, *Wherever You Go, There You Are: Mindfulness Meditation for Everyday Life* (Piatkus, 2004).

Emma Lucy Knowles, *The Power of Crystal Healing: Change Your Energy and Live a High-Vibe Life* (Pop Press, 2018).

Sushma Sagar, *Find Your Flow: Essential Chakras (Now Age series)* (Pop Press, 2020).

David A. Treleaven, *Trauma-Sensitive Mindfulness: Practices for Safe and Transformative Healing* (W. W. Norton & Company, 2018).

Bessel Van Der Kolk, *The Body Keeps the Score: Mind, Brain and Body in the Transformation of Trauma* (Penguin Books, 2015).

Dr Brian Weiss, *Many Lives, Many Masters: The true story of a prominent psychiatrist, his young patient and the past-life therapy that changed both their lives* (Piatkus, 1994).

Gary Zukav, *Spiritual Partnership: The Journey To Authentic Power* (Rider, 2010).

ACKNOWLEDGEMENTS

This book wouldn't be possible without my clients and the one-to-one sessions, workshops, classes and talk attendees. Thank you for trusting me and allowing me to help you carry whatever you bring into our work together. You inspire me every day with your willingness and unwavering dedication to showing up for yourselves. I'm endlessly grateful and forever in awe of you all. I love you.

Mum, Lystra, or dare I say Lys; the love of my life. There will never be enough words for me to thank you. You have held, inspired, supported me and made me laugh through every single one of these pages and every chapter in my life. It's a privilege to be your daughter.

My beloved grandparents, Euline and Conrad Holder, I adore you. Thank you for being my cheerleaders and showing me that I could create any life of my choosing and you would love me for it. I basically wrote this book so you can explain to people what I do for work.

Shannon Peter, my soul sister, you are my forever inspiration and greatest joy, wherever I am, whatever I'm doing, thinking about you always makes me smile – how lucky I am to have a best friend in you. Becky Symes, thank you for being my platonic life partner and the bravest, most resilient, dedicated and compassionate woman I've ever met. Thank you for holding my hand through life and letting me hold yours. Your unconditional love and support transcends every definition of friendship.

My favourite New Yorkers: Y.S, because of you I understand what peace is; it's my heart resting in the knowledge that somewhere in the world, there you exist, making this planet much more special. There are so many words I want to say, but for now, all I have is this: thank you. Claire Matern, the fact that we communicate on every single platform about every aspect of life from TV to astrology memes is proof of how much I love you. Thank you for always rooting for me.

Auntie Wilma, thank you for filling your bookcase and my mind from such an early age. I'm so grateful to have you in my life. Auntie Eleanor, my fairy godmother, our conversations and your never-ending wisdom and support have nourished me more than you'll ever know. To the La Pompe family, I am honoured to come from a lineage of such beautiful, wise, strong souls, thank you for trusting me with Mammy Sylvie's stories.

My therapist, Amanda, thank you for teaching me that there'll 'always be a way' and for guiding me back to the light even through the darkest days. Torsten Lange, Mary Neilson, Lindsay Mack, David Treleaven and Dr Linda Howe, thank you for your work, time, teachings and deep service in this world.

Anita Bhagwandas, Alex Nora Esculapio, Joanna Ellner, Sarah Massey, Jasmin Harsono, Tamara Driessen, Daniela

Morosini and Helen Morris: a million Thank Yous for your continued support, love, laughs and care.

To my incredible publisher and champion Olivia Morris, thank you for the unwavering trust, faith and belief in both myself and this book. My editor Bianca Bexton for being the kindest soul and always having my back and Dawn Bates for such care and reverence with my words. Thank you to Katie Cregg and Anna Bowen for your encouragement and enthusiasm and the entire team at Rider and Ebury for your endless support. Thank you to my agent Hayley Steed for everything you do and everyone at Madeleine Milburn Agency. So much gratitude for Catherine Cho for holding my ideas and seeing my potential as an author before I saw it myself.

ABOUT THE AUTHOR

Giselle La Pompe-Moore is a spiritual guide, trauma-sensitive meditation teacher, Reiki master teacher, speaker and writer. Prior to this, Giselle worked as a beauty and wellbeing writer and has written for *Stylist, Who What Wear, Elle, Red* and more. Taking a down-to-earth and practical approach to spirituality, she helps her clients through their life experiences and changes in one-to-one sessions and online group classes. Her work has been featured in *Vogue, Evening Standard, Sheerluxe, YOU Magazine*, and Channel 4 to name a few.